François Mauriac
The Making of an Intellectual

FAUX TITRE

290

Etudes de langue et littérature françaises
publiées sous la direction de

Keith Busby, M.J. Freeman,
Sjef Houppermans et Paul Pelckmans

François Mauriac
The Making of an Intellectual

Edward Welch

AMSTERDAM - NEW YORK, NY 2006

Photo cover: François Mauriac with Françoise Giroud and Jean-Jacques
Servan-Schreiber at *L'Express*, circa 1954. © D.R./L'Express/Editingserver.com

Cover design: Pier Post

ISBN-10: 90-420-2112-8
ISBN-13: 978-90-420-2112-9
© Editions Rodopi B.V., Amsterdam - New York, NY 2006
Printed in The Netherlands

Contents

Acknowledgements

Much of this book was written during a period of research leave granted by the University of Durham, and funded partially by the Arts and Humanities Research Council, whose support I gratefully acknowledge. It represents the culmination of a long engagement with Mauriac's work which has benefited from the advice, support and encouragement of various *mauriaciens* over the years, and in particular Toby Garfitt, my doctoral supervisor, Malcolm Scott and Margaret Parry. I would also like to thank Ron Naylor, who first introduced me to Mauriac and his world, and planted the seed of later research.

A number of people took the time and care to comment on earlier versions of the manuscript. My thanks go to Alex Harrington, Andrea Noble and Jean-Pierre Le Bourhis for several insightful and useful observations. Russell Goulbourne and Michael Hawcroft were particularly generous with their time, rigorous and incisive in their comments, and encouraging in their support. Their contribution is greatly valued. Thanks too to Karen Exell for her work on the index.

Finally, I wish to acknowledge the good-humoured and unfailing support offered by all my friends and family throughout the writing of the book. Lisa Downing, Katherine Lunn-Rockcliffe and Tom Westall are to be especially thanked, as are my parents, Derek and Christine, to whom this book is dedicated.

Conventions of Reference

Throughout the book, reference is made in the text to the following works by Mauriac.

BN	*Bloc-notes*, ed. by Jean Touzot (Paris: Seuil, coll. "Points", 1993), 5 vols
LV	*Lettres d'une vie*, ed. by Caroline Mauriac (Paris: Grasset, 1981)
MP	*Mémoires politiques* (Paris: Grasset, 1967)
NLV	*Nouvelles lettres d'une vie*, ed. by Caroline Mauriac (Paris: Grasset, 1989)
OA	*Œuvres autobiographiques*, ed. by François Durand (Paris: Gallimard, coll. "Bibl. de la Pléiade", 1990)
OC	*Œuvres complètes* (Paris: Fayard, 1952), 12 vols
ORTC	*Œuvres romanesques et théâtrales complètes*, ed. by Jacques Petit (Paris: Gallimard, coll. "Bibl. de la Pléiade", 1978-1985), 4 vols
SR	*Souvenirs retrouvés: entretiens avec Jean Amrouche* (Paris: Fayard/I.N.A., 1981)

References to all other works by Mauriac are footnoted.

Introduction

From Novelist to Intellectual

> Tous mes amis et moi nous le lisions et nous n'étions pas
> catholiques. Il atteignait en effet des milieux qui n'étaient pas de
> sa foi et qui considéraient ce qu'il écrivait non pas en liaison avec
> sa foi mais simplement avec sa raison.[1]

Suddenly, in the 1950s, François Mauriac emerged as one of France's
most influential and widely respected political commentators. Even
Jean-Paul Sartre, who had little time for Mauriac as a novelist, was
attentive to what he had begun to say in his new incarnation as a
political analyst. The writer best known for his novels of the 1920s
and 1930s – novels which helped him win the Nobel Prize for
Literature in 1952 – had gradually taken leave of fiction to devote
himself increasingly to journalism. This evolution in Mauriac's
activities is the subject of the present book. It investigates Mauriac's
role as a journalist, and more broadly as an intellectual, in the post-
war years, and traces the emergence of that role in the complex socio-
cultural context which shapes and informs it.

Mauriac's impact as a journalist in the 1950s was partly due
to the company he had started to keep. In 1954, he began a seven-year
involvement with *L'Express*, the newly-launched news weekly, whose
mission was to promote a radical, left-wing agenda for modernisation
and reform, and which was intent on co-opting what it saw as the most
eminent and influential players in French society to this end.
L'Express would secure the regular collaboration of emblematic
figures such as Sartre and Albert Camus throughout the 1950s; but
Mauriac, with the weekly column he entitled *Bloc-notes*, would be its

---

[1] 'Mauriac vu par Sartre, propos recueillis par Jean Touzot', in Jean Touzot (ed.),
François Mauriac, Cahiers de l'Herne, 48 (1985), 44-52 (p. 46).

main asset. He made a valuable contribution to its campaigning activity through his denunciation of torture and abuse in Algeria, or his mobilisation of the Catholic vote in support of Pierre Mendès France during the legislative elections of 1956.

The 1950s saw Mauriac assert himself as one of the major intellectual figures of the post-war period. He had joined that distinctive group of individuals in French society – writers, artists, philosophers, scientists – who make it their business to intervene in political debate, to judge political action and the social world, and who feel able to do so even if they lack any specific expertise in political matters. As Sartre puts it, 'l'intellectuel est quelqu'un qui se mêle de ce qui ne le regarde pas'.[2] The tradition was inaugurated in 1898 by Emile Zola during the Dreyfus Affair. His denunciatory article 'J'accuse' is widely recognised as marking the birth of the modern-day intellectual; and it is during the controversy provoked by his support of Dreyfus that the term 'intellectual' makes its first appearance.[3] Sartre points out that in the context of the Affair, the term was often used critically of those speaking out in favour of Dreyfus. Attempts were made to dismiss the interventions of Zola and the other *dreyfusards* on the grounds that they lacked the competence and the expertise to comment on the case: 'pour les antidreyfusistes, l'acquittement ou la condamnation du capitaine Dreyfus concernait les tribunaux militaires et, en définitive, l'*Etat-Major*: les dreyfusards, en affirmant l'innocence de l'inculpé, se plaçaient *hors de leur compétence*'.[4] However, as the role of the intellectual evolved, this lack of competence or specialist knowledge in fact came to be seen as an asset. It implied a critical distance from the worlds of politics and power which served to guarantee the value of what the intellectual had to say.

The intellectual operates by exploiting a status and authority acquired as a result of activities in a domain of intellectual endeavour like science, literature and the arts. Such domains, if their place in society can provoke controversy or dispute, are nevertheless broadly

---

[2] Jean-Paul Sartre, 'Plaidoyer pour les intellectuels', in *Situations, VIII* (Paris: Gallimard, 1972), pp. 375-455 (p. 377).

[3] Pascal Ory and Jean-François Sirinelli, *Les Intellectuels en France: de l'affaire Dreyfus à nos jours* (Paris: Perrin, 2004), pp. 7-12. See also Christophe Charle, *Naissance des 'intellectuels'* (Paris: Editions de Minuit, 1990).

[4] Sartre, 'Plaidoyer pour les intellectuels', p. 378. Sartre's emphasis.

respected for being governed by a set of principles distinct from those which shape other parts of the social world. They are characterised by their independence with respect to political and economic interests, by the disinterested pursuit of knowledge, understanding or beauty, and by a disavowal of – even disdain for – worldly glory and success. Intellectuals are defined as such by their decision to leave the autonomous realm of intellectual activity in order not just to enter the political realm, but to judge it according to the values and principles which govern the intellectual sphere, and in particular those universal principles such as truth, liberty and justice. At the same time, they present themselves as the rightful guardians and defenders of such values which they claim are eroded in a political world motivated by short-term interest and worldly power. For Pierre Bourdieu, the intellectual 's'affirme, contre les lois spécifiques de la politique, celles de la *Realpolitik* et de la raison d'Etat, comme le défenseur de principes universels'.[5] Intellectuals give themselves the tasks of scrutinising the actions of those who govern collective life and of raising the consciousness of those who are being governed, encouraging them to interrogate the world in which they live.

Mauriac's activities in the 1950s and 60s, and his rise to prominence as an intellectual, merit attention both because they can be seen to exemplify this understanding of the intellectual's role in society, and because they represent a striking contrast to the position of the novelist of the 1920s. Speaking in 1925, Mauriac not only made clear that he had no intention of venturing into the political arena, but he also expressed his bemusement at those who did: 'je n'éprouve aucun mépris pour ceux qui *font de la politique*, mais de l'indifférence. Ils me sont aussi étrangers que la corporation des hommes-sandwiches ou des croquemorts, et je n'ai pas envie de me mêler à eux'.[6] Moreover, when Mauriac's career as a journalist began to develop in the early 1930s, it was in newspapers which were staunchly conservative; and the political views he did express – fear of the threat posed by bolshevism, expressions of sympathy for the extreme Right protestors involved in the riots of 6 February 1934, a

---

[5] Pierre Bourdieu, *Les Règles de l'art: genèse et structure du champ littéraire* (Paris: Seuil, coll. "Points", 2nd edition, 1998), p. 217.
[6] Cit. in Jean Touzot, 'François Mauriac chez les "hommes-sandwiches" (1925-1935)', *Revue des lettres modernes*, série François Mauriac, 3 (Caen: Minard, 1980), 21-37 (p. 21). Mauriac's emphasis.

certain admiration for Mussolini when he first came to power – made
it clear that despite a flirtation with the left-wing Sillon movement in
his youth, the Mauriac of the 1930s was firmly on the political Right.
His views then were radically opposed to the ones he would articulate
some twenty years later, as he denounced colonial oppression and the
society which, when it did not actively condone it, continued tacitly to
accept it.

One of the aims of this book is to investigate Mauriac's
activities as a journalist and intellectual in the post-war years, and the
1950s and 60s especially. This period of his career was dominated by
the *Bloc-notes* column, which he published over an eighteen-year
period between 1952 and his death in 1970. After starting life as a
monthly column in the literary review *La Table ronde*, the *Bloc-notes*
appeared more or less every week from April 1954, first in *L'Express*
and then, from 1961, in *Le Figaro littéraire*. Its place as a significant
part of Mauriac's *œuvre* was signalled by its publication in volume
form during his lifetime. Gathering the articles together in this way
invited his readers to see them not as ephemeral pieces of commentary
on current affairs, but as an enduring engagement with contemporary
French politics and history.

In recent years, the *Bloc-notes* has taken on an even clearer
identity as a cohesive body of work thanks to Jean Touzot's new
critical edition published by Editions du Seuil in 1993. The
appearance of the *Bloc-notes* in Le Seuil's prestigious 'Points'
paperback series was doubly significant: it confirmed the status of the
Bloc-notes both as an important part of Mauriac's output, and as a
major body of work in the context of French thought more generally.
The decision by Le Seuil to republish a work which had long since
gone out of print, and to do so in a series which plays host to some of
France's key intellectual figures, can be seen to mark the consecration
of the *Bloc-notes* as one of the essential historical documents of recent
times. Not only does the *Bloc-notes* deserve to be kept in circulation,
it seems, but it is deemed sufficiently viable in economic terms for Le
Seuil to invest in a work of five volumes and some two thousand
pages.

The republication of the *Bloc-notes* has sparked a renewed
interest in his journalism among Mauriac specialists, after a period
during which it had been relatively neglected in favour of the novels.
Three book-length studies of the *Bloc-notes* have appeared over the

last ten years;[7] and attention has also begun to turn to other areas of Mauriac's journalistic output, from the articles of the 1930s to the television reviews of the 1950s and 60s.[8] All three studies of the *Bloc-notes* are largely text-based readings, and do much to reveal the literary significance and thematic unity of the corpus. While Bernard Chochon investigates the theme of time across the *Bloc-notes*, for example, Nathan Bracher reads it for Mauriac's reflections on history, and his understanding of the historical process. It seems to me important to add to such approaches a more rigorous consideration of Mauriac's journalistic activities in relation to the broader socio-cultural context.

Doing so is all the more necessary since Mauriac's work still tends to be overlooked by scholars of the period more generally. If Michel Winock devotes a chapter to what he calls 'le bel automne de François Mauriac' in his survey of the intellectual in France,[9] and Mauriac has a strong supporting role in Ory and Sirinelli's similar study,[10] the focus has remained on the more obviously exciting figures of the period such as Sartre, de Beauvoir and Camus. Comparatively little attention has been paid to Mauriac's role in the unfolding of events, or to the opinions he put forward.[11] The present study, by contrast, is motivated by the conviction both that his activities in the 1950s and 60s need to be resituated in their socio-cultural context, and

---

[7] Bernard Cocula, *Mauriac: le 'Bloc-notes'* (Bordeaux: L'Esprit du Temps, 1995); Bernard Chochon, *Le 'Bloc-notes' de Mauriac: une poésie du temps* (Paris: L'Harmattan, 2002); Nathan Bracher, *Through The Past Darkly: History and Memory in François Mauriac's 'Bloc-notes'*, (Washington, D.C.: The Catholic University of America Press, 2004).

[8] See Philippe Baudorre (ed.), *François Mauriac: un écrivain journaliste*, *Revue des lettres modernes*, série François Mauriac, 6 (Caen: Minard, 2003), and in particular the essay by Malcolm Scott, 'Pour recevoir le journalisme de François Mauriac', 151-187.

[9] Michel Winock, *Le Siècle des intellectuels* (Paris: Seuil, coll. "Points", 1999), pp. 635-650 and *passim*.

[10] Pascal Ory and Jean-François Sirinelli, *Les Intellectuels en France*.

[11] For example, Tony Judt, *Past Imperfect: French Intellectuals, 1944-1956* (Berkeley, Ca.: University of California Press, 1992), deals briefly with Mauriac, concentrating instead on the intellectuals of the Left and their relationship with the Communist Party. Likewise, in her study of decolonisation and modernisation in 1950s France, Kristin Ross offers us a tantalising glimpse of Mauriac at *L'Express*, but her main focus lies elsewhere. See Kristin Ross, *Fast Cars, Clean Bodies: Decolonisation and the Reordering of French Culture* (Cambridge, Ma.: The MIT Press, 1995).

that they illuminate and help us to understand some of the broader issues relating to that context.

In the later chapters especially, we shall see how Mauriac emerges as a sensitive and acute observer of the radical change – at political, social and cultural levels – affecting France in the 1950s and 60s. Chapter three analyses some of his most convincing interventions as an intellectual in the mid-1950s, as he denounces the torture and abuse being carried out by the French in North Africa. His criticism of the colonial regimes in Morocco and Algeria, and the incompetence of the metropolitan government, exemplify the ways in which we might expect an intellectual to function: he writes articles which interpolate their readers, confronting them with the moral and ethical problems raised by torture, inviting them to reflect on the society in which they live, and urging them to act in order to bring the practice of torture to an end.

Chapter four focuses on Mauriac's collaboration with *L'Express*, one of the most important periods in his career. Its significance is due in large part to *L'Express* itself, whose central place in the socio-cultural landscape of 1950s France has still to be fully recognised. I argue that Mauriac's association with *L'Express* plays a crucial role in confirming his status as an intellectual. Through his involvement with a magazine which is driving a radical agenda for change, he is exposed to, and directly caught up in, a socio-cultural order undergoing rapid mutation. Chapter five examines his increasing preoccupation with this change, and in particular with the consequences of the effort of *aménagement* which gathers pace under de Gaulle in the 1960s. Mauriac offers a valuable perspective on the period as someone being subjected to modernisation and attempting to articulate its often problematic consequences – consequences which were being subsumed in a narrative of progress. The chapter also explores the contradictions which arise from the fact that the change which alienates Mauriac takes place under the auspices of a President of whom he had become one of the most loyal and fervent supporters.

This book therefore sets out to consider Mauriac's post-war activity as a journalist and intellectual figure by resituating it in the socio-cultural context in which it unfolds. It also aims in turn to highlight the broader processes at work in that period which Mauriac's role helps to crystallise. However, if many of the texts discussed in the later chapters are drawn from the *Bloc-notes*, it is not intended principally to be a study of that body of work. While it sees the *Bloc-notes* as the most significant concrete manifestation of Mauriac's activity as a journalist, its focus is on Mauriac as an actor in the period, one whose action takes the form in particular of articles written with performative intent. It seeks to foreground the status of his weekly column as a series of acts or interventions which are bound up in, and are the product of, a particular historical moment. Conceiving of the *Bloc-notes* as a cohesive body of work and searching for its thematic or stylistic continuities over the months and years, risks eliding its inherent discontinuity – a discontinuity signalled precisely by the fragmentary form it often takes as a series of dated, diary entries – and the importance of each column as a response or reaction to a precise moment.

The status of the *Bloc-notes* as a series of interventions in, or responses to, a historical process, is underlined when we consider Mauriac's famous article on torture in Algeria, published in 1955, and read it not in the context of the first Seuil volume – that is to say, as part of a narrative unfolding over the five year period covered by the volume – but in the edition of *L'Express* in which it was originally published. In chapter three, I explore both the article itself and the way in which it was presented by the news weekly at the time. It becomes clear that Mauriac's intervention is not simply a matter of words on a page – the form it has for most readers today when they encounter it in a bound volume – but involves a whole set of framing discourses and devices (such as a powerful front cover featuring a moody portrait photograph of Mauriac and the headline 'Mauriac accuse') which are designed to ensure that his intervention has the greatest possible impact.

The way in which *L'Express* presents and frames Mauriac's article is also significant for what it reveals about the news weekly's perception of him. *L'Express* appears to take for granted that he has the status and authority to make an effective intervention, that he has a rightful place in the tradition of free-thinking and critical individuals who have the power to speak out and bring about change. Mauriac's status as an intellectual is assumed, in other words, and this assumption leads them to construct his identity as such through the images and words they use to present him to their readers.

It is noticeable that the critics who have so far engaged with Mauriac's post-war work share similar assumptions about Mauriac's status as an intellectual. They accept without question that Mauriac has perceptive things to say about the period, and that his perspective on events is a valuable one – that we can, for example, as Bracher's book suggests, turn to him in order to clarify our understanding of history. While I would certainly agree that Mauriac has valid and relevant things to say – that he raises the ethical issues foregrounded by torture in effective ways, for example – I would also argue that this should not prevent us from considering how he comes to have the power and authority to do so. We need also to investigate Mauriac's transformation from novelist to intellectual, and his emergence as a respected voice of moral conscience. Another aim of the book is to consider precisely these issues. It does not simply explore his post-war activities as an important columnist of *L'Express* intervening in political debate, but sets out to examine the means by which he acquires his intellectual status. Its subject is the *making* of an intellectual.

In doing so, the study draws on the work of Pierre Bourdieu and others in the domain of sociology who have considered the function and presence in society of figures such as intellectuals, artists and writers. Bourdieu has set out to examine the processes at work in the social sphere which allow certain individuals to obtain the legitimacy and authority to speak for and to others about the state of the world, and call their fellow citizens to account. The emergence of the intellectual as an identifiable social role can be seen as the result of a whole series of configurations and reconfigurations at the social, political and economic levels. Moreover, adopting the Bourdieusian perspective also allows us to understand how the intellectual has come to be such a prominent and distinctive feature of French culture and society in particular. While intellectuals are not a phenomenon unique to France, it is nevertheless the case that the organisation of French society has proved especially conducive to their development. Anna Boschetti observes that 'aucune autre nation n'a produit une organisation sociale aussi favorable, ni donc une représentation de l'intellectuel capable de rivaliser avec le modèle français'.[12] Her analysis is worth quoting at length:

---

[12] Anna Boschetti, 'Le mythe du grand intellectuel', in *Le Grand Atlas Universalis des littératures* (Paris: Encyclopaedia Universalis, 1990), pp. 244-247 (p. 247).

L'unification précoce et le centralisme politique et culturel ont permis très tôt la formation d'une société intellectuelle consciente de son importance sociale, ainsi que l'essor d'instances de diffusion et de consécration – académies, clubs, salons, cénacles, revues, maisons d'édition, presse périodique – et d'un système scolaire capables d'assurer l'existence et la croissance d'un marché culturel d'ampleur nationale. L'orientation démocratique, à partir de 1789, a contribué à l'autonomisation et au prestige de la culture, en favorisant la liberté du débat, le développement de l'enseignement public et, notamment, d'institutions de reproduction de l'élite intellectuelle, telles que l'Ecole normale supérieure: dans un ordre social qui fonde sur l'idéologie méritocratique sa légitimation, tout incline cette aristocratie de l'intelligence, relativement indépendante au pouvoir, à se penser comme totalement libre, lucide, désintéressée et, de ce fait, mandaté pour exercer une magistrature morale sur toute la société.[13]

If the process has its roots in the seventeenth and eighteenth centuries, it is the changes affecting the country in the nineteenth century – education reform, a rapid expansion of the liberal professions, fields of cultural production which were increasingly able to assert their independence from the State authorities and the dominant fractions of society – which proved decisive, as Boschetti suggests. I propose to insert Mauriac's own evolution into the broader narrative of the development of the intellectual and cultural fields as that narrative continues to unfold in complex ways in the twentieth century.

The most obvious place to locate Mauriac's transformation from novelist to intellectual is in the evolution of his own political views, and his increasing engagement with politics in the 1930s. His opinions shift rapidly during this time, as he frees himself from the conservative Right in the mid-1930s, somewhat paradoxically following his election to the Académie Française in 1933, and adopts progressively more liberal positions. This narrative of change has been told convincingly by Malcolm Scott in particular.[14] Scott highlights the key turning points of the election to the Académie Française, which Mauriac comes to realise is a stronghold of the extreme Right, and the attack on Franco and expression of support for the Basques in

[13] Boschetti, 'Le mythe du grand intellectuel', p. 247. See also Christophe Charle, *Naissance des 'intellectuels'*, ch. 1.
[14] Malcolm Scott, *Mauriac: The Politics of a Novelist* (Edinburgh: Scottish Academic Press, 1980).

1937. Mauriac's transformation is then further suggested during the Second World War by his activities as part of the intellectual Resistance.

While Scott's reconstruction of Mauriac's political and intellectual biography is an important starting point, it is nevertheless necessary to set the writer's evolution in a broader context, one which fundamentally shapes that evolution. It could be argued that Scott's account suffers from what Bourdieu terms the 'illusion biographique'.[15] It locates the motive force behind the unfolding of a life and career primarily at the level of individual consciousness, and asserts the primacy of that consciousness over the world in which it operates. Actions in the world or changes in direction are determined first and foremost by an individual's psychology, by changes in understanding as he or she reacts and responds to the world. Reconstructing these shifts in understanding, and linking them in a narrative of cause and effect, offers a way of comprehending the path people take, and accounting for their actions. Thus, for example, when Scott discusses Mauriac's move leftwards in the post-war years, and his emergence as an important intellectual voice, he interprets them principally in psychological terms. The evolution is a result firstly of Mauriac's changed perception of the political scene: 'the experience of war and occupation had lifted from the eyes the distorting filter through which he had instinctively surveyed men of the left during the period of the Popular Front'; and secondly of an increased confidence in his own abilities as a political commentator:

> Both in the proportion of his writing devoted to the public scene
> [...] and by the increasing confidence with which he expressed
> his opinions, it was plain that Mauriac had embarked on nothing
> less than a second career: that of political journalist.[16]

Yet we must always keep in mind that Mauriac's individual consciousness and his singular action unfold in particular socio-cultural configurations which inform and inflect them in important ways. Mauriac's emergence as an intellectual is a result not just of his own evolving political views or a developing political and moral

---

[15] Pierre Bourdieu, *Raisons pratiques: sur la théorie de l'action* (Paris: Seuil, coll. "Points", 1994), pp. 81-89.
[16] Scott, *Mauriac: The Politics of a Novelist*, p. 88.

conscience, but also the set of social and cultural conditions which help his transformation. If Mauriac can assert himself as an intellectual in the post-war period, for example, it is not just a result of an increased confidence on his part, but also because he is in a position to profit from the newly reconfigured cultural order which emerges after the Liberation. This new order is crystallised by Sartre's rise to prominence, and his successful attempt to impose a new definition of literary excellence and legitimacy based not on the autonomy and purity of literature – the criteria which had governed the field in the inter-war years – but on the writer's political commitment. Moreover, it was a shift in values which, if it had certainly been accelerated by the War and the crisis of the Occupation, had already begun to take shape in 1939: its first manifestation, in fact, was Sartre's savage critique of Mauriac's novelistic technique, a critique which confirmed the decline of Mauriac's fortunes as a novelist during the 1930s.

The book therefore traces what, from a Bourdieusian perspective, we would define as Mauriac's trajectory. Central to Bourdieu's approach is what he calls 'le mode de pensée relationnel'.[17] He argues that individual actions and decisions, and the ways in which they unfold over time, can only be properly understood when they are re-inscribed in the broader context in which they play themselves out; and by context, Bourdieu means more specifically a field of production. For Bourdieu, the social world is constituted by different fields of activity, each one structured by a series of different positions, and populated by actors and institutions holding those positions. The meaning and significance of each position is defined by its relationship to the others in the field. Bourdieu describes the field of cultural production in the following terms, for instance:

> Le microcosme social dans lequel se produisent les œuvres culturelles, champ littéraire, champ artistique, champ scientifique, etc., est un espace de relations objectives entre des positions – celle de l'artiste consacré et celle de l'artiste maudit par exemple – et on ne peut comprendre ce qui s'y passe que si l'on situe chaque agent ou chaque institution dans ses relations objectives avec tous les autres.[18]

---

[17] Bourdieu, *Raisons pratiques*, p. 68. See also *Les Règles de l'art*, pp. 297-303.
[18] Bourdieu, *Raisons pratiques*, p. 68.

Likewise, the significance of the choices made and the positions
adopted by individuals as they negotiate the field (seeking election to
the Académie Française, for example) only becomes clear when those
choices and positions are considered in the context of the field as a
whole, and the range of possible positions within it. As Bourdieu
observes, 'c'est par rapport aux états correspondants de la structure du
champ que se déterminent à chaque moment *le sens* et la valeur
sociale des événements biographiques, entendus comme des
placements et des *déplacements* dans cet espace'.[19]

The relationships between the different positions in the field
are above all relationships of power. Actors in a field are engaged in a
struggle for the capital specific to it, such as the values which define
it, or the definitions of excellence which pertain to it. They fight either
to obtain or to retain authority within it, an authority which gives them
the ability to distribute credit among the other actors in the field. As
Bourdieu puts it,

> Les luttes dont le champ est le lieu ont pour enjeu le monopole de
> la violence légitime (autorité spécifique) qui est caractéristique du
> champ considéré, c'est-à-dire, en définitive, la conservation ou la
> subversion de la structure de la distribution du capital
> spécifique.[20]

Throughout the inter-war period in the literary field, for example, the
power to define the terms of literary success and excellence lies in the
hands of the *Nouvelle Revue française* (*NRF*), a power it had seized
from existing bodies of legitimation such as the Académie Française;
but the *NRF* will itself lose this power to Sartre and *Les Temps
modernes* in years following the Liberation.

The more autonomy or independence a field has obtained
from the broader social sphere (and the fields of economic and
political power especially), the more it will function according to its
own specific logic, and the more it will shape the actions of those
operating within it. The most striking example of this is the field of
cultural production, which secures its autonomy from the field of
power during the latter half of the nineteenth century, and in doing so
takes the form of what Bourdieu describes as the 'economic world

[19] Bourdieu, *Les Règles de l'art*, p. 426. Bourdieu's emphasis.
[20] Bourdieu, 'Quelques propriétés des champs', in *Questions de sociologie* (Paris:
Editions de Minuit, 1984), pp. 113-120 (p. 114).

reversed': the dominant values at work in the fields of art and literature are those which disavow economic profit and worldly glory in favour of recognition by one's peers and the pursuit of art for its own sake. [21] Such values are the ones embodied by the group at the *NRF* in the inter-war years, whose members oppose themselves explicitly to the longstanding guardians of literary orthodoxy in the Académie Française.

Making use of these Bourdieusian perspectives, my aim in the first two chapters is thus to track Mauriac's trajectory in the inter-war years, and trace his negotiation of a literary field polarised by the opposing forces of the *NRF* and the Académie Française. It is in Mauriac's activities during this period that we find some of the key factors contributing to his emergence as an intellectual. The two chapters take as their starting point the decade of the 1930s, which is marked by some of the most decisive turning points in Mauriac's career. Firstly, the 1930s is defined by a startling change in his fortunes as a novelist. 1932 sees the publication of *Le Nœud de vipères*, hailed by critics at the time as his masterpiece. Writing in the *NRF*, Ramon Fernandez argues that 'l'art de M. Mauriac ne s'est jamais affirmé avec plus de maîtrise'. [22] Moreover, confirmation of Mauriac's success in the literary field comes the following year, in the form of his election to the Académie Française. Yet in 1939, again in the pages of the *NRF*, Mauriac's work as a novelist would be subject to a famous and devastating critique by Sartre who, having found fault with the God-like omniscience of his narrators, would conclude that 'Dieu n'est pas un artiste; M. Mauriac non plus'. [23] In doing so, he would apparently serve notice rather brutally on Mauriac's existence as a novelist.

Secondly, the period sees Mauriac's increasing involvement in the political domain, itself related to a journalistic career which had begun to take off in the summer of 1932, when he signed as a columnist to *L'Écho de Paris*. His activity as a journalist would

---

[21] Bourdieu, 'The Field of Cultural Production, or: The Economic World Reversed', trans. by Richard Nice, *Poetics*, 12 (1983), 311-356. I explore this process in more detail in chapter one.

[22] Ramon Fernandez, 'François Mauriac, *Le Nœud de vipères*', *La Nouvelle Revue française*, 223 (April 1932), p. 761.

[23] Jean-Paul Sartre, 'M. François Mauriac et la liberté', *La Nouvelle Revue française*, 305 (February 1939), p. 232.

culminate during the Spanish Civil War in his unequivocal support for the Basque people and the Republican cause. In the aftermath of the bombing of Guernica in 1937, Mauriac would be the lead signatory of a petition 'pour le peuple basque', and write a series of articles in *Le Figaro* and elsewhere, condemning Franco's actions and a Spanish Catholic Church which he saw as complicit with the regime. This would be his first intervention in the political domain as a voice of moral conscience, and would signal his break with the Right.

The first two chapters explore these broad trends and examine the evolution of Mauriac's position in the field which they reflect. Chapter one focuses on the motives behind his return to journalism in the early 1930s, and on his election to the Académie Française in 1933. It situates them in the context of his earlier trajectory in the field, and considers how they prepare the ground for effective interventions in the political field as an intellectual. We can see how Mauriac begins to exploit in new ways the prestige or symbolic capital accrued as a result of his success as a novelist in the 1920s. Chapter two, in contrast, turns to consider his declining fortunes precisely as a novelist during the period, as Mauriac tries to negotiate, and fights to keep, his position in the literary field – a battle which seems lost after Sartre's intervention in 1939.

While not suggesting that there is a simple, causal connection between Mauriac's decline as a novelist and his emergence as a journalist and an intellectual – a deliberate strategy of re-conversion, for example, by which he would move into one domain because of difficulties in the other – I argue that both aspects of his trajectory, and his dramatic change of fortunes as a novelist especially, are symptomatic of broader changes at work at the time. The instability of Mauriac's position can be seen as an indication of a similar instability affecting the literary field as a whole. More specifically, Sartre's symbolic execution of Mauriac simultaneously marks the decline of a certain conception of literature more generally, and signals the emergence of a new critical framework. It also points to a restructuring of the field from which, ironically, Mauriac will be in a position to benefit, as he possesses resources (in terms of symbolic capital and his own dispositions) which are adequately adapted to the field in its new configuration, and which allow him to operate successfully as an intellectual within it. In particular, the moralistic stance for which he was repeatedly criticised as a novelist in the 1930s would prove ideally suited to his developing role as a moral authority.

If, in the immediate post-war years, Mauriac proves resistant to the new model of excellence represented by Sartre and the notion of 'committed literature' – a resistance he articulates in his new literary review, *La Table ronde*, which styles itself as both an alternative to Sartre's *Les Temps modernes*, and a replacement for the defunct *NRF* – it is a model which he will in fact come to exemplify as his career as a political journalist develops. Chapter three explores Mauriac's motivations for his return to the political fray in the early 1950s. It draws attention especially to what it terms the 'ethical shock' experienced by Mauriac when violent oppression by the colonial forces in Casablanca coincides with his trip to Stockholm to receive the Nobel Prize. We see how the collision of these two events obliges Mauriac to interrogate, in ways new to him, the role of the writer and the place of culture in society. Indeed, as he responds to the crisis in the Maghreb, and attempts to articulate his own role and position as a writer, it is a Sartrean language of responsibility and commitment he will use in order to do so.

At the same time, I will argue that Mauriac's emergence as an intellectual in the post-war years is related not just to the evolution of his own position, but also to changes at work in the field of cultural production more generally. In the post-war period, we can see the status of the intellectual itself entering a new phase. The change is operated by intellectuals themselves, as a result in particular of the imposition of the Sartrean paradigm of the 'total' intellectual; but it is fostered too by broader cultural shifts, and the rapid evolution of mass culture especially, which responds to newly-dominant intellectual figures by transforming them into media stars. We will see how Mauriac himself is caught up in, and illustrates, these complex processes during the 1950s, and his seven-year collaboration with *L'Express*.

Bourdieu's insistence on the need for relational thinking is important for the double perspective it opens up: tracing the trajectory of a specific actor through the field in which he operates also allows us to grasp the structure of that field, both at a particular moment in its existence, and as it changes over time. Bourdieu reminds us that the field is 'un espace lui-même en devenir et soumis à d'incessantes transformations'.[24] Indeed, in France especially, change in the fields of cultural production has taken the form of a series of revolutions or symbolic coups, as individuals and groups have imposed their own artistic tastes and judgements at the expense of others. Moreover, while all actors in the field are caught up in the changes which shape it, some are more exposed to their effects than others. If, as we shall see at various points, Mauriac's trajectory is particularly useful for the light it sheds on the broader changes affecting the field during the twentieth century, it is because he emerges as one such actor. The different positions he is led to adopt in the field mean that he is subjected to the effects of change more than he engineers or provokes change himself. The most obvious example of this is the moment when he is singled out for attack by Sartre in 1939. Not only is the attack a clue to Mauriac's position in the field as a novelist at the time, and the way in which he is perceived by the other actors within it, but it also makes Mauriac one of the main vectors through which changes in the field begin to emerge and crystallise. In the wake of Sartre's critique, it soon becomes clear that what is at stake is not just Mauriac's reputation as a novelist, but a certain understanding of literature more generally, one which had dominated the literary field for twenty years, but which now found itself under threat.

The Bourdieusian perspective is valuable and productive because it stresses contextualisation and historicisation, both in terms of the need to resituate individual lives in an evolving field of forces, constraints and possibilities, and in terms of understanding social and cultural phenomena as products of a particular set of social processes, structures and configurations. It also brings with it a further benefit. In his analysis of the fields of cultural production, Bourdieu identifies a fundamental property they all share, namely 'la logique proprement magique de la production du producteur et du produit comme fétiches'.[25] One of the most important effects of the fields of cultural production is the way in which artists and their work are transformed into fetish objects. They are invested with an almost mystical power to bewitch and charm by a society which seems happy to succumb to the myth of the creative individual, and to accept that great artists or writers have some sort of natural ability or genius that transcends

---

[24] Bourdieu, *Raisons pratiques*, p. 88.
[25] Bourdieu, *Les Règles de l'art*, p. 300.

social and historical contingencies. When such figures venture into the political realm, the status which derives from this belief accords an intrinsic and automatic significance to what they have to say.

The aim of Bourdieu's approach, on the other hand, is precisely to engage with that myth, to identify and account for its origins. For Bourdieu, it is the historical development of the cultural field that has provided the conditions in which notions of the creative genius, the great mind, and the universal and transcendent nature of what they say and do, can develop: 'l'histoire ne peut produire l'universalité transhistorique qu'en instituant des univers sociaux qui, par l'effet de l'alchimie sociale de leurs lois spécifiques de fonctionnement, tendent à extraire de l'affrontement souvent impitoyable des points de vues particuliers l'essence sublime de l'universel'.[26] Certainly, one of the things made clear by Mauriac's trajectory, as we shall see in the next two chapters, is that literary or artistic excellence is as much acquired as it is innate. It depends on being aligned sufficiently with the dominant perceptions of literary merit and value, and of being recognised as a legitimate writer or artist by those who possess the legitimacy to make such recognition. In other words, the Bourdieusian perspective is a demystifying one. It invites us to recognise and interrogate the machinery at work in society which produces and sustains cultural figures, great minds and intellectuals, and simultaneously cloaks them in myth. In doing so, it offers an understanding of the role of culture in society which is more rigorous and more complex than, as Bourdieu puts it, 'la croyance dans les vertus miraculeuses du génie créateur'.[27]

Our exploration of Mauriac's adventures in the literary field begins with a discussion of his shifting fortunes during the inter-war period. It considers his emergence and decline as a recognised and successful novelist, and the gradual changes and reorientations which see him begin to acquire a new status as an intellectual.

---

[26] Bourdieu, *Raisons pratiques*, p. 80.
[27] *Raisons pratiques*, p. 80.

Chapter One

Choices and Positionings

Making a mark: literary success and the (re)turn to journalism

Mauriac's career as a journalist began to develop in July 1932, when he started to write a regular chronicle for *L'Écho de Paris*. He joined *Le Figaro* in 1934, shortly after his friend Pierre Brisson had taken over as its director, and was one of its leading editorialists for twenty years. He was also an occasional contributor to other newspapers, travelling to Rome for *Le Journal* in December 1934 to cover Pierre Laval's meetings with the Fascist regime; and, as his political views evolved in the mid- to late-1930s, he began to make regular contributions to the progressive Catholic journal *Sept*, and its replacement *Temps présent*.

Journalism was not something new for Mauriac. Indeed, he had been a frequent contributor to reviews and newspapers in the 1910s, writing for the *Journal de Clichy* in 1914, and for *Le Gaulois* between 1919 and 1921; but the author of these pieces was very much, as Jean Touzot puts it, 'Mauriac avant Mauriac'.[1] In spite of a promising entry into the literary field in 1910, when his first volume of poems, *Les Mains jointes*, was enthusiastically reviewed by Maurice Barrès, Mauriac had struggled to establish himself as a writer during the first ten years of his career. His novels failed to make a mark either commercially or critically, and his attempt in 1912 to establish a literary review which might rival the *NRF* – the first of three such efforts – came to nought. The publication of *Les Cahiers de*

---

[1] François Mauriac, *Mauriac avant Mauriac*, ed. by Jean Touzot (Paris: Flammarion, 1977). This volume contains a selection of articles and texts from the period up to 1921.

l'Amitié de France was interrupted by the First World War, and the journal would never reappear.[1]

The writer who signed to *L'Écho de Paris* in 1932, however, was a rather different beast from the one who had taken his leave of journalism in 1921. The intervening period, of course, is marked by his dramatic success as a novelist, which begins with *Le Baiser au lépreux* in 1922, and culminates in *Le Nœud de vipères* in 1932. Moreover, this success manages to be at once commercial – with *Le Baiser au lépreux*, Mauriac notes in 1965, 'je rompis pour la première fois le cercle étroit des trois mille exemplaires et j'atteignis le grand public: les éditions se succédaient' (OA 815) – and, above all, critical.

If *Le Baiser au lépreux* marks the beginnings of Mauriac's artistic success, it is because it represents the moment when his novels enter the circuits of legitimation and consecration, that is to say the processes by which a literary text (or any cultural product) is acknowledged and celebrated as having some sort of artistic merit. This happens in particular when an author's work begins to earn the recognition and respect of peers in the field, attracting the attention, and holding the interest, of other writers whose literary worth or value is already well established. In a letter to his wife shortly after the publication of *Le Baiser au lépreux*, Mauriac writes that 'toutes les lettres crient au chef-d'œuvre. *Même Valéry* trouve que c'est bien' (LV 117, Mauriac's emphasis). Moreover, like all well-adjusted actors in a field, Mauriac had clearly internalised and understood the rules of the particular game he had chosen to play: in a later letter to his wife, he shows himself to be acutely aware of the importance of such acts of recognition, and the symbolic or transformative power they possess, describing the enthusiastic critical reception of *Le Baiser au lépreux* as 'cet instant de mue entre le gigolo de lettres et le romancier' (LV 400).

The processes of consecration and recognition (as, also, of disavowal and rejection) are formalised in the review pages of literary journals, where writers assess and pass judgement on the work of their peers, and establish their current value. One particularly important measure of Mauriac's success was the increasingly warm reception given to his work by the *NRF*. As the 1920s progress, we can trace

---

[1] See Jean Touzot, 'Les trois avatars de la revue rivale', *Nouveaux Cahiers François Mauriac*, 8 (2000), 199-210. I discuss the other two attempts (*Vigile* and *La Table ronde*) below and in chapter 3.

how Mauriac's stock begins to rise, and he comes to be seen by the review as a complex and important writer. In his review of *Le Fleuve de feu* of 1923, for example, Jacques Rivière concludes that

> Chacun de ses romans non seulement est en progrès sur le précédent, mais encore contient de quoi faire rêver au delà de lui-même. C'est le signe d'un talent en pleine croissance et qui n'a pas fini de nous donner d'heureuses surprises.[2]

Just under two years later, Charles Du Bos would open his review of *Le Désert de l'amour* by arguing that Mauriac's work now required longer and more careful analysis: 'ce n'est pas en une note, mais dans l'étude que désormais son œuvre exige, qu'il conviendrait de parler de Mauriac'.[3] He went on to demonstrate this in an article which, at over five pages, was the longest the journal had yet devoted to Mauriac; and the study he calls for would be published in its pages five years later[4] (his own would follow in 1933[5]). Finally, after the triumph of *Le Nœud de vipères*, Marcel Arland could announce in 1933 that Mauriac's artistic talent was beyond doubt: 'il est peu de romanciers aujourd'hui dont le talent [...] soit moins discuté que celui de M. François Mauriac; et c'est à bon droit'.[6]

If the approbation of the *NRF* is especially significant, it is because of the peculiarly powerful role it played in the field at the time. In his discussion of the literary field, Pierre Bourdieu argues that central to its economy is not just the process of consecration, but also the possession of the monopoly on that process, in other words being acknowledged as the most important agent of legitimation and consecration. The history of the literary field can be read as an on-going struggle over the right to judge – judge, that is to say, who is a writer, what makes a good writer, and so on – and a struggle to

---

[2] Jacques Rivière, 'François Mauriac, *Le Fleuve de feu*', *La Nouvelle Revue française*, 118 (July 1923), p. 101.

[3] Charles Du Bos, 'François Mauriac, *Le Désert de l'amour*' *La Nouvelle Revue française*, 140 (May 1925), p. 936.

[4] Jean Prévost, 'De Mauriac à son œuvre', *La Nouvelle Revue française*, 198 (March 1930), 349-367.

[5] Charles Du Bos, *François Mauriac et le problème du romancier catholique* (Paris: Corréa, 1933)

[6] Marcel Arland, 'François Mauriac, *Le Mystère Frontenac*', *La Nouvelle Revue française*, 234 (March 1933), p. 519.

maintain that monopoly on judgement and consecration in the face of potential rivals. As Bourdieu puts it,

> Un des enjeux centraux des rivalités littéraires (etc.) est le monopole de la légitimité littéraire, c'est-à-dire, entre autres choses, le monopole du pouvoir de dire avec autorité qui est autorisé à se dire écrivain (etc.) ou même à dire qui est écrivain et qui a autorité pour dire qui est écrivain.[7]

I shall be discussing in more detail later how the *NRF* quickly began to win this struggle on its entry into the field in 1909, challenging and to a large extent usurping the existing systems of consecration (and in particular that represented by the Académie Française and the salons, which continued to dominate literary life in Paris into the early twentieth century). Following its return to the literary field in 1919, having been in suspended animation during the First World War, it would continue to hold the monopoly on the power of consecration for the whole of the inter-war period.

As Mauriac himself was well aware, the entry of the *NRF* into the literary field was nothing short of a revolution. Looking back on the period in *La Rencontre avec Barrès*, he observes that

> Les jeunes écrivains d'aujourd'hui auront peine à imaginer, [...] lorsque Alfred Capus régnait sur Paris, et que les grands écrivains de l'Académie ne se glorifiaient plus que de "servir", le prestige de ce petit groupe pur autour d'une revue en apparence modeste et comme nous passionnait son scrupule devant l'œuvre d'art. (OA 191)

He returns again to its significance in his interviews with Jean Amrouche in 1952: 'c'était la Loi et les Prophètes, et cela correspondait à mon sentiment profond. En ce sens, *La Nouvelle Revue française* a été importante, elle a été vraiment l'expression d'un besoin de notre génération' (SR 124). Its importance for him lay in the way it instigated a necessary correction or realignment of the values operating in the field: 'il s'agissait de remettre en place les vraies valeurs, et c'est ce qu'elle a fait' (SR 124). In the face of a literary establishment which had become distracted by the lure of political

---

[7] Pierre Bourdieu, *Les Règles de l'art*, p. 366. As Bourdieu's parentheses suggest, this analysis can be applied to all fields of cultural production.

power and worldly success (Mauriac is doubtless thinking of Maurice Barrès, first elected to the Assemblée nationale in 1889), and a market dominated by commercially successful but artistically mediocre writers (exemplified for Mauriac by the long-forgotten Capus), the *NRF* refocused attention on the proper business of literary creation.

Its efforts would be devoted to fostering a climate in which literary talent could be expressed and developed; and essential for this, as Mauriac's reference to the 'purity' of the group suggests, was maintaining the review as an environment free of any influence or hindrance from outside forces. For Jacques Rivière, writing in the review on its reappearance in 1919, the founding group of the *NRF* had set out to 'écarter les broussailles de toute sorte, j'entends les préoccupations d'ordre utilitaire, théorique ou moral, qui pouvaient gêner ou déformer la végétation spontanée du génie ou du talent'.[8] The relaunched *NRF* would continue in this vein, he argued: 'il reste nécessaire de purifier et de maintenir exempte de toute influence étrangère, l'atmosphère esthétique'.[9]

To put it another way, the importance of the *NRF* lies in the way it sets out to reassert the autonomy of the literary field within the broader field of power. I discussed briefly in the introduction how, as Bourdieu and others have argued, the mid- to late-nineteenth century in France sees the growing autonomy of the literary field within the larger field of political and economic power; that is to say, actors within the field can increasingly assert their own set of values, which are often independent from, not to say directly opposed to, the values and ideals which dominate in the field of power.

More precisely, a dualistic structure begins to emerge within the field, opposing two distinct poles around which coalesce rather different values and actors. At what Bourdieu terms the 'pôle hétéronome', or heteronymous pole, we find those writers who associate most closely with the dominant elements in the field of power. They are writers who are willing to submit to the demands and the tastes of the dominant fractions of society, and who are often rewarded as a result with commercial success (authors of best-selling fiction or boulevard theatre, for example); or those, such as Barrès and Henry Bordeaux, who signal their proximity to the dominant order by

---

[8] Jacques Rivière, 'La Nouvelle Revue française', *La Nouvelle Revue française*, 69 (June 1919), p. 2.
[9] Ibid., p. 3.

accepting honours and political positions, or seeking election to state-sponsored institutions such as the Académie Française. While such writers might achieve worldly glory and fame, it is less likely that they will have acquired artistic credibility.

At what Bourdieu terms the 'autonomous' pole, on the other hand, we find precisely the opposite ethos at work. The autonomous pole is defined above all by what he calls 'l'indépendance à l'égard des demandes externes'.[10] This independence is often asserted as a form of asceticism or disavowal, whereby what is seen as success in the dominant social sphere (commercial success, consecration by the dominant order in the form of election to the Académie, for instance) is seen as a sign of failure (moral as much as aesthetic) in the literary world. In effect, the 'economy' of the literary field at the autonomous pole is a mirror image of that in the broader social sphere: 'elle exclut la recherche du profit et elle ne garantit aucune espèce de correspondance entre les investissements et les revenus monétaires; elle condamne la poursuite des honneurs et des grandeurs temporelles'.[11] As we have seen, it is precisely these sorts of values to which the *NRF* lays claim, and which are expressed in various ways: firstly, in literary or artistic terms, through a manifesto or agenda based on the primacy and purity of the aesthetic, free from 'distorting' influences such as politics or morality; secondly, in terms of a broader ethos or position in the world which meant not just the disavowal, but the active denigration of worldly or social success.

The group was dismissive of those in the field who gravitated towards the heteronymous pole, and the existing systems of consecration, as Mauriac himself knew only too well. For if, in his early years in the field, Mauriac had failed to associate himself with the *NRF* group, it was due in part because of his frequenting of the literary salons. As he says in his interview with Jean Amrouche, 'j'étais aussi pour eux un petit-bourgeois salonnard sans intérêt' (SR 121); and as he points out in the same breath, Gide rejected *À la recherche du temps perdu* for similar reasons when Proust first

---

[10] *Les Règles de l'art*, p. 356.
[11] Ibid. For further discussion of the opposition between the heteronymous and autonomous poles of the literary field, see pp. 353-365 ('Le champ littéraire dans le champ du pouvoir'). On the position and role of the Académie Française in the literary field, see Gisèle Sapiro, *La Guerre des écrivains* (Paris: Fayard, 1999), pp. 250-261.

submitted it to the *NRF*: 'Gide a ouvert le manuscrit et l'a écarté parce qu'il avait cette idée préconçue que Proust était un salonnard' (SR 121).[12] In the light of this, the crowning success of *Le Nœud de vipères*, and Mauriac's recognition and final consecration by the *NRF* – both in terms of its acknowledgement of his work's interest, and in terms of his appearance in its pages as a reviewer and contributor – might seem to be something of a victory for him, especially in the way it appears to confirm his proximity to the autonomous pole of production.[13]

Moreover, if Mauriac can develop his journalistic career so rapidly and so successfully in the 1930s, it is precisely because he can capitalise on the prestige he had acquired during the 1920s. He does so in two distinct ways. Literally, first of all: journalism presents him with an opportunity to convert the symbolic capital represented by the acclaim and recognition of his peers into economic capital. When Mauriac returns to the field, it is very much as a 'grande plume', a well-known name whom papers are willing to attract to their columns.[14] Nor should this financial motive be overlooked or dismissed when considering Mauriac's reasons for returning to the journalistic field, as he himself acknowledges both at the time and when he looks back: 'une vocation de journaliste comme la mienne naît de la rencontre d'une exigence très haute et d'une exigence, sinon très basse, du moins très médiocre' (MP 17). The 'exigence très haute', the lofty demands made of him, are those which he will start to feel during the time of the Spanish Civil War in particular.

However, it is the other, rather less glamorous motives which drive him initially:

---

[12] Cf. Gide's comments to Proust himself in a letter from January 1914, describing his initial impressions of Proust as 'un snob, un mondain amateur, quelque chose d'on ne peut plus fâcheux pour notre revue'. *Autour de* La Recherche: *correspondance Marcel Proust-André Gide*, ed. by Pierre Assouline (Paris: Editions Complexe, 1988), p. 10.

[13] On his contributions to the review, see John Flower, 'Mauriac's contributions to the *Nouvelle Revue française*', in John Flower and Bernard Swift (eds), *François Mauriac: Visions and Reappraisals* (Oxford: Berg, 1989), pp. 117-131.

[14] Mauriac's Rome articles for *Le Journal* in December 1934 are perhaps the best example of this. The paper had a habit of inviting famous writers to carry out *reportages* for them: Colette would sail on the inaugural voyage of the liner *Normandie* six months later, for example.

> Quant à l'exigence médiocre, c'est celle qui oblige un écrivain
> [...] à arrondir, comme on dit, ses fins de mois. Eh oui, il ne faut
> pas avoir honte, à l'heure du bilan, de mettre en lumière ces
> motifs de notre action qui ont compté plus que les sublimes peut-
> être pour nous mettre une plume de journaliste à la main. (MP 17)

Indeed, in his correspondence with Louis Brun (general manager of the publishing house Grasset) during the early 1930s, as he attempts to renegotiate his contract, Mauriac makes several references to his financial difficulties. In May 1932, he writes: 'j'aurais aimé causer avec vous au sujet de mon traité: vous constatez avec moi que ce succès ne diminue guère le fardeau de ma dette' (NLV 147). He had already somewhat gloomily predicted in September 1931, in the face of Brun's resistance, that 'je commencerai à quarante-six ans une carrière de journaliste et de nouvelliste' (NLV 143). Ironically, it could be said that during this period, Mauriac finds himself having to deal with the consequences of the inversed economic logic working at the autonomous pole, whereby artistic success, if it generates symbolic capital in the short term, in the form of recognition from one's peers, tends to bring true economic success only in the longer term.[15] While the texts he produces in the 1920s coincide sufficiently with the dominant understanding of literariness in place at the autonomous pole to earn him the interest and respect of his peers, their commercial success was not quite enough, in the short term at least, to give him complete financial security: it was only in the 1950s that Mauriac could be considered a wealthy man.[16]

The second way in which Mauriac exploits his newly-acquired prestige is to negotiate or stake out his own position in the field. For it is noticeable that despite winning the recognition of the *NRF* during the 1920s, he does not automatically align himself with it. Indeed, it soon becomes clear that his trajectory during the 1930s will be defined in particular by a largely antagonistic relationship with the autonomous pole. A striking indication of Mauriac's attitude comes in

---

[15] See *Les Règles de l'art*, pp. 235-236.
[16] See Jean Lacouture, *François Mauriac*, 2 vols (Paris: Seuil, coll. "Points", 1990), II, pp. 11-12. Lacouture notes that 45,000 copies of *Le Nœud de vipères* were printed in its first year. While a significant increase on his first novels, such a print run was modest when compared to his contemporaries. Bernanos' *Sous le soleil de Satan* sold 140,000 copies in its first year, for example; and at the heteronymous pole, writers such as Henry Bordeaux could usually expect print runs in excess of 600,000.

his first few months as a columnist for *L'Écho de Paris*, when he devotes two articles to an attack on Gide, perhaps its most iconic or prominent representative.

The first article, 'Qui triche?', published in July 1932, focuses on the question of sincerity and its relationship with religious faith.[17] The article opens with a critical discussion of Gide's conception of the self, which Mauriac compares unfavourably with that of Barrès. He argues that Barrès' efforts to reconcile his inner discordances represent a more sincere form of existence than Gide's attitude that sincerity – if such a thing is possible – lies in the recognition and cultivation of the conflicting desires and facets of the self. He then mounts a defence of faith in the face of Gide's criticism of religion as a discipline imposed on the self, and therefore an obstacle to sincerity, accusing Gide of hypocrisy in the process. If anyone is guilty of cheating, says Mauriac, it is Gide, who wilfully misunderstands the nature of religious belief. As Gide well knows, argues Mauriac, faith is not simply a question of a discipline to which one must submit, but of love for a real individual in the form of Christ. The second article, published in September 1932, condemns Gide's recently proclaimed 'conversion' to Communism, and his enthusiastic support for the USSR, in scathingly ironic terms: 'Moscou attire plusieurs Messieurs écrivains, fort délicats et subtils – et le premier de tous, M. André Gide, que le plan quinquennal plonge dans le plus curieux délire'.[18]

What lies behind Mauriac's attack on Gide at this point? The relationship between Mauriac and Gide is a long, complex and often tense one.[19] Broadly speaking, it was marked in the early 1930s by Mauriac's increasing hostility towards Gide's position. Central to this was the two writers' radically different conceptions of the self. Mauriac's understanding, of course, had been shaped since childhood by the moral framework of the Catholic faith, and structured around the oppositions of good and evil, body and soul. For him, an

---

[17] François Mauriac, 'Qui triche?', *L'Écho de Paris*, 16 juillet 1932, p. 1. Repr. in André Gide, François Mauriac, *Correspondance (1912-1950)*, ed. by Jacqueline Morton, *Cahiers André Gide*, 2 (Paris: Gallimard, 1971), pp. 152-155.
[18] François Mauriac, 'Les esthètes fascinés', *L'Écho de Paris*, 10 September 1932, p. 1. Repr. in André Gide, François Mauriac, *Correspondance (1912-1950)*, pp. 156-160.
[19] For a detailed comparative study of the work of the two men and their relationship, see Malcolm Scott, *Mauriac et Gide: la recherche du Moi* (Bordeaux: L'Esprit du Temps, 2004).

individual's efforts should be directed towards self-knowledge, which meant primarily a lucid awareness of the perils posed by the body and its desires. With this lucidity comes moral responsibility, a requirement to police the self, to regulate and control its problematic urges. Moreover, lucidity and self-control are vital because they bring with them the possibility – though not, for a Mauriac whose Catholicism had a distinctly Jansenistic edge, the guarantee – of salvation.[20] As a result, Mauriac could be nothing other than deeply troubled by the Gidian conception of the self, which he saw as celebrating moral dissolution and encouraging the exploration of corrupting desires in the name of sincerity.

He was increasingly angered too by Gide's persistent interrogation of ideas and institutions which were central to Mauriac's essentially conservative morality. What attracts Gide to Communism, notes Mauriac in 1932, is that he sees it sweeping away religious faith and traditional family structures, two things against which he had always struggled: 'la seule contrainte qu'il redoute, cette loi morale que fortifient, contre nous-même, la religion et la famille, il la croit vaincue enfin; victoire que, selon lui, on ne saurait payer trop cher!'.[21] In Mauriac's eyes, Gide's enthusiasm for Communism is motivated more than anything by his fundamental antagonism towards Christianity, which Mauriac in turn feels called upon to defend. As he explains in a letter to Jean Paulhan, 'je n'attacherais aucune importance au bolchevisme de Gide, si ce qui l'y attirait n'était précisément, l'*antéchrist*, ou, pour être plus exact, l'antireligion – si, pour lui, la question n'était avant tout religieuse'.[22]

Mauriac was also disturbed by what he saw as the growing anti-Christian tone of the *NRF* more generally during this period.

---

[20] For further discussion of Mauriac's moral position, and the ways in which it is shaped by his upbringing and education, see Edward Welch, 'A "Catholic Novelist" in Context: suggestions for a reassessment of the work of François Mauriac' (unpublished doctoral thesis, University of Oxford, 2000), pp. 45-57. See also Malcolm Scott, *Mauriac: The Politics of a Novelist*, pp. 41-48. On the influence of Jansenism, see Margaret Mein, 'François Mauriac and Jansenism', in John Flower and Bernard Swift (eds), *François Mauriac: Visions and Reappraisals*, pp. 147-164.
[21] François Mauriac, 'Les esthètes fascinés', p. 159.
[22] François Mauriac, Jean Paulhan, *Correspondance (1925-1967)*, ed. by John Flower (Paris: Editions Claire Paulhan, 2001), p. 107. Mauriac's emphasis. On Gide's flirtation with Communism, see also Malcolm Scott, *Mauriac et Gide*, pp. 108-116, and Michel Winock, *Le Siècle des intellectuels*, pp. 272-283.

Writing to Claudel in 1929, he comments that 'chaque numéro de la
NRF soufflette Jésus. Ils vont publier dans quelques mois je ne sais
quel chapitre de Flavius Josèphe, retrouvé par les Soviets d'où il
ressort que le Christ était bossu!!' (LV 154). His sensitivity to this is
itself the result of recent events in his own life, namely the moral and
spiritual crisis of late 1928 which led to his 'conversion', or more
accurately, the reassertion of his faith. Mauriac emerges from this
period a newly fervent, even zealous Christian, keen to combat what
he sees as nothing less than the moral delinquency of Gide and the
NRF.[23]

Mauriac's response to the challenge posed by the *NRF* is a
bold and interesting one: he persuades Grasset to let him set up a new
review, *Vigile* (that he can do this is itself a result of his recently
acquired prestige, and his status as one of Grasset's most successful
authors), which he fully intends will serve as a counterweight to the
NRF and even, he hopes, challenge its pre-eminence. 'Il s'agit de faire
contrepoids à l'esprit *NRF*', he says to Claudel in a letter setting out
his aims (LV 153). The journal would provide a rallying point for
Catholic writers. Indeed, its pages would be open only to practising
Catholics, and their submissions would be scrutinised by a censor, the
abbé Altermann, who had been Mauriac's spiritual mentor and
confessor during his crisis. Moreover, in the same way that the *NRF*
orbited around the figure of Gide, Mauriac was intent on securing the
patronage and collaboration of Claudel, the dominant Catholic writer
of the time, who would be the centre of gravity of *Vigile*: 'vous
comprenez que dans notre esprit, cette revue sera *votre* revue' (LV
153, Mauriac's emphasis). The first number would be published in
1930, and feature texts by Claudel, Mauriac and Charles Du Bos; but
the review would prove to be short-lived, running out of steam in
1933 after thirteen issues, having been described by Gide as a
'monument d'ennui'.[24] Nearly twenty years after *Les Cahiers de
l'Amitié de France*, a review led by Mauriac had once again failed to
impose itself in the field.[25]

---

[23] On the spiritual crisis of 1928, see Jean Lacouture, *François Mauriac*, I, ch. 11, and
below.
[24] André Gide, *Journal (1926-1950)*, ed. Martine Sagaert, (Paris: Gallimard, "Bibl. de
la Pléiade", 1997), p. 187.
[25] On *Vigile*, see also Jean Touzot, 'Les trois avatars de la revue rivale'.

Looking back in 1965, Mauriac expresses indifference at the failure of *Vigile*, obscured for him by his successes: 'le ratage de *Vigile* était compensé dans ma vie par trop de réussites pour que j'en souffrisse vraiment' (OA 749); but the adventure, and its failure, remain significant for two reasons, both of which illustrate aspects of the literary field at this time. Firstly, Mauriac's attempt to challenge the dominant position of the *NRF* by launching a rival review shows once again, at one level, an intuitive understanding of the rules governing the field in which he is operating. For as Anna Boschetti has pointed out, and as we have seen in relation to the *NRF*, one of the most significant developments in the literary field in the twentieth century is the growing importance of the review as a way of intervening in the field and shifting its balance of power, particularly in order to establish new and avant-garde positions.[26]

At the same time, if Mauriac's review fails, it does so in part at least because it misreads the nature of the field at another level. Writing to Claudel in 1932, Mauriac acknowledges one of the key problems faced by *Vigile*: 'en effet, du moment que nous nous soumettons à un censeur ecclésiastique, il devenait par le fait même le maître absolu de la publication' (LV 189). In submitting freely to the will of its censor, *Vigile* goes against the principle of literary autonomy which is enshrined at the autonomous pole as the guarantor of artistic integrity. By abandoning literary freedom, and surrendering to external ideological pressures, the review loses all likelihood of usurping the *NRF* from its position of dominance in the field.[27] Moreover, as Mauriac himself admits with hindsight, the collaborators

---

[26] Anna Boschetti, 'Des revues et des hommes', *La Revue des revues*, 18 (1994), 51-65.

[27] This is certainly the case given the nature of the field during the inter-war period. However, while the bipolar structure of the field identified by Bourdieu persists throughout the twentieth century, the criteria by which literary excellence is judged at the autonomous pole vary over time. As we shall see in chapter 3, the fate of the *NRF* itself illustrates the often rapid changes in the perception and definition of literary excellence which take place in the field. In the wake of the Liberation, when the disappearance of the *NRF* had left the way open for Sartre and *Les Temps modernes* to lay claim to the autonomous pole, it is precisely the notion of literary autonomy which will be called into question. Literary success and excellence will be defined by a work's political and ideological intent, the degree to which it engages with the world; and writers who fail to do this will be deemed 'irresponsible'.

themselves soon realised the damage being done to literature by Altermann in the name of religion:

> Il éplucha le premier numéro ligne par ligne, et tous les autres, sans aucun scrupule d'ordre littéraire, ce qui faisait horreur à Du Bos aux yeux de qui il n'y avait pas de pires attentats que ceux perpétrés contre les textes. (OA 748)

The reasons for *Vigile*'s failure help to crystallise the crucial and inescapable point of conflict between Mauriac and the *NRF*, itself related to an irreconcilable contradiction facing Mauriac himself. On the one hand, we see here that Mauriac and Du Bos recognise, and to a certain extent subscribe to, the principle of literary and aesthetic autonomy (Du Bos, after all, had been a long-time collaborator of the *NRF*); but the on other hand, the primacy of the aesthetic over all other concerns – and moral concerns especially – was one Mauriac had always struggled to accept, and was finding it increasingly difficult to do so. Where Gide would argue that the ethical derives from the aesthetic, Mauriac would argue the precise opposite. For him, the moral must always govern and inform the aesthetic. From *La Vie et la mort d'un poète* of 1924, Mauriac's writing about literature is dominated by the theme of the writer's moral responsibility. The idea finds one of its clearest expressions in the *Mémoires intérieurs* of 1959, appropriately enough in the context of a discussion about sexuality in the work of Gide: 'plus j'y songe et plus je me persuade que l'esthétique appelle l'éthique. La maîtrise, c'est le mot même qui s'impose à l'artiste et à l'homme' (OA 553). Just as the individual has a moral duty to work towards lucidity and self-knowledge, so too the writer must keep himself in check and govern what he writes. The failure or unwillingness to do so is nothing less than criminal and moral neglect.[28]

Ironically, though, not only was such neglect to be found in the work of Gide or in the pages of the *NRF*, but it was also something he had been forced to confront in his own novels. For the roots of Mauriac's strong moral conservatism of the early 1930s lie in his

---

[28] On Mauriac's conception of the relationship between the moral and the aesthetic, and its impact on his writing practice, see Welch, 'A "Catholic Novelist" in Context', pp. 57-66. His concerns can be seen to translate into a mode of writing imitating that of the authors of the seventeenth century, whose understanding of the passions of man, for Mauriac, derived from the clarity of their style and its precision.

artistic success in the 1920s. The work he produces during this period
– morally ambiguous, sensuously and sexually charged – brings him
into conflict not just with the religious authorities and the Catholic
Establishment[29] but also with himself, as he grapples with the problem
that artistic creation can overwhelm moral intention, and as such can
be quite simply incompatible with the demands of the Christian faith.

The tension of this contradiction, and the pressures it places
on Mauriac, will be famously articulated by Gide in his open letter to
him, published in the *NRF* in June 1928. Mauriac's work, he suggests,
is marked by a desperate attempt to find a compromise between the
irreconcilable demands of art and faith:

> En somme, ce que vous cherchez, c'est la permission d'écrire
> *Destins*; la permission d'être chrétien sans avoir à brûler vos
> livres; et c'est ce qui vous les fait écrire de telle sorte que, bien
> que chrétien, vous n'ayez pas à les désavouer. (ORTC II 833)

The cruel irony for Mauriac is that a tension which he comes to see as
an irresolvable problem is precisely what, for Gide, makes Mauriac's
novels an artistic success:

> Tout cela (ce compromis rassurant qui permet d'aimer Dieu sans
> perdre de vue Mammon), tout cela nous vaut cette conscience
> angoissée qui donne tant d'attrait à votre visage, tant de saveur à
> vos écrits. (ORTC II 833)[30]

The moody and disconcerting texts which he finds himself writing are
the key to his recognition and consecration by the autonomous pole.
Indeed, the publication of Gide's letter in the pages of the *NRF* can be
seen to mark a significant stage in that process, proof that his work
merits the sustained attention of the autonomous pole's most eminent

---

[29] See Jean Touzot, 'Quand Mauriac était scandaleux...', *Œuvres et Critique*, 2
(1977), 133-144.

[30] I argue elsewhere that this tension emerges particularly in the insistent presence of
the body in his fiction. Indeed, the distinctive 'flavour' Gide identifies can be traced
to a disjunction in Mauriac's writing practice between its syntactic and lexical
dimensions. While Mauriac's syntax is invested with a moral force aimed at
articulating and therefore neutralising desires and urges, the words he uses to describe
the body foreground its materiality and draw it forcefully to our attention. See 'Le
carnaval perverti de François Mauriac', in Edward Welch (ed.), *Masque et carnaval
dans la littérature européenne* (Paris: L'Harmattan, 2002), pp. 39-53.

representative. At the same time, however, the publication of Gide's letter will also bring to a head the spiritual crisis and conversion which will lead Mauriac to reassess his artistic practice, and reassert the primacy of the moral over the aesthetic. Mauriac's increasing hostility towards the corrupt and corrupting work of his contemporaries is coupled with a conscious effort to write more 'Catholic' novels which, *Le Nœud de vipères* apart, marks the beginning of his less successful period, not to say decline as a novelist.[31]

Mauriac's attacks on Gide in 1932 signal a definitive shift in position in the early 1930s in the wake of his moral and spiritual crisis, and a desire to signal his distance from the autonomous pole represented by the *NRF*. He repeatedly declines Jean Paulhan's frequent invitations to contribute to the review during this period, for example.[32] That he has the confidence to stake out his position in this way is due, ironically, to his recent consecration by the *NRF*; but his reluctance to accept its ethos, and his concomitant insistence on subordinating the aesthetic to the demands of the moral, mark out a boundary which separates him from it. Moreover, the irreducible distance between them would soon be articulated and confirmed in other ways.

Making a choice: Mauriac and the Académie Française

'J'étais classé à droite', observes Mauriac in the *Nouveaux mémoires intérieurs*, as he looks back at the early 1930s (OA 815). Despite a rather sly use of the passive to imply that this was a label imposed on him, Mauriac certainly did enough to merit it during the period. There was no more telling signal of Mauriac's political position than the choice he made on his return to the journalistic field. By writing in *L'Écho de Paris*, even if only a handful of his articles were overtly

---

[31] On the novels of the 1930s, see Marie-Françoise Canérot, *Mauriac après 1930: le roman dénoué* (Paris: SEDES, 1985). Mauriac's efforts in this direction will be praised by Claudel in 1929, whose criticism of the increasing 'perversity' of his novels during the 1920s provides a instructive counterpoint to Gide's opinion. The voice of the moral order condemns and casts out the devil of aesthetic and artistic freedom: 'depuis *Le Fleuve de feu* déjà si inquiétant, si votre talent n'a cessé de s'affirmer, votre sentiment de la moralité n'a cessé de s'obscurcir, jusqu'à ce que nous arrivons dans *Destins* à une véritable perversité. Je suis heureux de penser que cette phase est finie.' Paul Claudel, François Mauriac, *Correspondance (1911-1954)*, ed. by Michel Malicet and Marie-Chantal Praicheux (Paris: Minard, 1988), p. 20.
[32] François Mauriac, Jean Paulhan, *Correspondance (1925-1967)*, pp. 108-109.

political, he aligned himself clearly with the Catholic and conservative establishment. In joining the newspaper, he was following in the footsteps of some of the key figures of the intellectual right, such as Barrès and Paul Bourget. Moreover, the political opinions he did express, both in *L'Écho de Paris* and in *Le Figaro*, to which he moved in 1934, echoed those of the conservative bourgeoisie of the period: hostility towards parliamentary democracy;[33] fear of the threat posed by Communism;[34] a certain admiration for the right-wing dictatorships in Italy and Spain in their early days.[35]

Another important indication of Mauriac's political position at this time, and beyond that, his sense of his place in the social order, comes when he is elected to the Académie Française in June 1933. This will prove to be a crucial moment in his trajectory, one which produces unexpected consequences. His election to an institution which, through its relationship to the State and the social status of its constituting members, is located firmly at the heteronymous pole of the literary field and therefore in the orbit of the dominant pole of the field of political and economic power more generally, would seem to locate Mauriac definitively within the literary field. It suggests a certain choice made, a certain orientation in the form of his increasing alignment with the heteronymous pole. Inversely, it would also seem to stand as a concrete manifestation of the ideological differences

---

[33] 'Le peuple et les penseurs', *L'Écho de Paris*, 14 April 1934, repr. in MP 43-46.

[34] 'Qui triche?', 'Les esthètes fascinés', and 'La voix de Thorez', *Le Figaro*, 22 April 1936, repr. in MP 56-58.

[35] 'Les beaux jours de Rome', *Le Figaro*, 18 January 1935, repr. in *Journal*, II (OC XI 144-146), and 'L'Internationale de la haine', *Le Figaro*, 25 July 1936. The fate of both these articles illustrates the way in which the later Mauriac, who had broken with the Right and adopted more liberal views, was not averse to a certain amount of historical revisionism in order to elide his initial political positions. Jean Touzot notes that when 'Les beaux jours de Rome' came to be republished in 1937, Mauriac removed the warm praise for Mussolini which closes the original article, to take into account changes in both world politics and his own political position. See Jean Touzot, 'Mauriac chez les "hommes-sandwiches" (1925-1935)', p. 36, n. 40. Similarly, the second article, in which Mauriac supports Franco's actions and condemns the attempts of the *Front populaire* government to intervene in the Spanish Civil War, was also quietly forgotten when he came to compile his *Mémoires politiques* in 1967, failing as it did to conform to the straightforward narrative of support of the Basques and the Republican cause which he wanted to underline. For an overview of Mauriac's political views during the early to mid-1930s, see Jean Lacouture, *François Mauriac*, II, pp. 11-23, and Malcolm Scott, *Mauriac: The Politics of a Novelist*, pp. 67-72.

which separate him from the autonomous pole represented by the *NRF*. Yet we shall see that, contrary to expectations, his membership of the Académie Française is in fact responsible for inflecting his trajectory in an entirely different direction. If Mauriac's political views and position-takings become increasingly radical as the 1930s progress, it is due in no small part to his membership of this body.

One of the most crucial influences on Mauriac's trajectory throughout his career is in fact the result of a historical accident. His entry into the literary field happens to coincide with a significant turning point in its history, for 1909 marks not just the publication of *Les Mains jointes*, his first volume of poetry, but also the launch of the *NRF*. I indicated above that the importance of the *NRF* lies in the way it challenges and usurps the dominant systems of consecration represented by State-sponsored institutions such as the Académie Française, and the more informal social networks of the literary salons. Success would depend no longer on a reputation established in the literary salons and the patronage of a social elite, but on recognition by a literary and artistic elite which acted as the guardian of values protected from, and at odds with, those of the social and political order. While the *NRF* was not the first journal of its type – it has important predecessors in the *Mercure de France* and Péguy's *Cahiers de la quinzaine*, for example – we can see its launch as marking the point at which the new system had acquired sufficient momentum and capital (both economic and symbolic) finally to displace the existing order.

As Anna Boschetti has argued, this moment of transition can be seen as the culmination of the rapid evolution affecting the literary field since the late nineteenth century as it acquired its autonomy within the broader field of power, a process which is itself the result of a complex series of historical, social and cultural changes affecting the economy of literary production.[36] Boschetti identifies the growth in readership during the mid to late nineteenth century (the consequence of social and educational reforms which contribute to the expansion of the professional classes) as being a key factor in this change. The expansion in the number of readers during this period in turn enables and supports an expanding market of literary reviews, which become

---

[36] Anna Boschetti, 'Légitimité littéraire et stratégies éditoriales', in *Histoire de l'édition française*, ed. by Roger Chartier, 4 vols (Paris: Promodis, 1984-86), IV, pp. 481-527.

increasingly important in the late Nineteenth Century as places where
new and young writers can publish. The increasing financial security
afforded by a more readily accessible income allows some reviews,
such as the *Mercure de France*, to branch out into publishing by
setting up their own *comptoirs d'édition*.

Another important development during this period is the
emergence of literary 'entrepreneurs' such as Bernard Grasset, who
establishes his publishing house in 1907. Grasset sets out to exploit
the expanding readership and encourage it further, in particular by
seeking coverage in the literary pages of the mainstream press. At the
same time, he shows himself willing to promote and make speculative
investments in new, young writers such as Mauriac, who would sign
to Grasset in 1922. A significant consequence of his approach, and in
particular the appeal to a wider public and the courting of press
coverage, is the by-passing of the established circuits of legitimation
and consecration represented by the literary salons.

The *NRF* combines both these strands when it appoints
Gaston Gallimard in 1911 to manage and develop its own *comptoir
d'éditions*. Creating an in-house publishing operation proves to be a
potently successful idea. Not only does it provide a way of exploiting
the symbolic resources of the group, but its resultant economic
success further ensures the review's independence and protects its
values from outside interference. That the complete autonomy of the
field has been achieved at this point is arguably signalled by the
founding of publishing houses which, by subscribing to – and in the
case of Gallimard, symbolising – the values at work at the
autonomous pole, and by acquiring significant economic power, can
act as its guarantors. At the same time, the existing system of
legitimation and consecration, which was dependent upon the
dominant social and political classes for its operation, can be
definitively abandoned as the field acquires sufficient autonomy to
regulate itself. Boschetti observes that

> C'est tout le système de légitimation jusqu'alors dominant qui
> s'écroule peu à peu, tout le circuit des agents et des institutions
> qui, ayant partie liée avec la classe dominante, sont l'expression
> d'une ingérence directe de celle-ci au sein de la vie littéraire. La
> *Revue des deux mondes*, Anatole France, voire l'Académie, font

de plus en plus figure de survivants dès lors que le champ peut à lui seul assurer la gloire à ses élus.[37]

As we saw earlier, the arrival of the *NRF* triggers a radical polarisation of the field between the autonomous pole it represents, and the heteronymous pole embodied by the Académie Française and the literary salons. That their rivalry is conscious is clear from the way in which they confront each other openly: the demonisation of the *NRF*, and Gide in particular, by those at the heteronymous pole is repaid by hostile or dismissive reviews of their work by the opposing camp.[38] This mutual antagonism can be understood as the sign of a struggle for power which is provoked by the emergence of the *NRF*, and its creation of a new position in the field. The rivalry between the two institutions illustrates the cycles of innovation, displacement and decline through which the history of the literary field is created.

The *NRF*'s seizure of the autonomous pole, to position itself at the avant-garde of literary production, has the effect of dating all existing positions and relegating them to the past: they are the old against which the new defines itself. As Bourdieu puts it, 'chaque acte artistique qui fait date en introduisant une position nouvelle dans le champ "déplace" la série toute entière des actes artistiques antérieurs'.[39] The emergence of the *NRF* gives new meaning to the existing positions and the institutions (such as the Académie Française) which embody them, and changes the existing relationships of power in the field. With the triumph of the new comes a threat to the pre-eminence of the old, and the beginning of its decline.[40]

---

[37] Anna Boschetti, 'Légitimité littéraire et stratégies éditoriales', p. 491.

[38] Reviewing an novel by Henry Bordeaux in 1914, for example, Albert Thibaudet writes that 'il est vrai que M. Bordeaux est, en bien des points, un auteur faible'. Cit. in Gisèle Sapiro, *La Guerre des écrivains*, p. 221.

[39] Pierre Bourdieu, *Les Règles de l'art*, p. 266.

[40] For Bourdieu, 'lorsqu'un nouveau groupe littéraire ou artistique s'impose dans le champ, tout l'espace des positions et l'espace des possibles correspondants, donc toute la problématique, s'en trouvent transformés: avec son accès à l'existence [...] c'est l'univers des options possibles qui se trouve modifié, les productions jusque-là dominantes pouvant, par exemple, être renvoyées au statut de produit déclassé ou classique'. *Les Règles de l'art*, p. 384. Pinto points out that artistic innovations define themselves against both the 'bourgeois' art of the heteronymous pole, and the existing avant-garde. Thus, the *NRF* rivalled not only the Académie Française, but also the established avant-garde represented by Symbolism. See Louis Pinto, *Pierre Bourdieu et la théorie du monde social* (Paris: Seuil, coll. "Points", 2002), pp. 114-116.

Mauriac was well aware of this in 1955, when he wrote that the pre-war literary field was defined by 'une constante montée des valeurs défendues par la *Nouvelle Revue française* et d'une baisse non moins continue, suivie d'un total effondrement, de celles que prônaient l'Académie française et la *Revue des Deux Mondes*'.[41] Moreover, this newly polarised and remodelled field is what he himself had to negotiate when he made his entrance in 1909; and like a magnet attracted by two opposing forces, the first part of his career will be marked by his oscillation between them.

In March 1910, Mauriac's first volume of poetry is the subject of an enthusiastic article by Barrès in *L'Écho de Paris*.[42] The moment will take on a totemic status for the rest of his life as marking the start of his career, his birth as a writer. He comments in 1968 that 'c'était comme si m'avait touché la baguette d'un enchanteur, et je crois bien aujourd'hui que Barrès en eut conscience lui-même' (BN V 16). The article signals Mauriac's recognition not just by an established figure, but one with a great amount of prestige. Barrès stood as a dominant cultural force at the time, above all because of the way he had managed to accumulate success across the different literary, political and social domains, being at once a successful author, a parliamentarian and a member of the Académie Française.

Recognition by Barrès also brings with it both a certain fame and access to the Parisian salons, where the literary men were still keen to mingle with and cultivate the social aristocracy, and in which Mauriac was happy to circulate. Writing in *Du côté de chez Proust*, he observes that, 'influencé par Balzac, je croyais naïvement aux "salons" comme seul un provincial peut y croire' (OA 275); and he recalls Lucien Daudet saying to him, 'je vais faire pour vous une chose très importante: je vais vous présenter à la marquise d'Aryragues' (OA 275). While Mauriac's early career moves would have been unproblematic in the previous state of the field, they are rather less of a guarantee of success in its new configuration, when a new set of rules are at work.

Mauriac gets a taste of this in 1912, when he publishes an article in *La Revue hebdomadaire* on 'La Jeunesse littéraire', which

---

[41] François Mauriac, 'Histoire politique de l'Académie française. 3: le nouveau chef', in *La Paix des cimes*, ed. by Jean Touzot (Paris: Bartillat, 2000), p. 553.
[42] Reprinted in *La Rencontre avec Barrès*, Mauriac's account of the early years of his career in Paris. See OA 194-197.

offers a survey of the trends in the field at the time. 'Jamais on ne vit jeunesse si férue d'ordre et de discipline', he suggests, having identified Maurice Barrès and Paul Bourget as two of the most important influences on the new generation of writers.[43] More pertinent than this tendentious analysis is the almost simultaneous reply to his piece published by Alain-Fournier in *Paris-Journal*, which opens with a pithy and dismissive account of Mauriac's poetry: 'c'est la poésie d'un enfant riche et fort intelligent qui ne se salit jamais en jouant, qui a la croix chaque samedi et qui va à la messe tous les dimanches'.[44] If Alain-Fournier's response is important, it is because, as Jacques Rivière's brother-in-law, he serves here as the voice of the autonomous pole, disowning Mauriac and putting him firmly in his place.[45] Mauriac is little more than the 'salonnard' who will have to wait ten years before he produces work interesting enough to warrant their attention.

One of the key problems facing Mauriac is that while he enters a field which has undergone a fundamental change, he does so with a perception and understanding of it formed during, and adapted to, its previous state. As the older and wiser Mauriac suggests in the quotation above, the literary salons in the mind of the young Mauriac, his imagination fuelled by nineteenth-century myths of the conquest of Paris and worldly glory, are still places where reputations are made rather than damaged. Also interesting, however, is the fact that he will continue to invest in this outmoded perception of the field as his career evolves, and the changing nature of the field has emerged. For even as he seeks and starts to receive the recognition of the *NRF* in the early 20s, his sights remain firmly set on the Académie Française.

During this period, we can see him engage actively in what Gisèle Sapiro terms a strategy of 'double jeu'.[46] By this, she means that Mauriac attempts to maximise the profits available from both poles – worldly success on the one hand, recognition from his artistic

---

[43] François Mauriac, 'La Jeunesse littéraire', *La Revue hebdomadaire*, 6 April 1912, p. 60.

[44] Alain-Fournier, 'Une enquête sur la jeunesse littéraire', *Paris-Journal*, 5 April 1912.

[45] Alain-Fournier receives Rivière's approbation in a letter shortly afterwards: 'je trouve très bien sa note sur Mauriac (lequel nous embête avec son ordre et sa discipline)'. Jacques Rivière, Alain-Fournier, *Correspondance (1904-1914)*, ed. by Alain Rivière and Pierre de Gaulmyn, 2 vols (Paris: Gallimard, 1991), II, p. 472.

[46] Gisèle Sapiro, *La Guerre des écrivains*, p. 219.

peers on the other. This strategy is revealed most strikingly when Mauriac declines Jacques Rivière's offer to write an article for the *NRF* on Paul Bourget, one of the most emblematic figures of the old guard, and above all, a member of the Académie Française. As he says in a letter to Rivière, 'il me semble que je serais capable d'écrire sur lui une bonne étude dans le genre féroce – mais mon devoir et mon intérêt s'accordent pour une fois à m'en détourner' (LV 123). Mauriac knowingly keeps his options open by avoiding an article which would have signalled his proximity to the *NRF*, especially since, as he implies, it would have to be suitably critical in tone. Moreover, the strategy is arguably a successful one, Mauriac being one of very few writers in the interwar period to be recognised and consecrated both by the *NRF* and by the Académie Française, and the only one to whom this happens more or less simultaneously.[47]

To understand why Mauriac's hesitation between the two poles of the field is ultimately resolved in favour of the Académie Française, we must take into account his own complex and contradictory nature, which he frequently acknowledges, and the way in which this is influenced by his background. Mauriac's oscillation is provoked not just by the polarised field in which he is operating, but also by the coexistence of conflicting dispositions making up what Bourdieu would term his 'habitus' (the socially acquired system of attitudes and perceptions which shape his vision of the world and his actions).[48] Its resolution will be determined to a large extent by which of these dispositions prove to be the strongest or the most influential.

On the one hand, he demonstrates the values and attitudes which align him with the autonomous pole, chief among which is an indifference to worldly success and a desire simply to express his poetic vision. As he puts it in 1968, '*réussir, arriver*, j'ai toujours su au fond de moi et dès 1910 que c'était dérisoire, que ce ne serait rien, que seul comptait le témoignage qui m'était demandé, que le

---

[47] Though it is true that, to a certain extent, Mauriac's election to the Académie in 1933 is a case of anticipated consecration: at 48, he was a relatively young Academician. Suffering from a potentially life-threatening illness at the time, Mauriac stood unopposed. Paul Valéry, the other writer of the inter-war period to be consecrated by both the *NRF* and the Académie, elected towards the end of his career in 1925, illustrates a more typical trajectory in this respect; and it is in the post-war period when Mauriac will be joined at the quai Conti by other figures of the interwar *NRF*, including Jean Paulhan.

[48] Cf. Pierre Bourdieu, *Le Sens pratique* (Paris: Editions de Minuit, 1980), pp. 88-91.

balbutiant poème des *Mains jointes* apportait déjà' (BN V 17, Mauriac's emphasis). Yet on the other, he recognises the influence of his provincial, bourgeois upbringing and the legacy of bourgeois values with which he is left, one of the most important of which is precisely the need to display the familiar signs of a successful career. If Mauriac is drawn to the Académie Française and the heteronymous pole, it is because he wants to convince his family that he has achieved the right goals:

> Il faut tout de même en revenir au fait que j'étais un jeune bourgeois, de tradition bourgeoise, appartenant à une famille bourgeoise, qui croyait donc aux valeurs auxquelles croyait sa famille et qui, en tout cas, s'il n'y croyait pas, si au fond, il y croyait assez peu, voulait convaincre sa famille et rassurer sa famille, rester dans le droit fil de ce que sa famille considérait comme la réussite. (SR 108)

The visible and worldly glory represented by Mauriac's election to the Académie Française coincides most closely with their perception or understanding of success.

As such, it is the dispositions and values acquired from his milieu which ultimately prevail and inflect his career in the 1930s; and for the Mauriac of 1968, analysing his trajectory with a sociologist's sensitivity, its governing principle was a certain sense of caution or prudence, 'cette prudence héritée d'eux qui me gardait de tout excès, de toute folie' (BN V 16). This socially acquired sense of caution is reinforced by a religious faith which, as we have seen, tends towards Jansenism in what Mauriac terms its 'inquiétude', its fear that everything gained can be lost at the last moment (SR 304).[49] It is in the moral realm in particular where prudence is essential. Indeed, we have seen how this prudence translates, especially in the wake of a spiritual crisis which reasserts his faith, into the conservatism of his politics, and his equally conservative understanding of the relationship between morality and aesthetics. Ironically, however, the membership of the Académie Française to which it leads will produce some unexpected consequences, as the opposing set of dispositions once

---

[49] As he puts it in his interviews with Jean Amrouche, 'je crois qu'arrivé au soir de sa vie, c'est le moment pour le chrétien, de se rappeler que jusqu'à la fin nous sommes menacés; que le chrétien joue une partie qu'il peut perdre à la dernière minute, et c'est cela qui est terrible' (SR 305).

more start to prevail, and Mauriac's position in the context of the Académie Française becomes increasingly complicated. What might have been a move condemning Mauriac to a gradual artistic decline and the increasing indifference of his peers and audience, in fact provides him with a situation which will be crucial for his emergence as an intellectual figure.

The mid-1930s, then, see Mauriac move increasingly from the political Right with which he had aligned himself on his return to the journalistic and political field. Moreover, he begins to do so shortly after his accession to an institution which embodied the Right in the literary field. In her excellent discussion of Mauriac's activities during this period, Gisèle Sapiro has underlined the important role played by his election to the Académie Française in provoking Mauriac's change of political direction.[50] Mauriac soon realises that the Académie is a highly politicised institution, and in particular that the extreme Right was intent on taking it over and using it as a powerbase for its own political ends.

This is made clear in 1935, when the minor novelist Claude Farrère is elected over Claudel, much to Mauriac's anger. Outraged at such blatant disregard for Claudel's literary merits, he recognises that his fellow Academicians also wanted to inflict defeat on the political system of which Claudel, as a high-ranking diplomat, was a representative:

> L'aspect littéraire du scandale, cette honte d'avoir préféré Farrère
> à Claudel, si je la ressentais jusque dans mes entrailles, c'est que
> j'avais discerné, dès ce moment-là, que c'était moins le poète
> qu'ils exécraient dans Claudel (bien qu'il incarnât tout ce qu'un

---

[50] Gisèle Sapiro, *La Guerre des écrivains*, pp. 209-241. However, I would argue that Sapiro is a little hasty in suggesting that Mauriac's religious conversion of 1928 provides the main key to his political conversion in the mid-1930s (p. 229). After all, nearly ten years stand between the religious crisis and his interventions over the Spanish Civil War, and as we have seen, its initial effect was to *confirm* Mauriac's position on the Right through the way it reinforced his artistic, moral and political conservatism. Religious faith undoubtedly informs the position he adopts over the Civil War (condemnation of the complicity of the Spanish Church with Franco's regime); but I would suggest that Mauriac's election to the Académie Française is more immediately important in bringing about a change in his political position and inflecting his trajectory.

Henri Bordeaux ou un Abel Bonnard haïssaient) que le
fonctionnaire de la Troisième République. (MP 19)[51]

Suddenly, as Sapiro points out, Mauriac finds himself in the position
of defending what, in the context of the Académie, has become the
autonomous pole of literary excellence represented by Claudel (a
long-standing collaborator of the *NRF* and a Gallimard author) against
the heteronymous pole represented by Bordeaux and Bonnard. In
defending these values against the Academic right, and opposing their
decisions, Mauriac puts himself on what is effectively the left wing or
radical margin of the Académie Française, in a position homologous
with that of the left-wing intellectual in the broader political field.

For when he enters the Académie in 1933, Mauriac is subject
to what can be termed an 'effet de champ'.[52] While it represents one
position in the literary field, the Académie is not a homogenous entity.
Rather, like any social structure or organisation, it has properties
similar to those at work in the field of which it is part, in that it is
constituted by a set of positions whose meanings are defined by the
relationships, forces and conflicts existing between them.
Furthermore, and as Mauriac demonstrates, actors entering and
operating within such institutions are exposed to their own distinct set
of forces, which can influence or disrupt those at work in the larger
field, and so inflect trajectories in unexpected ways.

It seems that being confronted at close quarters by the
fascistic tendencies of the political and cultural Establishment
represented by the members of the Académie serves to rid Mauriac of
what he terms his 'naivety' (MP 18), and clarify his own political
conscience, allowing him to grasp in particular the incompatibilities
between certain right-wing ideologies and his own worldview. It
provokes the inflection in his trajectory which will lead him to adopt
increasingly liberal and even – in the 1950s especially – leftist
political positions. This inflection is itself expressed in a series of

---

[51] See also François Mauriac, 'Histoire politique de l'Académie française. 1: André
Chaumeix', in *La Paix des cimes*, pp. 540-544, and Gisèle Sapiro, *La Guerre des
écrivains*, p. 230. Mauriac offers a subtle analysis of the history of the Académie,
sketching out its trajectory since the nineteenth century, and tracing its shift from
focal point of liberal opposition during the Second Empire to bastion of conservatism
in the Third Republic.
[52] Cf. Alain Viala, 'Effets de champ, effets de prisme', *Littérature*, 70 (May 1988),
64-71.

displacements around the journalistic field, as he writes for journals and reviews which are more in accordance with his evolving views: hence his collaboration with the progressive Catholic reviews *Sept* and *Temps présent* in the mid- to late-1930s; his move from *L'Écho de Paris* to the more liberal (or less conservative) *Le Figaro* in 1934; and above all, as I shall be discussing at length in chapters three and four, his collaboration with the radical news weekly *L'Express* in the 1950s.[53]

Mauriac's suspicions over the political direction being taken by the Académie were confirmed when the election of Charles Maurras, leader of the extreme-right Action Française, was engineered in 1938; but by this time, Mauriac had for some time been what Sapiro appropriately terms a 'heretical academician', in conflict with the dominant order at the literary and above all political levels. The first signs of his break with the Right come in 1935 when he criticises the racist mockery of the Ethiopians in the wake of Italy's invasion of the country.[54] It is then made strikingly clear in May 1937, when Mauriac is the lead signatory of the 'Manifeste pour le peuple basque', published by the progressive, Catholic newspaper *L'Aube*.[55] In the months which follow, he publishes an outspoken series of articles in *Le Figaro* and *Sept* condemning the Franquist regime's suppression of the Basque people, and its attempts to justify its actions by claiming to be engaged in a 'holy war'.[56] The extent to which he is at odds with the political mood of the Académie Française more generally is confirmed later that year when several of his fellow members sign a counter-manifesto, 'Manifeste aux intellectuels espagnols', in which they express their support for the Franquist regime.

At the same time, Mauriac's position on the radical fringe of the Académie Française can be seen as a strikingly faithful translation

[53] On Mauriac's movements around the journalistic field during the 1930s, see also Marie-Chantal Praicheux, 'Le journaliste François Mauriac: une question de tribunes', *Revue des lettres modernes*, série François Mauriac, 6 (Caen: Minard, 2003), 19-37. On his collaboration with *Sept* and *Temps présent*, see Jacques Monférier, 'Les "Billets" de François Mauriac dans *Sept* et *Temps présent* (1934-1940)', *Revue des lettres modernes*, série François Mauriac, 3 (Caen: Minard, 1980), 67-80.
[54] 'Un dessin de Sennep', *Le Figaro*, 24 September 1935 (MP 54-55).
[55] *L'Aube*, 8 May 1937, p. 1.
[56] See in particular 'Le membre souffrant' (MP 81-82), 'Pour le peuple basque' (MP 82-84) and 'Mise au point' (MP 89-93). See also Slava Kushnir, *Mauriac journaliste* (Paris: Minard, 1979), pp. 62-70.

or concretisation of the conflicting dispositions which constitute his habitus, articulating as it does the hesitation or oscillation which had been the defining feature of his trajectory up to that point. It is no surprise to find Mauriac take up a liminal position in the field, one on the radical fringe of the cultural orthodoxy, but not entirely in accordance with the autonomous pole. Yet it is significant too that while he may be on the margins of the Académie, he nevertheless remains within its boundaries, and as such signals his fundamental allegiance to the established social and cultural order which it represents. As he says in a letter to Emmanuel Mounier in 1937, 'je ne suis pas, je ne serai jamais pour la révolution' (NLV 181). Nevertheless, while he was not perhaps about to start a revolution, Mauriac was clearly beginning to embark on a form of rebellion, tentatively at first over the Spanish Civil War, then with increasing confidence during the Occupation and in the 1950s, as France grappled with the problem of decolonisation.

Mauriac's signing of the petition in May 1937 marks the point at which he begins to use his existing prestige or symbolic capital in a new way. His aim is not to consolidate his position within the literary field, as was the case in the early 1930s, but to make an effective foray into the political field. He takes on for the first time the prophetic status which, as I discussed in the introduction, is the hallmark of the intellectual. His provenance from the autonomous realm of the literary field becomes the guarantee of his independence of mind and free-thinking nature, as he sets out to interpret the signs which remain hidden to others, or denounces what others attempt to hide. Writing to Drieu La Rochelle in July 1941 about his interventions during the Spanish Civil War, he argues that

> C'est contre le *mensonge de l'idée de croisade* que Maritain, Bernanos et moi nous sommes dressés; l'identification de la cause du Christ en Espagne et dans le monde entier avec celle des généraux qui faisaient mitrailler leur peuple par des avions allemands et italiens, voilà contre quoi nous nous sommes dressés. (LV 252, Mauriac's emphasis)

Moreover, the fact that he is the lead signatory of the petition published in *L'Aube*, his name alone occupying the first line in the list, is itself an indication that his status and importance as a voice of moral conscience had by now been acknowledged.

Of crucial importance too, I would suggest, is that when he
signs the petition, it is as 'François Mauriac de l'Académie française'.
For I would argue that one of the keys to Mauriac's effectiveness as
an intellectual will lie precisely in his distinctive position as a
'heretical' Academician, and the persistent disjunction which ensues
between what he says – his increasingly radical *prises de position* over
a range of sensitive issues – and the position in the field from which
he says it. It is not just that he establishes himself in the late 1930s as
an outspoken, critical and free-thinking voice, but that he does so as a
member of the cultural institution which is most closely associated
with the established order and the dominant fraction within the field of
power. Moreover, this disjunction will be underlined each time
Mauriac writes an article or signs a petition, for as tradition and
protocol dictate, he will always do so with the mention 'de
l'Académie française'. That Mauriac's membership of the Académie
is perceived to give his activities a distinctive symbolic weight
becomes clear during the Occupation especially. The importance of
his participation in the intellectual Resistance is seen to lie not just in
his publication of texts such as *Le Cahier noir*, but also in the very
fact that he was the only member of the Académie to join Resistance
movements such as the Front National and the Comité Nationale des
Ecrivains.[57]

By saying and doing things which would not normally be
associated with the position in the field from which he does them,
whether it be as a member of the Académie Française or as a
columnist for a conservative newspaper such as *Le Figaro*, Mauriac
rapidly accumulates significant amounts of symbolic capital, capital
which is specific to his own position, which defines its distinctiveness,
and above all, which can itself be exploited to make further
interventions. 'M. Mauriac, vous trahissez votre classe!', he is told in
1938 by the mayor of Bordeaux (MP 28). In a relatively short period
of time, Mauriac had come to be seen as a rebel voice condemning the
interests of his own class, the dominant order; but as he goes on to
say, 'je la trahissais, mais en 1938, je ne lui faisais pas peur' (MP 28-
29). That point would come in the post-war period as Mauriac
becomes increasingly implicated in the debates over the future of the

---

[57] See Jacques Debû-Bridel, *La Résistance intellectuelle* (Paris: Julliard, 1970), pp.
96ff.

North African colonies, and starts threatening interests closer to home. We will be considering later the various ways in which the symbolic capital he had begun to acquire towards the end of the 1930s would be used – both by himself and others – and how he becomes increasingly practised at performing the function of the intellectual. The next chapter, however, focuses on the problems faced by Mauriac in the literary field as he begins to establish himself as an intellectual in the political field.

Chapter Two

Death and Resurrection

'M. Mauriac n'est pas un romancier'

If the 1930s is a period of transition for Mauriac, this is so not just in terms of his developing career as a journalist and his emergence as an intellectual, but also with respect to his activity and status as a novelist. It is striking that his triumphs of 1932 and 1933 (the commercial and critical success of *Le Nœud de vipères*, his election to the Académie Française) simultaneously mark the beginning of his decline. A decline in productivity first of all, as Mauriac's novelistic output slows down noticeably. Whereas *Le Nœud de vipères* was his eighth novel in ten years, complemented by a series of short stories, the next ten years saw the appearance of only five more.

It marks a decline too in the sense that Mauriac's creative powers appeared to falter. The root cause of this, as I discussed in the previous chapter, was the religious crisis of late 1928 and its aftermath. Mauriac's 'conversion' leads him to attempt a form of self-censorship, as he makes an effort to write more overtly 'Catholic' novels which demonstrate the redemptive effect of God's love on human lives. The first of these is *Ce qui était perdu*, published in 1930.

Mauriac's new direction is immediately obvious to Marcel Arland. In his review of the novel for that September's *NRF*, Arland describes it as 'l'histoire de la misère de l'homme quand il s'éloigne de Dieu, de sa renaissance quand il se retourne vers lui'.[1] Arland recognises the novel as a defining moment in Mauriac's career, above all because of the gamble it represents. In surrendering to the demands

---

[1] Marcel Arland, 'François Mauriac, *Ce qui était perdu*', *La Nouvelle Revue française*, 204 (September 1930), p. 410.

of his faith, Mauriac had willingly and dramatically sacrificed what had made his earlier work so distinctive, and had been the key to his success: 'c'est une situation pathétique que celle de cet auteur dont le talent brillait avant tout dans une sensuelle peinture du monde et à qui la foi impose de renoncer à cette peinture'. In wanting to write more obviously 'Catholic' novels, which lead their main characters – and so, it is intended, their readers – to God, Mauriac must abandon what Arland terms a 'certaine complicité avec sa création, qui n'est pas la moindre source de sa puissance et de saveur'.[2] Arland demonstrates the problems this causes as he highlights various flaws in the novel.

One of the most significant, for him, is the change in Mauriac's relationship with his characters: 'ce qui peut-être a le plus nui à ce livre, c'est que M. Mauriac, en se rapprochant de Dieu, s'est éloigné, s'est détaché de ses personnages'. Mauriac's theological intentions, he suggests, interfere with character development. Many seem mainly to have an allegorical function, helping to illustrate his spiritual lesson:

> Les meilleurs eux-mêmes, cette Irène un peu trop uniformément touchante, cette vieille mère que Mauriac aurait jadis poussée au premier plan, semblent plutôt des allégories que des êtres véritables. Ce sont les moyens employés par le romancier pour communiquer son enseignement.[3]

Above all, Arland implies, Mauriac's biggest gamble had been to abandon what he possessed without really knowing what would replace it:

> On a l'impression que M. François Mauriac a quitté la terre familière à son pied pour pénétrer dans des régions qui lui sont encore inconnues. [...] Il a perdu tels biens, il ne connaît pas encore ceux qu'il a gagnés.[4]

The creative stakes were clearly high for Mauriac: would he be able to discover and develop the new dimension his work needed?

---

[2] Arland, 'François Mauriac, *Ce qui était perdu*', p. 412.
[3] Ibid., p. 411. In Arland's criticism, we can also see re-emerge the aesthetic orthodoxy of the *NRF*, its suspicion of writers who subordinate the literary to non-literary concerns.
[4] Ibid., p. 412.

His next novel, *Le Nœud de vipères*, published in 1932, indicated that he could. The novel traces the emergence of religious consciousness in the central character, Louis – a vengeful, misanthropic and atheistic individual – and culminates in his suggested conversion at the end of his life. The key to its success lies in the use, rare for Mauriac, of the first-person narrative voice. The text takes the form of a letter written by the central character to his wife, and intended to be read by her after his death; but her unexpected death leaves it without its intended addressee, and it begins to take the form of a journal whose focus increasingly becomes Louis' evolving understanding of himself and those around him. This technique allows Louis' turn towards God to be implied rather than stated explicitly, clues to his conversion lying in subtle shifts in vocabulary and emphasis. Ramon Fernandez highlights its effectiveness in his review of the novel, calling it a 'manière oblique et souple qui permet de suggérer plutôt que de dérouler un roman balzacien dans les libres et rapides visions d'une conscience fiévreuse',[5] having already declared *Le Nœud de vipères* to be Mauriac's 'chef-d'œuvre'.[6]

Yet despite seeming to have found a solution to the problem raised by Arland a year previously, Mauriac would not manage to repeat this success, and as the 1930s progressed, critical attitudes towards his work would start to shift. The *NRF*'s reviewers still display good will towards his novels, appreciating and acknowledging the elements which make it recognisably *mauriacien*. In keeping with the ethos of the *NRF*, their concern is to judge his work in terms of its contribution to his particular artistic enterprise. Thus, while *Les Anges noirs* may not be Mauriac's best novel, according to Arland writing in 1936,

> C'est à coup sûr l'un des livres les plus curieux, les plus étonnants qu'il ait écrits. On aime qu'il l'ait écrit; [...] Et peut-

---

[5] Ramon Fernandez, 'François Mauriac, *Le Nœud de vipères*', *La Nouvelle Revue française*, 223 (April 1932), p. 761.
[6] Ibid., p. 759. On *Le Nœud de vipères*, see also James Reid, 'Mauriac: the ambivalent author of absence', *Studies in Twentieth-Century French Literature*, 11 (1987), 167-188.

être n'est-on sensible à ses défauts que dans la mesure où ils
paraissent le signe d'un élargissement.[7]

At same time, though, the reviewers become increasingly aware of his
work's problems and limitations.

The most significant of these will in fact prove to be
Mauriac's narrative technique. For rather than persisting with the first-
person narration which defines *Le Nœud de vipères*, Mauriac reverts
to his more usual third-person narrative technique in later novels, or
combines third- and first-person perspectives in the case of *La Fin de
la nuit*. While not in itself problematic, critics notice that there is a
growing tendency for the authorial voice to intervene in his narrative
in order to pass judgement on the characters and express his own
opinions, something first detected by Arland in his review of *Le
Mystère Frontenac* in 1933: 'la voix de M. Mauriac, que l'on
percevait derrière tous ses autres romans, s'élève ici, directe, grave;
[...] il entre en scène, juge les personnages, oppose, rapproche,
anticipe, et dit enfin sa croyance'. Arland concludes with a salutary
observation: 'c'est une très belle et très dangereuse entreprise'.[8] The
same problem reappears in *Les Anges noirs*, where once again the
hand of the author is too obviously at work:

> On résiste, on reste parfois incrédule devant ce drame et ces
> personnages. Non parce qu'ils sont trop noirs; mais leur noirceur
> semble voulue par l'auteur; il a besoin d'elle, afin de rendre plus
> éclatante la lumière qu'il dispense aux dernières pages.[9]

We can see here how Arland, as befits a critic affiliated to the
NRF, judges Mauriac's work principally on aesthetic and technical
grounds. The problem posed by his novels lies not necessarily with the
technique he adopts *per se* – though Arland clearly considers it to be a
risky one – as with its execution. It needs to be used with great skill,
he implies, if the dangers it poses are to be avoided; and the evidence
would suggest that Mauriac has failed properly to master it. For
Arland, in effect, Mauriac is increasingly being let down by his

---

[7] Marcel Arland, 'François Mauriac, *Les Anges noirs*', *La Nouvelle Revue française*,
271 (April 1936), p. 587.
[8] Marcel Arland, 'François Mauriac, *Le Mystère Frontenac*', *La Nouvelle Revue
française*, 234 (March 1933), p. 521.
[9] Marcel Arland, 'François Mauriac, *Les Anges noirs*', p. 587.

craftsmanship: his interventions are too clumsy, upsetting the harmony of his texts, and so interfering with the reader's investment in the imaginary worlds they create.

Tacit recognition that his talents as a novelist might be in decline also comes from Mauriac himself in the title of an article from 1937, 'Le romancier peut se renouveler par le théâtre et le cinéma' (OC XI 257-258). Mauriac is referring here to the imminent launch of his first play, *Asmodée*, performed at the Comédie Française for the first time in November that year. Although the play was a success with the public, this came after a laborious writing process (involving the collaboration of Edouard Bourdet and Jacques Copeau, the play's producer) and a trenchant critical response. Reviewing the play for the *NRF*, Benjamin Crémieux observed that

> Il y a seulement dix ans, la technique adoptée dans *Asmodée* eût paru le comble de l'art. Aujourd'hui ces présentations de biais des personnages, ces sentiments en filigrane non seulement ne sont plus à la mode, mais font *démodé*. Nous souhaitons des héros de théâtre plus directs, plus affirmés.[10]

Once again, the *NRF*'s readers were left with the unmistakeable impression that Mauriac was losing ground.

This impression of decline would be confirmed – irrevocably, for many – when the *NRF* published Sartre's famous essay, 'M. François Mauriac et la liberté', in February 1939. Its fame lies not just in Sartre's devastating critique of Mauriac's novelistic technique, based on his reading of *La Fin de la nuit* of 1935, but in the virulence of its expression. By the end of the article, one is left with the distinct impression of having witnessed a summary execution, as Sartre takes it upon himself to announce famously that 'M. Mauriac n'est pas un romancier'.[11] Beyond its polemical dimension – and indeed because of it, to a certain extent – the article also represents a crucial moment both in terms of Mauriac's trajectory and in terms of the evolution of

---

[10] Benjamin Crémieux, '*Asmodée*, cinq actes de François Mauriac à la Comédie-Française', *La Nouvelle Revue française*, 292 (January 1938), p. 147. Crémieux's emphasis. On the difficult genesis of the play, see Mauriac's letters to Copeau (LV 224-226), and Jean Lacouture, *François Mauriac*, II, pp. 86-90.

[11] Jean-Paul Sartre, 'M. François Mauriac et la liberté', *La Nouvelle Revue française*, 305 (February 1939), p. 231.

the field as a whole, something signalled, as we shall see, by the controversy it provoked at the time.

The main target of Sartre's criticism is in fact a problem which had already been identified by other critics, and Marcel Arland in particular – namely, Mauriac's intrusive narrative technique, which leads him to judge and define his characters, and speak about them with omniscient certainty. Arland himself had already highlighted the problem in his review of *La Fin de la nuit*, noting 'certains épisodes où l'on sent trop nettement la main de l'auteur, certains propos qui sont de François Mauriac plus que de ses héros'.[12] What is new, however, is the significance Sartre affords this problem, and the critical assumptions which inform his judgement of it. His shift in perspective is signalled clearly by the title of the article, which focuses attention on the theme of freedom in Mauriac's novel. It quickly becomes clear that what, for Arland, had fundamentally been an aesthetic problem becomes, for Sartre, a philosophical one, and that it is because of Mauriac's failings on this level that Sartre questions his competence as a novelist.

Sartre argues that a successful novel works by generating the illusion of freedom. It gives its readers the impression that its characters, like them, are projecting forward into their own undecided future, and share their own potentiality. When we read, says Sartre, we slip into a character's life and share his drama with him. As he engages with the story of Rogojine in Dostoyevsky's *The Possessed*, Sartre suggests, 'je me glisse en lui et le voilà qui s'attend avec mon attente, il a peur de lui *en moi*; il vit'.[13] However, this process of absorption can only take place if we feel the characters' future remains unknown to us and them, and their development is shrouded in ambiguity: 'voulez-vous que vos personnages vivent? Faites qu'ils soient libres'.[14] The best way to ensure this is not to define or analyse characters and their states of mind, but simply to present them and their actions to the reader: like those around us in real life, they should remain inscrutable. As soon as he feels that a character's future is pre-determined, whether through heredity, social influences, 'ou quelque autre mécanisme', the spell is broken for Sartre. He drops out of the

---

[12] Marcel Arland, 'François Mauriac, *La Fin de la nuit*', *La Nouvelle Revue française*, 258 (March 1935), p. 451.
[13] Jean-Paul Sartre, 'M François Mauriac et la liberté', p. 213. Sartre's emphasis.
[14] Ibid.

novel's world, for it can no longer support his own consciousness, his own potentiality.[15]

The problem is exemplified, for Sartre, by *La Fin de la nuit* (which continues the story of Thérèse Desqueyroux, whom Mauriac had left roaming the streets of Paris in 1927), and it has its roots in Mauriac's narrative technique. By adopting her point of view in the opening pages of the novel, Mauriac encourages his readers to identify with Thérèse and slip into her consciousness; but their attempt to do so is thwarted, Sartre argues, by Mauriac's continual oscillation between presenting her as a subject and an object of consciousness. Sartre highlights how Mauriac shifts rapidly from one perspective to the other. We may begin by seeing the world, and Thérèse herself, through her own eyes, privy to her thoughts and experiences, and knowing only what she knows; but we are then jolted into another position, find ourselves with the narrator observing her from the outside, and we are given insights into her character of which she herself is seemingly unaware:

> Elle entendit sonner neuf heures. Il fallait gagner un peu de temps encore, car il était trop tôt pour avaler le cachet qui lui assurerait quelques heures de sommeil; non que ce fût dans les habitudes de cette déseperée prudente, mais ce soir elle ne pouvait se refuser ce secours. (ORTC III 83)

Thus, the reader's position is a peculiar one, being at once the accomplice of Thérèse and her judge. As Sartre asks in relation to this passage, 'qui juge ainsi Thérèse une "désespérée prudente"? ce ne peut être elle. Non, c'est M. Mauriac, c'est moi-même: nous avons le dossier Desqueyroux entre les mains et nous rendons notre arrêt'.[16] We are repeatedly placed not at the level of the characters, but at that of the narrator, a narrator whose role it is to bring insight and clarification; not at the level of the human or subjective, but of the absolute or divine. 'Toutes les bizarreries de sa technique s'expliquent par ce qu'il prend le point de vue de Dieu sur ses personnages', concludes Sartre. 'Dieu voit le dedans et le dehors, le fond des âmes et les corps, tout l'univers à la fois'.[17]

---

[15] Ibid.
[16] 'M. François Mauriac et la liberté', p. 219.
[17] Ibid., p. 221.

It emerges once again, therefore, that Mauriac's stance as a moralist, as a God-like observer and judge of the human character, is the major cause of his limitations as an artist; but the problems this poses for Sartre are rather different from those perceived by the *NRF*. Sartre's concern is not with the way in which Mauriac's omniscience may infringe on the aesthetic qualities of his text, or limit his artistic freedom, but with the philosophical, or more accurately theological, implications of his position. Drawing on ideas he would develop further in *L'Etre et le néant*, Sartre takes issue first of all with Mauriac's habit of defining or clarifying aspects of his characters' personality. In doing so, Sartre argues, he transforms them into little more than objects with a fixed essence: 'les appréciations définitives que M. Mauriac est toujours prêt à glisser dans le récit prouvent qu'il ne conçoit pas ses personnages comme il le doit. Avant d'écrire, il forge leur essence, il décrète qu'ils *seront* ceci ou cela'.[18] His desire to do this is itself informed by his understanding of man, and the notion of freedom which accompanies it.

In the eyes of Mauriac, informed by Christian theology, freedom is defined principally in terms of free will, the struggle to overcome or escape from our essential nature, a nature which is basically corrupt, and which leads us to do ill. Moreover, it is precisely Thérèse's engagement in this struggle which Mauriac had wanted to depict in *La Fin de la nuit*. If this conception is problematic for Sartre, it is because the individual's capacity for free will is seen as an adjunct to a pre-existing essence. For Sartre, however, freedom is inherent in our very being, the basis on which we forge our existence:

> Entendons que, pour M. Mauriac, la liberté ne saurait *construire*; un homme, avec sa liberté, ne peut point se créer lui-même, ni forger son histoire. Le libre-arbitre n'est qu'une puissance discontinue qui permet de brèves évasions, mais ne produit rien, si ce n'est que quelques événements sans lendemain[19].

If Mauriac's novels fail to convince, it is because his understanding of freedom, and beyond that, his vision of man, preclude him from

---

[18] 'M. François Mauriac et la liberté', p. 222. Sartre's emphasis.
[19] Ibid., p. 224. Sartre's emphasis. See also 'La liberté cartésienne', in *Situations, I* (Paris: Gallimard, 1947), pp. 314-335.

conceiving them in terms of his characters' becoming and projection into the future.

Secondly, Sartre asserts that Mauriac's omniscient position, and the philosophy which underpins it, are themselves an anachronism. They show that he has failed to take into account the fact that our understanding of the world has changed, and that consequently, the ways in which artists and writers represent that world must also evolve:

> Il a voulu ignorer, comme font du reste la plupart de nos auteurs, que la théorie de la relativité s'applique intégralement à l'univers romanesque, que dans un vrai roman, pas plus que dans le monde d'Einstein, il n'y a de place pour un observateur privilégié.[20]

Mauriac has not realised the significance of the fact that he is writing in a post-Einsteinian world. It is no longer realistic to adopt a position from which to make absolute judgements when the possibility that such a position exists has so recently been called into question. Nor, by extension, is it appropriate to model oneself on God in a world where God no longer exists, or at least where God's existence has been radically interrogated, and where the dominant philosophical models are increasingly those which take as a given the absurdity of the human condition. Mauriac, it seems, inhabits a world which he is no longer qualified to represent, and which requires a new poetics and a new philosophy – and both of these, it is implied, are what Sartre himself is best placed to articulate.

Our overriding impression of Sartre's article is of its rhetorical force and tone. Mauriac's technical errors and philosophical blind spots disqualify him as a novelist, Sartre proclaims, using the twin techniques of accumulation and apostrophe to encourage the reader to share his judgement:

> *La Fin de la nuit* n'est pas un roman. Appellerez-vous "roman" cet ouvrage anguleux et glacé, avec des parties de théâtre, des morceaux d'analyse, des méditations poétiques? Ces démarrages heurtés, ces coups de frein violents, ces reprises pénibles, ces pannes, pouvez-vous les confondre avec le cours majestueux de la durée romanesque?[21]

---

[20] 'M. François Mauriac et la liberté', p. 231.
[21] Ibid., p. 231.

At best, Mauriac serves as a counter-example whose mistakes might be instructive, and Sartre's criticisms of his technique are indeed combined with normative assertions about literary method: 'il est temps de le dire: le romancier n'est point Dieu. [...] Je soutiens qu'il n'a pas le droit de porter ces jugements absolus. Un roman est une action racontée de différents points de vue'.[22] By the end of the article, we are left in no doubt that notice has been served by Sartre on Mauriac's career as a novelist.

Mauriac's reaction to Sartre's intervention was mainly one of surprise: 'j'ai été frappé, si vous voulez, par l'attaque de Sartre', he would say in an interview thirty years later.[23] Why did Mauriac merit such attention from Sartre, and why did Sartre invest so much energy in attacking him? Sartre's assault on Mauriac is a particularly interesting and revealing moment in recent literary history, as Mauriac gets caught up in one of the periodic revolutions which reshape the field. The four-year gap between the publication of *La Fin de la nuit* and Sartre's critique makes clear that his article is not a spontaneous response to Mauriac. Rather, as Caroline Casseville has pointed out, it forms part of a broader campaign orchestrated by Jean Paulhan to help launch Sartre's career. Having spotted Sartre's talent, Paulhan had charged himself with stage-managing the young and still relatively unknown author's entry into the literary field.[24] Writing a provocative and sophisticated essay on a well-established and broadly respected author was clearly one way in which this could be done; but more was at stake than a simple desire to generate publicity and mark his arrival on the literary scene.

Paulhan's aims were in fact twofold: not only was he keen to promote a writer whom he recognised as the most significant of his generation, but he also aimed to sustain the *NRF*'s pre-eminence at a time when he felt it was losing its edge. In Sartre, he saw a writer who could both re-establish the *NRF*'s reputation for literary innovation, and reinvigorate the literary field. Judging by his revealing comments

---

[22] Ibid., p. 221

[23] *France-Soir*, 28 février 1969, cit. in Michel Contat and Michel Rybalka, *Les Ecrits de Sartre* (Paris: Gallimard, 1970), p. 72.

[24] Caroline Casseville, 'Mauriac et la critique sartrienne', *Nouveaux Cahiers François Mauriac*, 1 (1993), 77-95. On Paulhan's management of Sartre's *entrée en jeu*, see pp. 79-81, and Anna Boschetti, *Sartre et 'Les Temps modernes'* (Paris: Editions de Minuit, 1985), ch. 2.

in a letter to Roger Martin du Gard, this latter task was all the more urgent for Paulhan given that a writer such as Mauriac could be perceived, beyond the vicinity of the autonomous pole at least, as one of the field's most important figures:

> Je tâche d'aiguiller Sartre vers une "campagne romanesque". Je ne connais pas de jeune écrivain qui en soit plus capable que lui. Et *tout* est à dire. Je ne sais quel journaliste (au fait si, c'est Rousseaux) écrivait l'autre jour dans *Le Figaro* que Mauriac domine tout le roman contemporain – j'aurais dit, tout au plus, qu'il domine le genre du poème-en-prose-à-rallonges. Vraiment, tout est ici à recommencer.[25]

Sartre's eruption into the literary field in the late 1930s is an exemplary illustration of the way in which the field evolves and its history takes shape. As Anna Boschetti notes in her study of Sartre's rise to power in the field, Mauriac is one of a number of writers he targets at the time, each of whom occupies a specific position in the field, and so has a certain symbolic value:

> Des maîtres dont le jeune écrivain se réclame (Faulkner, Dos Passos); des auteurs de son âge auxquels il se confronte (Camus, Blanchot, l'ami Nizan); des aînés plus ou moins célèbres, influents, discutés (Mauriac et Giraudoux, Ponge et Parain, Drieu La Rochelle et Charles Morgan).[26]

Commenting on these writers, defining and analysing their work, is one of the ways in which Sartre can begin to sketch out his own position.

In effect, his aim is to 'faire date', as Pierre Bourdieu would put it. Bourdieu highlights the way in which the emerging avant-garde of a new generation (artistic, literary, and so on) makes its mark by

[25] Jean Paulhan, *Choix de lettres*, ed. by Dominique Aury, Jean-Claude Zylberstein and Bernard Leuilliot, 3 vols (Paris: Gallimard, 1986-96), II, p. 56. Paulhan's emphasis. On Paulhan's editorial strategy at the *NRF* during this period, see Martyn Cornick, *Intellectuals in History: the 'NRF' under Jean Paulhan, 1925-1940* (Amsterdam: Rodopi, 1995), pp. 41-43 and Gisèle Sapiro, *La Guerre des écrivains*, pp. 388-389. Ironically, of course, in promoting Sartre, Paulhan is also preparing the ground for the revolution in the field which, in the wake of the Occupation, will allow his protégé to establish himself and his review as the dominant force at the autonomous pole in the field.
[26] Anna Boschetti, *Sartre et 'Les Temps modernes'*, p. 63.

defining itself against existing positions, and underlining its difference
from what has gone before: 'faire date, c'est inséparablement *faire
exister une nouvelle position* au-delà des positions établies, en *avant*
de ces positions, *en avant-garde*, et, en introduisant la différence,
produire le temps'.[27] Distinguishing oneself from existing positions
has the simultaneous effect of making those positions look dated and
relegating them to the past, making them the old against which the
new can stand out.

Thus Mauriac interests Sartre as much for what he symbolises
or the position he holds as for the particular problems the work itself
may pose. Mauriac represents an enticing target for two reasons. His
status, first of all: Mauriac stands as a respected and prominent figure,
but one whose value is by no means uncontested, as Paulhan's
remarks to Martin du Gard make clear. Secondly, Mauriac is one of
the field's most obvious exponents of a certain sort of literature, the
traditional psychological novel. His work is traditional both in the
sense that the psychological novel is a long-established genre in
French literature, and in the sense that, as Sartre demonstrates,
Mauriac's understanding of human psychology has its roots in the
philosophical tradition represented by Pascal and Descartes. Through
a critique of Mauriac's work, not only can Sartre call for a renewal of
novelistic technique, which he will himself attempt by drawing on
American fiction in particular (signalled by his articles on Faulkner
and Dos Passos), but he can also begin to articulate his own
philosophy of human subjectivity which rejects the premises of the
Judeo-Christian tradition.

One of the effects of Sartre's article is to bring about a crisis
in Mauriac's relationship with the literary field, as it reveals the
precarious nature of his position within it. Sartre's attack on Mauriac
represents a crucial moment in a writer's trajectory, one which all
writers will face at some point – including Sartre himself – and which
determines their future in the field. In the wake of Sartre's article,
Mauriac is suddenly confronted with the realities of ageing in the
literary field. The creation of new positions by the next artistic
generation serves, as we have seen, to displace existing positions and
relegate them to the past. They become dated. This displacement into
the past usually has one of two outcomes, according to Bourdieu. On

---

[27] Pierre Bourdieu, *Les Règles de l'art*, p. 261. Bourdieu's emphasis.

the one hand, writers can acquire the status of 'classique': they become an accepted part of the history of the field, or what Bourdieu terms 'l'éternel present de la *culture* consacrée',[28] remaining a constant presence within it beyond their biological or artistic lifetime. Some writers, on the other hand, will become 'déclassé', fading from view or no longer being considered valid members of the field.[29]

It is precisely the resolution of this fate which is at stake for Mauriac when Sartre publishes his article. Indeed, Sartre's decision to target Mauriac is itself a reflection and result of the already uncertain nature of Mauriac's place in the field. The ambivalence which marks Mauriac's own perception of the field, and translates into his oscillation between its two poles, is mirrored in the divided critical opinion of his work and status. Despite the consecration of his peers in the wake of his successes of the 1920s, he remains a contested figure. In the eyes of more conservative critics, such as André Rousseaux of *Le Figaro*, Mauriac's status as classic is beyond doubt. Similarly, the tone of Marcel Arland's reviews in the *NRF* suggests that the conservative elements of the established avant-garde also seem willing to accept his place in the field and see him accede to the status of classic.

However, it is also apparent that conservative opinion of Mauriac lacks the weight with which to impose itself. Within the *NRF* especially, we can see that the authority of judgement is distributed unequally among its contributors, and that it is the more radical among them, such as Jean Paulhan, whose opinion will hold sway. As early as 1930, for example, Paulhan was disagreeing with Arland's sympathetic treatment of *Ce qui était perdu*:

> Les habiletés littéraires passées de Mauriac m'agaçaient, mais je me disais: peut-être sera-t-il un jour tellement habile que ça ne se verra plus. Il a renoncé à être habile et n'y a rien gagné. Même ta note ne me réconcilie avec lui.[30]

By 1938, as we have seen, Paulhan had decided that Mauriac represented the ideal scalp for a new talent looking to impose himself in the field. In this way, the debate around Mauriac offers an insight

---

[28] Pierre Bourdieu, *Les Règles de l'art*, p. 259. Bourdieu's emphasis.
[29] Ibid. For further discussion of the processes of ageing and change in the field, see pp. 259-264.
[30] Jean Paulhan, *Choix de lettres*, I, p. 191.

into the way in which the field produces and sanctions its history, the power to decide who can become part of the field's 'eternal present' lying principally with those who drive change within it.

Sartre's opinion is of crucial importance in this respect, because it represents the judgement of the next generation of actors in the field. Not only that, but it is the judgement of the actor already acknowledged by the established avant-garde to be its most important figure. As such, Sartre is in a position to benefit from the complex dynamic of recognition which operates in the field. Sartre gains the recognition of the established avant-garde in the form of Paulhan, and has his blessing as he sets out to carve out a new position in the field; but in acquiring legitimacy in this way, he also acquires the power to decide on the fate of the previous generation. As the future of the field, he can decide who deserves to be remembered, and who will be forgotten; who accedes to the status of classic, and who will be 'déclassé'.[31] At stake for Mauriac, in other words, is whether or not he will have a place in the new literary order Sartre looks set to create, whether or not he will be able to survive in the field after Sartre's arrival; and Sartre's judgement would seem to confirm this as more than unlikely.

Yet it is also true that Sartre's concerns extend far beyond Mauriac's position in the field, or the problems posed by his narrative technique. In reality, Mauriac is no more than a means to an end for him, an unfortunate but ultimately dispensable casualty of the symbolic coup he stages in order to establish himself at the literary avant-garde; but neither is this coup an empty gesture, a mere marketing campaign by which he can increase his profile. Rather, his aim is quite simply to provoke a revolution in the literary field, to bring about change not just in literary practice, but also in the criteria for understanding and judging literary success.

As we saw above, the power of Sartre's critique lies not just in his analysis of Mauriac's narrative technique, but in the way a new poetics emerges out of it. His rejection of orthodox literary practices is combined with the case for a new approach and a new set of techniques. First, the rejection of an omniscient narrator in favour of a technique which either adopts a character's point of view, or presents

---

[31] On the field's production and sanctioning of its past, see also Louis Pinto, *Pierre Bourdieu et la théorie du monde social*, pp. 114-115.

characters in a way which leaves their opacity and indeterminacy intact:

> Les êtres romanesques ont leurs lois, dont voici la plus rigoureuse: le romancier peut être leur témoin ou leur complice mais jamais les deux à la fois. Dehors et dedans. Faute d'avoir pris garde à ces lois, M. Mauriac assassine la conscience des personnages.[32]

Second, the need to respect and generate a sense of the passage of time, and the individual's becoming in time:

> Il est visible d'ailleurs que M. Mauriac n'aime point le temps, ni cette nécessité bergsonienne d'attendre "que le sucre fonde". [...] Le vrai romancier se passionne pour tout ce qui résiste, pour une porte, parce qu'il faut l'ouvrir, pour une enveloppe, parce qu'il faut la décacheter.[33]

Hence the strongly normative tone of the article as Sartre lays down a new aesthetics, and the rhetorical force which gives it the character of a manifesto.

Sartre's other intention emerges in this normative gesture. For the very act of setting out certain rules or laws is an attempt to redefine the criteria for assessing literary merit, the standards against which an author's work is to be measured. Furthermore, the criteria he puts forward are radically and provocatively new. We have seen him argue in relation to Mauriac that literary technique should be informed by philosophical understanding, and that the success of a text is dependent on the veracity and validity of the philosophy which underpins it. Indeed, this philosophy itself needs to take into account recent changes in our understanding of the world. In the post-war years, of course, Sartre would develop further his theory of literature, focusing in particular on its role and function in the world. He would underline the political function of writing, and call for writers to recognise that their position – or, to use the Sartrean term, their situation – in society brings with it certain powers and responsibilities. Failing to do so, he would say in 1945, is quite simply irresponsible.[34]

---

[32] Jean-Paul Sartre, 'M. François Mauriac et la liberté', p. 223.

[33] Ibid., p. 227.

[34] Jean-Paul Sartre, 'Présentation des *Temps modernes*', in *Situations, II* (Paris: Gallimard, 1948), pp. 9-30.

In other words, Sartre is proposing what amounts to nothing less than a reversal of the understanding of literature and literary excellence which had dominated the autonomous pole since the arrival in the field of the *NRF*. He is calling into question the autonomy of the aesthetic in literary practice, and arguing that it is no longer appropriate to disassociate the aesthetic from other demands and concerns. The literary should be aware of, and informed by, its relationship to the realms of politics and philosophy especially. Sartre's article on Mauriac represents one of the first moves in his campaign to challenge and depose the existing holders of the monopoly on consecration, and the vision of literature they promote – the existing holders of that monopoly being, of course, the group at the *NRF*. As we shall see later, his campaign will be helped by the Occupation which, in the way it disrupts the established order of the literary field, and leads especially to the disappearance of the *NRF*, paves the way for Sartre to seize control of the autonomous pole in 1945 with the launch of his own review, *Les Temps modernes*.

Moreover, the controversy provoked by the article in the aftermath of its publication suggests that the actors in the field are themselves aware of its significance, and the extent to which it represents a challenge to the established order. The reaction of conservative critics is predictably hostile. Among the first to respond is André Rousseaux, who had so irritated Paulhan by identifying Mauriac as one of the most important writers of the period. Having criticised Sartre for being too schematic in his argumentation, which allows him to present a caricatured version of it, Rousseaux takes Sartre to task for suggesting that art can only concern itself with surface realities, and that the hidden truths of man are beyond its purview: 'le sens de ce que pense M. Sartre semble être à peu près ceci: l'art n'a pas pour objet que les réalités apparentes, et il n'y a pas, pour l'art, de réalités intérieures'. If this were the case, Rousseaux goes on to argue, then it would invalidate the work of all those writers whose main aim has been precisely to investigate such inner realities: 'voilà qui atteint – ou qui atteindrait, si c'était fondé – toute une littérature pour qui l'art, au contraire, n'a souci que de réalités intérieures'.[35] The conservatism of Rousseaux's argument emerges

---

[35] André Rousseaux, 'La vie littéraire', *La Revue universelle*, 15 February 1939, p. 485.

clearly in the assumptions which underpin it, which ascribe to literature the proper and timeless vocation of exploring and articulating human complexities – or more precisely, the essence of mankind – for lesser mortals. The doubts he expresses about Sartre's argument serve above all to articulate his own unwillingness, or inability, to grasp the new perspective from which Sartre is analysing Mauriac's text.[36]

The dismissive way in which Paulhan responds to Rousseaux's article is equally predictable, the brief note he publishes under the pseudonym of Jean Guérin in the *NRF* of March 1939 describing it as 'si légère, et si faible'.[37] In doing so, Paulhan reasserts the hierarchies of power at work within the field by rejecting any claim Rousseaux might have to critical authority. A more revealing indication of the disruptive nature of Sartre's intervention comes in May 1939, when Marcel Arland reviews Mauriac's latest novel, *Les Chemins de la mer*. Reflecting on the recent controversy in his opening paragraph, Arland acknowledges the broader significance of Sartre's article: 'c'est qu'à travers M. Mauriac, le sort du roman français, ou du moins d'une de ses tendances essentielles, semblait en

---

[36] Rousseaux's hostility is shared by many modern *mauriaciens*, who continue to mount an impassioned defence of Mauriac by attempting to refute or dismiss Sartre's critique. They have seized in particular on his criticism of Mauriac's interventions and his omniscience, pointing out that it is a charge which can be levelled at several authors, such as Balzac, whose reputation goes unquestioned. See Caroline Casseville, 'Mauriac et la critique sartrienne', for example. To argue this, of course, is to miss the crucial point of the article, for Sartre is not suggesting that the techniques of omniscience and intervention are wrong *per se*, but that they are wrong in a contemporary context. Another tactic has been to confront Sartre's opinion with that of other authorities whose status, in their eyes, is as great if not greater. In 1988, the *Cahiers François Mauriac* published a letter from Henri Bergson to Mauriac, in which the philosopher comments favourably on Mauriac's narrative technique in *La Fin de la nuit*, and the skill with which he combines interpretation and observation. In other words, it could be reported, Bergson 'loue Mauriac sur le point précis où Sartre le critiquera âprement dans la *NRF* de 1939. De ce fait, le procès intenté depuis près d'un demi-siècle par Sartre et les sartriens contre *La Fin de la nuit* perd beaucoup de sa valeur'. *Cahiers François Mauriac*, 15 (1988), p. 13. The hope, perhaps, is that Mauriac can be re-established as a credible author in the eyes of a broader and increasingly indifferent critical public, for whom his status as *déclassé* is taken increasingly for granted.

[37] Jean Guérin [Jean Paulhan], 'A propos du 'François Mauriac' de Sartre', *La Nouvelle Revue française*, 306 (March 1939), p. 535.

jeu'.[38] He realises that what is at stake is not just Mauriac's future, but the future direction of the field as a whole; and it quickly becomes clear that Arland's article in turn is more than just a review of Mauriac's novel. It is the response of the established avant-garde, or at least its more conservative element, to Sartre's radical new vision of literature, and takes issue with him on two fronts.

Firstly, Arland defends 'le roman français' in the wake of Sartre's call for French writers to learn from the Anglo-Saxon tradition exemplified by Faulkner, Hemingway and others. The sense of duration and liberty Sartre demands can already be found in several French novels, he argues:

> Quelques-uns des meilleurs parmi les romans français offrent ce double caractère de la complexité et du choix, de la durée et de la concision, tout comme ils offrent cette spontanéité des actions, ce libre cours de la vie, ce refus de juger enfin, que l'on admire tant dans les littératures étrangères.[39]

As for other novelists, he wonders, 'si leurs œuvres sont plus particulières d'aspect, dira-t-on que ce ne sont pas des romans?'[40]

This latter comment points to the second important theme of Arland's review, as he sets out to dispute the criteria by which Sartre aims to judge literary merit, and his conception of literature more broadly. He takes issue with Sartre for neglecting what he terms 'l'apport original de Mauriac', and the fact that his work carries 'la marque très nette d'un homme et d'un artiste'.[41] In doing so, he articulates once more the understanding of literary practice and literary merit holding sway at the autonomous pole under the auspices of the *NRF*. In appreciating a work of literature, our focus should be on the distinctiveness of its vision or the atmosphere it generates. As Arland puts it, 'ce chant, tout à la fois ample et rauque, cette sombre ardeur, cette intime union de la sensualité et de l'esprit [...] voilà bien la marque de Mauriac'.[42]

---

[38] Marcel Arland, 'François Mauriac, *Les Chemins de la mer*', *La Nouvelle Revue française*, 308 (May 1939), p. 875.

[39] 'François Mauriac, *Les Chemins de la mer*', p. 880.

[40] Ibid.

[41] Ibid., p. 875.

[42] 'François Mauriac, *Les Chemins de la mer*', p. 875.

Moreover, the critic's role is not to lay down prescriptive rules, but to determine a writer's particular artistic project, and to assess the way in which it develops. Mauriac is noteworthy and interesting for Arland because he is trying to take his work in a new direction, even if it is not always with success, when he could quite easily have stayed faithful to a well-practised formula:

> Il semble que l'auteur, à mesure qu'il avance dans son œuvre, se sente requis par de nouvelles figures et de nouveaux problèmes. Il ne veut point *fermer* son roman, comme il lui serait aisé de faire; il se tourne vers ce qui le sollicite, il l'aborde, il se sent entraîné.[43]

Finally, Arland reverses one of the most resounding assertions of Sartre's essay in order to reassert the supremacy of the aesthetic: 'un personnage est vivant parce qu'il est libre, dit M. Sartre. Il nous paraît libre ici parce qu'il est vivant'.[44] For him, our impression of the characters' liberty derives not from some preconceived or abstract notion of freedom which they then embody, but from the writer's artistic abilities, the skill with which they are painted and the reality evoked.

Arland's article is a vigorous defence of a conception of literature which the *NRF* had imposed on the field since its launch; but given Arland's position within the *NRF*, and the shift in its balance of power towards a young avant-garde being promoted by Paulhan, his defence can only look like the rearguard action of a perspective which has been relegated from its position of authority and finds its power ebbing away. That decline would be confirmed in the aftermath of the Occupation and Liberation, both of which would have a crucial impact on the literary field.

However, it is a nice irony that Mauriac's own moment of crisis – a crisis around which the future direction of the field itself had begun to crystallise – is resolved by the same historical events which will provoke the radical restructuring of the literary field around the avant-garde position represented by Sartre. Damage to Mauriac's reputation as a novelist is undoubtedly done by Sartre's intervention; but the reconfiguration of the field provoked by the Second World

---

[43] Ibid., p. 877. Arland's emphasis.
[44] Ibid., p. 878.

War means other possibilities and positions become available to him. Indeed, it is thanks in particular to the new system of values imposed in the cultural field by the young avant-garde that Mauriac can capitalise on certain aspects of his profile and trajectory to complete the transformation from novelist to intellectual which had begun more haphazardly in the 1930s. Having executed Mauriac as a novelist, Sartre was about to provide him with the means to stage his Second Coming as an intellectual.

'Nous avions besoin de toutes nos armes. Mauriac était de celles-là'

Mauriac's wartime activities and his role in the literary field during the Occupation have already been comprehensively and convincingly analysed by Gisèle Sapiro, among others.[45] We can retain a series of key moments from the narrative of the period. In August 1940, the spokesman of the Resistance forces gathered around de Gaulle in London, Maurice Schumann, makes a direct appeal to Mauriac during a radio address:

> Ces ondes auxquelles je n'oserais pas confier un message pour ma mère, je leur demande ce soir, de porter ma voix jusqu'à vous, François Mauriac [...] si grand que vous soyez par l'esprit ou par le cœur [...] nous pensons à vous comme à une image douloureuse de la France lointaine.[46]

His designation by the Free French as an emblem of the nation's suffering, and by implication as a vital voice of hope and moral authority, coincides with his designation as an enemy by the collaborationist press, for whom his work exemplifies the moral decadence which had led France to the catastrophe of defeat, and which required the 'redemptive' reign of Pétain to put right. In June 1941, he is the subject of a public debate, 'Un agent de désagrégation: François Mauriac', which is successfully disrupted by a number of

---

[45] Gisèle Sapiro, *La Guerre des écrivains*. On Mauriac's wartime activities, see also Jean Lacouture, *François Mauriac*, II, ch. 4, Jean Touzot, *Mauriac sous l'Occupation* (Bordeaux: Editions Confluences, 1995), and Malcolm Scott, *Mauriac: The Politics of a Novelist*, pp. 88-96.

[46] Cit. in Jean Lacouture, *François Mauriac*, II, pp. 118-119.

friends and allies, including Jean Paulhan;[47] and in September of the same year, he is the subject of a critical article by Drieu La Rochelle in an *NRF* he had revived as a collaborationist journal after it had ceased publication in June 1940.[48]

The attacks from the collaborationists in particular serve to sharpen Mauriac's awareness of his role and position:

> Je leur en suis reconnaissant parce qu'ils m'ont aidé à prendre conscience de ce que j'étais, car au début, comme pour beaucoup de Français [...], le maréchal Pétain représentait pour moi Verdun, une victoire de la France, enfin un homme indiscutable.[49]

In 1941, he joins the most important organisation of what became known as the 'Résistance intellectuelle', the Comité National des Ecrivains, and publishes in its clandestine journal *Les Lettres françaises*, putting aside ideological differences to collaborate with the Communists in doing so.[50] In 1943, he makes his most significant contribution to the intellectual Resistance, with the publication of *Le Cahier noir* by Les Editions de Minuit under the pseudonym Forez. He spends much of his time in the occupied zone, and puts himself in real danger of arrest as a result. For as Sapiro points out, 'c'est le propre de cette situation de crise que d'avoir transformé le risque symbolique associé à la prise de position en risque de vie et de mort'.[51]

The Occupation will play a determining role in Mauriac's emergence as an intellectual figure, as he finds himself in a position to benefit from the specific conditions it puts in place. It serves to disrupt the established order of things in every domain of existence, and the literary field is no exception, as the rules which had governed its workings up to that point are abruptly suspended. In particular, the

---

[47] Paulhan recounts the meeting and its sabotage in a letter to Mauriac. See François Mauriac, Jean Paulhan, *Correspondance (1925-1967)*, pp. 143-147.
[48] Drieu La Rochelle, 'Mauriac', *La Nouvelle Revue française*, 331 (September 1941), 343-350. Drieu attacks Mauriac for his position over the Spanish Civil War before turning to Mauriac's latest novel, *La Pharisienne*, and rehearsing once again some of the familiar criticisms of his narrative technique.
[49] Cit. in Jacques Debû-Bridel, *La Résistance intellectuelle*, p. 97.
[50] On the Comité National des Ecrivains and *Les Lettres françaises*, see Gisèle Sapiro, *La Guerre des écrivains*, ch. 7.
[51] Sapiro, *La Guerre des écrivains*, p. 233.

feature which defines the modern literary field more than any – its relative autonomy from the broader field of power – is put into abeyance as the political impinges suddenly and dramatically on its operation and its direction.

This manifests itself most clearly in the surveillance and interference by the propaganda department of the occupying forces, and is illustrated by the events surrounding the *NRF* in the months following the Occupation. Wound down by Paulhan in September 1940, the review is re-launched in December of that year under the editorship of Drieu La Rochelle with the support of the Nazi authorities in Paris. Aware of the importance and prestige of the *NRF* in the French cultural domain, they encouraged its reappearance as part of the process of normalisation of the occupation.[52] Drieu secures the freedom of the review from censorship on the understanding that it will express no hostility towards the Germans, and indeed it becomes openly collaborationist in tone. This *ersatz NRF* would function for three years, but its clear political allegiances, and the desertion of many of the key figures who had acted as the guarantors of its authority during the inter-war period, meant that its legitimacy had all but disappeared.

Schumann's interpellation of Mauriac itself signals a desire on the part of the Free French to mobilise the forces, material or symbolic, available to them. Their decision to single out Mauriac is an indication of his status beyond the confines of the autonomous pole. The Gaullists in London are in no doubt as to his importance as a novelist and cultural figure. In their eyes, he possesses a huge amount of symbolic capital which they want to exploit. As Schumann puts it, 'nous avions besoin de toutes nos armes. Mauriac était de celles-là...'[53] In other words, a writer whose legitimacy and future as a literary figure had been called into question only a year previously now finds himself asked to play a role in the fight for the liberation of his country, one which will depend in large part precisely on the status and talents he is perceived to have as a writer.

This rapid shift in fortunes is a direct result of the intriguing changes in the position of the literary field brought about by War and Occupation, and the loss of its autonomy especially. Suddenly, it

---

[52] Cf. Martyn Cornick, *Intellectuals in History: the 'NRF' under Jean Paulhan*, pp. 181-182.
[53] Cit in Jean Lacouture, *François Mauriac*, II, p. 119.

seems that the power of consecration, the power to designate the most important figures in the field, lies not within the field but outside it; not with a self-regulating peer group at the autonomous pole, but with literary laymen in the political sphere who are beginning to conceive of the field and its actors in strategic terms. Moreover, these laymen have a perception of the field, and Mauriac's place within it, which appears to be aligned more with that of Arland and Rousseaux than that of Sartre.

A clue to the change in both Mauriac's status and the values defining the field can also be found in the shifting attitude of Jean Paulhan during this period. In the 1930s, as we have seen, he was increasingly dismissive of Mauriac's abilities as a novelist; but in the new circumstances represented by the Occupation, Paulhan is prepared to recognise his broader importance and role. The most striking evidence of this comes in 1942, when he starts to draw up secret plans for a new editorial board to take over the running of the *NRF* from Drieu, who had expressed a desire to resign as editor (the plans would in fact come to nothing, and publication of the review would instead cease in 1943).

The participation of Mauriac, alongside Valéry and Gide, is seen as essential for the success of the project. As Paulhan says in a letter to Mauriac, 'je commence à me sentir plein de confiance, si vous êtes là. Il arrive à Valéry d'être faible. Gide est bien loin. Fargue est léger. Mais je compte sur votre rigueur, pour nous sauver tous'.[54] While there may be an element of flattery in Paulhan's remarks here, another indication of his acknowledgement of Mauriac's status comes in a letter to Drieu during the same period. Arguing for Mauriac's place on the committee in the face of Drieu's resistance, Paulhan writes: 'au demeurant, Mauriac a collaboré régulièrement à la *nrf*, et a toujours été tenu pour l'un des plus grands de nos étrangers'.[55] For the moment at least, it seems that Paulhan has put to one side his previous, and rather more brutal, assessment of Mauriac's literary talents. What matters now, and what earns Mauriac the right to be counted among the established heavyweights of the field, is the status he has begun to acquire as a result of his activities and membership of the Resistance.

---

[54] François Mauriac, Jean Paulhan, *Correspondance (1925-1967)*, p. 163. See also pp. 160-162.
[55] Jean Paulhan, *Choix de lettres*, II, p. 274.

Indeed, Mauriac's role in the intellectual Resistance crystallises an important irony, one which offers a key to understanding his emergence as a voice of national and moral conscience. I would argue that those things which cause him difficulties as he negotiates the literary field prove to be central to his success as an intellectual; that what is seen as problematic within the confines of the literary field shows itself to be an asset when he ventures out into the political field and intervenes in worldly affairs. This is true firstly of the position he occupies in the literary field and the social order as a member of the Académie Française. As we saw in the previous chapter, it is precisely his membership of the Académie which makes him a valuable addition to the Resistance. As Jacques Debû-Bridel puts it, 'c'était pour nous, vu sa personnalité, son talent, sa situation politique, une grande victoire, un grand réconfort; le seul, l'unique académicien du CNE jusqu'en 1944'.[56]

It is true too in terms of his ethos, and in particular his stance as a moralist. Writing in 1937, in fact, Jean Grenier had already suggested that it was the role of moralist which seemed to suit him well, and for which he would be most remembered: 'probablement beaucoup plus encore que le romancier, demeurera de lui le psychologue et le moraliste'.[57] Mauriac's habit of adopting an omniscient, God-like position from which to scrutinise and judge human behaviour compromises him repeatedly as a novelist, whether in the eyes of the *NRF* or Jean-Paul Sartre; but this is exactly the quality which befits an intellectual figure. The intellectual is called upon to perform a prophetic function, to divine and interpret events and the motives which drive them, to act as a voice of conscience reminding those around him of their duties and responsibilities.

Moreover, *Le Cahier noir* will demonstrate that he clearly has the means to carry out the task he is called upon to perform. In this thunderous text, he expresses his belief in France's victory over the forces of oppression, while simultaneously calling on his readers to play their part in the on-going struggle:

> Se tenir au-dessus de la mêlée? Regarder de haut les multitudes
> torturées? En tout cas, pas de plus haut que la croix. Il faut

---

[56] Jacques Debû-Bridel, *La Résistance intellectuelle*, p. 45.
[57] Jean Grenier, 'François Mauriac, *Journal (II)*', *La Nouvelle Revue française*, 287 (August 1937), p. 344.

demeurer à la hauteur du gibet – et nous savons que celui où le Christ rendit l'esprit était très bas puisque les chiens souvent dévoraient les pieds des esclaves crucifiés.[58]

At the same time, Mauriac can also profit from the fundamental changes which affect the literary and cultural fields both during the years of crisis marked by the Occupation, and in the aftermath of the War, as they are reconfigured in important new ways. Not only does Mauriac possess the qualities which are essential for the role of intellectual, but he will begin to assume that role at a time when it becomes the subject of extensive reflection and theorisation, and is seen as the most legitimate position available to writers – one, indeed, they are virtually obliged to adopt.

Central to these changes, of course, is the successful way in which Sartre secures a hegemonic position in the field, consolidated by the launch of his journal *Les Temps modernes* in October 1945. His accession to the autonomous pole marks a vital moment, and a properly revolutionary moment, in the history of the field. The key to his power lies in the unprecedented status he manages both to acquire and to impose as a model of excellence, that of the 'total intellectual'. Sartre shows himself capable of intervening and excelling in various domains of intellectual activity simultaneously, and those of literature and philosophy especially. Not only does he establish himself as an important new philosopher, thanks to *L'Etre et le néant* (1943), but he asserts himself too as a novelist and playwright, both with *La Nausée* (1938), and *Les Mouches* (1943). Crucially, too, the significance of his literary works lies precisely in their exploration of the new philosophy he is proposing; and in the theatre especially, he finds a radical way of taking that philosophy beyond the closed circuits of the academic world and disseminating it to a wide range of audiences. As Anna Boschetti observes,

> Sartre s'impose à l'attention du monde philosophique et du monde littéraire, au monde de la culture noble et à celui des grands quotidiens, et il franchit ainsi les deux barrières – qui caractérisent le fonctionnement du champ pendant toute son histoire – entre circuit philosophique et circuit littéraire, entre succès légitime et divulgation.[59]

---

[58] François Mauriac, *Le Cahier noir* (Paris: Desclée de Brouwer, 1994), p. 41.

[59] Anna Boschetti, *Sartre et 'Les Temps modernes'*, p. 18.

With Sartre's totalising gesture, his drawing together of these different disciplines, it suddenly seems as if mastery of both is the essential criterion of legitimacy and success. It is not just that Sartre is the new Bergson or the new Gide, but that he is both simultaneously. Moreover, being the new Bergson is what gives him the necessary distinctiveness to establish himself as the new Gide; and his sense of the literary gives him the means to present his philosophy in a newly vivid and concrete way. Another consequence of his evident competence and success in both fields is that actors operating in just one domain will appear limited as a result, as Boschetti remarks:

> L'intellectuel complet fait paraître tous les autres en défaut. Son plus proche rival en littérature, Camus, est un amateur sur le terrain philosophique par rapport à l'auteur de *L'Etre et le néant*. Et Merleau-Ponty, le seul concurrent sérieux en philosophie, n'est que philosophe.[60]

However, Sartre intends his sphere of action to be far broader than these two disciplines. In making his totalising gesture – that is to say, in eliding the artificial barriers put in place between domains of knowledge, and demonstrating the interdependence which exists between them – he is laying claim to the power and authority to intervene across the whole spectrum of intellectual, cultural and political activity. After all, performed as it is in the context of the Occupation, *Les Mouches* has a political point as much as a philosophical one. Or rather, Sartre sets out to demonstrate how his philosophy of existence necessarily implies a politics, one which is radical and contestatory.

The position of the Sartrean intellectual is thus undoubtedly one of privilege, but this also makes it one of obligation; and the political dimension of the intellectual's activity will be one of the most important issues of the post-war years. It will be a central theme of the essay which sets the agenda for *Les Temps modernes* in its first issue, published in October 1945. If we should have learned one thing from the Occupation, argues Sartre, it is the distinctive nature of the writer's role in society. He calls on writers to recognise their position in the world, and in doing so, to measure their responsibilities, the

---

[60] Ibid., p. 176.

power their words can have: 'l'écrivain est *en situation* dans son époque: chaque parole a des retentissements'.[61] In 'Qu'est-ce que la littérature?' two years later, Sartre would theorise further his notion of the committed writer. Commitment would be firmly established as the new criterion of excellence for the writer. Where partisanship and intervention in the world could still be called into question during the inter-war period (by Julien Benda in *La Trahison des clercs*, for example), it is now a writer's refusal to engage with the world which is seen as a fault. Furthermore, this engagement is understood as central to a writer's very being. A writer must be an actor, not a spectator; he must use the tools at his disposal – namely language and his linguistic abilities – in order to try to change the world. Or, as Sartre would put it, 'parler, c'est agir'.[62]

By the mid-1950s, Mauriac would come to exemplify Sartre's notion of the committed intellectual, intervening forcefully via his column in *L'Express* to condemn the ineffectual governments of the Fourth Republic, and in particular their handling of the deteriorating situation in North Africa. Yet his path from key figure of the intellectual Resistance to militant journalist is not a straightforward one. Indeed, his position is initially one of opposition to the agenda being put forward by *Les Temps modernes*.

Mauriac undoubtedly emerges from the Occupation with new status and prestige, playing an important role in the intellectual and political debates which mark the Liberation. As the major editorialist of *Le Figaro*, he publishes a resounding article celebrating de Gaulle on the day of the liberation of Paris.[63] He becomes heavily involved in the debate surrounding the *épuration*, intervening in an attempt to save the collaborationist writers Henri Béraud and Robert Brasillach from execution, successfully in the case of the former, not so in the case of the latter. Nicknamed 'Saint François des Assises' by *Le Canard enchaîné*, he is caught up in a notorious polemic with Albert Camus over the legitimacy of the *épuration*, which Camus would characterise as a debate between Justice and Charity, arguing that Mauriac's desire for Christian charity should not stand in the way of

---

[61] Jean-Paul Sartre, 'Présentation des *Temps modernes*', in *Situations, II*, p. 13. Sartre's emphasis.
[62] Jean-Paul Sartre, 'Qu'est-ce que la littérature?', in *Situations, II*, p. 72.
[63] 'Le premier des nôtres', *Le Figaro*, 25 août 1944, repr. in OC XI 389-391.

the need for earthly justice.[64] Another polemic with the Communists, his provisional allies of the Resistance period, would provoke his relative disengagement from the political scene at the end of 1946.[65] Reflecting on the period in *Nouveaux mémoires intérieurs*, he remarks that 'j'avais été pris dans les remous de la Libération, j'avais reçu des coups de toutes parts [...]. J'en avais assez de la politique' (OA 819).

His decision was helped by fact that the government of the new Fourth Republic was dominated by the Christian Democrats of the Mouvement Républicain Populaire (MRP), Mauriac's preferred party at the time: 'la Résistance était au pouvoir. Le vieux silloniste en moi se réjouissait de cette montée au zénith de la démocratie chrétienne' (MP 26). Indeed, when he does intervene in political debate, it is to lend his support to the government. This includes backing French action in Indochina, where the first of the country's wars of decolonisation broke out in 1947, and expressing his loyalty to France's colonial enterprise.[66] His position during this period sits uncomfortably with the vigour of his campaigns against the colonial conflicts in North Africa in the 1950s, and which he would later regret (MP 26).

Although the late 1940s would be marked by something of a return to the novel, Mauriac's most notable activity during this time is centred on *La Table ronde*. This new literary journal was launched in 1948 by the eponymous publishing house, with Mauriac and Thierry Maulnier as its directors. It is hard not to read Mauriac's involvement in *La Table ronde* as an attempt to capitalise on the authority and prestige he had acquired during the War years. As we have seen, both the *NRF* and *Les Temps modernes* demonstrate the vital importance of the review as a way of establishing a position in, and exerting an influence on, the modern literary field. One of the attractions of *La*

---

[64] 'Chaque fois qu'à propos de l'épuration, j'ai parlé de justice, M. Mauriac a parlé de charité'. *Combat*, 11 January 1945, repr. in Albert Camus, *Actuelles: écrits politiques* (Paris: Gallimard, 1950), p. 59. On Mauriac's polemic with Camus, and his role in the debates surrounding the *épuration*, see Sapiro, *La Guerre des écrivains*, pp. 601-611, and Georges Montheillet, 'Mauriac et Camus: la justice et la charité', *Travaux du Centre d'Etudes et de Recherche François Mauriac*, 32 (December 1992), 27-45.

[65] On Mauriac's polemic with the Communists, see Malcolm Scott, *Mauriac: The Politics of a Novelist*, pp. 102-105. For an overview of his activities during this period, see also Jean Lacouture, *François Mauriac*, II, pp. 172-219.

[66] See 'Le bourreau de soi-même' from September 1947 (MP 443-445), and 'La dure vérité' from October 1950 (MP 447-448), for example.

Table ronde for Mauriac was that it brought him into contact with some of the talented young writers emerging on to the scene, and in particular the group of writers around Roger Nimier and Jacques Laurent, who would become known as the Hussards. As Patrick Louis puts it, 'nul doute que Mauriac n'éprouve un grand plaisir à se retrouver, au travers de *La Table ronde*, [...] le parrain de la jeune génération'.[67] Like Paulhan at the *NRF* in the pre-war days, he could play the role of figurehead and mentor to the next generation, and through them, perhaps, have a bearing on the history of the field.

Certainly, Mauriac's stated aim for *La Table ronde* is an ambitious one: nothing less than to fill gap left by disappearance of the *NRF* in 1943, to take over where it had left off as the leading literary journal in the field: 'l'idée me vint à ce moment-là [...] que puisque *La Nouvelle Revue française* ne reparaissait pas, on pouvait tenter de prendre sa place' (OA 819). The review lays claim to the governing principles which had proved the key to the success of the *NRF* in the inter-war period. *La Table ronde* would be a literary journal above all else, a place where writers from all parts of the political spectrum could disengage from their political positions and focus on the business of literary creation. Writing in 1949, Mauriac defines the role of *La Table ronde* as 'le regroupement des écrivains français dignes de ce nom et que les sinistres conjonctures de la plus récente histoire avaient séparés'.[68] As an indication of the review's intentions, Camus will participate in the first issue; but he will not reappear, and nor will any other writer from the political left. Instead, the influence of the Hussards will increasingly assert itself, and *La Table ronde* will be seen as a review of the Right.

Indeed, fifteen years after the debacle of *Vigile*, *La Table ronde* will prove to be another misadventure for Mauriac, as the review fails to impose itself in the field. Just as he misreads the field in the early 1930s, underestimating the hegemony of the *NRF* and its ethos, so too in the post-war period, he fails to appreciate the significance of the field's recent reconfiguration. The problem lies not so much in the fact that Mauriac wants *La Table ronde* to take the place of the *NRF*. His desire to emulate it is understandable, given the

[67] Patrick Louis, *'La Table ronde': une aventure singulière* (Paris: Editions de la Table Ronde, 1992), p. 84.
[68] François Mauriac, 'Notre raison d'être', *La Table ronde*, août-septembre 1949, p. 1235.

success with which it dominated the field during the inter-war period. However, he is attempting to replicate its position in a field which, since its disappearance, has been restructured around an autonomous pole incarnated by *Les Temps modernes*.

Les Temps modernes asserts such influence in the post-war period because, like its director in the intellectual field, it performs a totalising gesture, devoting itself not just to literature, but to all domains of intellectual activity: philosophy, politics, the human sciences. The effect is to make other reviews appear outmoded or limited in their scope. As Boschetti observes,

> Tous ces prétendants, qui sont retenus sur le terrain de la *NRF*, la littérature, par une propension à reproduire compréhensible après un règne de vingt ans, apparaissent tout à coup comme les copies attardées et imparfaites d'une réalité dépassée par rapport à une position qui semble à la fois conserver et aller de l'avant.[69]

La Table ronde may set itself up as the inheritor of the *NRF*'s mantle, and borrow the terms in which it articulated its vision of literature; but if it fails to establish itself, it is because those terms and that vision are outmoded. The very presence of *Les Temps modernes* in the field means that the significance of the position represented by the *NRF* and its successors also changes.

That the team at *La Table ronde* are aware of having to negotiate a new and challenging environment is suggested by their constant reference to *Les Temps modernes* as they put forward their own agenda. In fact, the aim of *La Table ronde* is as much to counter the dominance of Sartre's journal as to replace the *NRF*. The review's hostility is signalled almost immediately when an article by Thierry Maulnier attacking Sartre's theories of literature appears in its second number.[70] It re-emerges the following year when Mauriac outlines the review's philosophy. While *Les Temps modernes* is not named explicitly in his article, there is no doubt from its focus that its programme is dictating his thinking. Indeed, his piece can be seen as a riposte to Sartre ten years after his attack on *La Fin de la nuit*.

Mauriac asserts that the review's main intention is to resist some of the recent trends in literary practice, and as he does so, he

---

[69] Anna Boschetti, *Sartre et 'Les Temps modernes'*, p. 187.
[70] Thierry Maulnier, 'J.-P. Sartre et le suicide de la littérature', *La Table ronde*, février 1948, 195-210.

establishes its position as the guardian of the long-standing model of literary excellence incarnated by the *NRF*. Firstly, he takes issue with the notion of committed literature, arguing – precisely as Jacques Rivière had done in the *NRF* thirty years previously – that literature should be kept free from the utilitarian requirements of politics. Its function is not to engage with the transitory concerns of the period, he says, but to explore the timeless and universal aspects of the human condition: 'elle a une mission certes "dans les siècles et dans les cieux", qui est de rendre témoignage à l'homme'.[71] Likewise, while a writer can certainly bear witness, 'ce témoignage se doit d'être désintéressé, gratuit. Pour aucun artiste né cela ne souffre discussion'.[72] Secondly, he reasserts the autonomy of the aesthetic, rejecting the idea that literary practice should be dictated to by other disciplines, and philosophy in particular. We can make out a sardonic retort to Sartre in Mauriac's comments, as he responds to the criticisms levelled at him in 1939:

> Un catéchisme a cours touchant la manière dont il faut introduire le temps dans le roman, les droits et les devoirs du romancier à l'égard de ses personnages, la liberté qu'il doit leur concéder […]. Toute une génération d'écrivains a dû subir les effets stérilisants de ce protocole arbitraire imposé par des philosophes "qui ont volé l'outil".[73]

Mauriac's remarks are a direct challenge to the new model of excellence which Sartre and *Les Temps modernes* is attempting to impose, whereby the most legitimate actors in the field are those who draw on expertise from a range of disciplines.

However, to argue for the political disengagement of the writer and the autonomy of literature in a field dominated by *Les Temps modernes* is different from doing so in one where the aim is to reassert the autonomy of the field in the face of literary institutions too closely allied to the dominant fractions in the field of power. The arrival of *Les Temps modernes* in the field has the effect of politicising the position adopted by *La Table ronde* in a way which was not the case when it was occupied by the *NRF* in the inter-war period. The group of writers at *La Table ronde* may want to keep literature apart

---

[71] François Mauriac, 'Notre raison d'être', p. 1237.
[72] 'Notre raison d'être', p. 1238.
[73] Ibid.

from politics; but in a world where Sartre is arguing that writers need to be aware of the political power their writing can have, this gesture itself takes on political significance. The configuration of the field in the late 1940s and early 1950s means that *La Table ronde* assigns itself to a reactionary position, one which is marked politically as being on the right, precisely because it attempts to argue that literature should remain disengaged from politics.

Moreover, the position *La Table ronde* adopts in the field is one of intrinsic weakness. While it may attempt to establish itself as a place of resistance to the new and dominant order, its constant reference to Sartre's position as it does so is an acknowledgement that the agenda is being set by *Les Temps modernes*. Mauriac's review defines itself on the basis that it is what *Les Temps modernes* is not. This is in striking contrast to Sartre's journal which, having positioned itself 'en avant', beyond the existing positions, can define its agenda on its own terms. The weakness of *La Table ronde*'s position in the field is further confirmed when the *NRF* is re-launched in January 1953, firstly by the ease with which the *NRF* can supplant its new rival, and secondly by the fact that the *NRF* itself will fail to reclaim the prestige and authority it had enjoyed in the inter-war period. The position it represents had become a dominated one in the field.[74]

Ironically, Mauriac himself would soon become aware of the weakness of *La Table ronde*'s position, and be obliged to leave it behind. In April 1954, Mauriac took his leave of the review after an increasingly tense relationship with the other members of its editorial board. The reason for his departure lay in his sudden and dramatic

---

[74] On the return of the *NRF*, see Martyn Cornick, 'Jean Paulhan et la résurrection de la *NRF* en 1953', *La Revue des revues*, 29 (2001), 30-53. As Cornick notes, Mauriac greeted the return of the *NRF* with notorious hostility, devoting the first four of his monthly 'Bloc-notes' columns to it in 1953, and describing it infamously as 'cette chère vieille dame tondue, dont les cheveux ont mis huit ans à repousser', in reference to the punishment meted out to women accused of 'horizontal collaboration' with the enemy. See François Mauriac, *D'un bloc-notes à l'autre, 1952-1969*, ed. by Jean Touzot (Paris: Bartillat, 2004), pp. 24-32, and Martyn Cornick, 'Jean Paulhan et la résurrection de la *NRF*', pp. 44-49. Mauriac's attitude is an indication as much as anything of his recognition that *La Table ronde* had failed to secure its position in the field, that is to say mobilise sufficient resources (and in particular an appropriately diverse group of contributors with the requisite amount of symbolic capital) to counter a review which could draw on its historical importance and iconic status: 'il reste qu'elle a l'ancienneté, le prestige', he acknowledges in 1952 (*D'un bloc-notes à l'autre*, p. 25).

return to politics, and in particular his intervention in the debate over the future of Morocco. His comments in both the editorials he continued to write for *Le Figaro*, and the 'Bloc-notes', the monthly column he began for *La Table ronde* in late 1952, were taking a distinctly anti-colonialist tone, and this sat uneasily with the political position of both journals.

The trigger for his return to politics was an important event late in 1952, one which would prove to be the final and decisive step in his emergence as one of the key intellectual figures of the period. In November 1952, Mauriac is awarded the Nobel Prize for literature. When he travels to Stockholm the following month to receive the prize, he is struck by a troubling coincidence, as the day of the ceremony coincides with unrest in Casablanca, which is repressed violently by French troops. The impact on Mauriac is dramatic: 'désormais je fus engagé' (BN I 303). During 1953, he would begin to take an increasingly radical line on the situation in Morocco, criticising French settlers and condemning what he terms 'ce racisme né du lucre et de la peur' (MP 453), and beginning a period of militancy which would continue during the 1950s.

The shock Mauriac receives from the collision of these two events will have several significant, and ironic, consequences. Firstly, it encourages in him exactly the sort of reflection Sartre had been demanding of his fellow writers, and which Mauriac and the rest of the writers at *La Table ronde* had initially resisted. Mauriac is driven in particular to recognise and interrogate his status and position in society as a writer, something which provokes an abrupt artistic silence as he engages with the events unfolding in the world around him. Even more ironically, when he makes his return to politics, he will use a Sartrean language of commitment and responsibility to articulate his position; and in his activities as a journalist, he will provide a convincing demonstration of Sartre's notion of the committed intellectual.

Mauriac's departure from *La Table ronde* also confirms the review's incompatibility with the requirements of the field in its current configuration. As Mauriac adapts himself to that configuration in his return to militant politics, *La Table ronde* proves unable to provide him with an effective platform from which to perform the function of committed intellectual. He requires a different position in the field from which to articulate his views, one which he will find in

L'Express, the news weekly launched in 1954. Indeed, such is his change in direction that Sartre can even envisage approaching him to write an article for *Les Temps modernes* later that same year.[75] In the next chapter, we examine more closely Mauriac's motivations for returning to the political domain in the 1950s, the interventions he makes, and the complex effects of the broader socio-cultural configuration in which he finds himself operating.

---

[75] 'Mauriac vu par Sartre, propos recueillis par Jean Touzot', in Jean Touzot (ed.), *François Mauriac*, *Cahiers de L'Herne*, 48 (1985), p. 46.

Chapter Three

Responsibility and Commitment

Having received the award of the Nobel Prize for Literature in late 1952, Mauriac made an abrupt return to the political realm as a voice of contestation. His attention was caught by the increasingly troubled situation in the French colonies of North Africa, and Morocco especially. During the conflict in Indochina – France's first war of decolonisation, which broke out in 1947 – Mauriac continued to express his support for the colonial enterprise, and dismiss those who questioned French attempts to hold on to power.[1] However, as instability spread to North Africa, and his disillusion grew with the ruling Christian Democrats of the MRP, he was himself about to emerge as an important critic of French colonialism.

The political situation in Morocco had worsened dramatically during 1952, as the colonial authorities attempted to control a growing nationalist sentiment. The crisis culminated in the Casablanca riots of early December, which had coincided with the Nobel Prize ceremony in Stockholm. On his return from Stockholm, Mauriac was approached by Robert Barrat, the left-wing Catholic militant who ran the Centre Catholique des Intellectuels Français (CCIF). Barrat presented him with evidence that the riots had been in large part provoked by the authorities in order to justify the subsequent repression and deportation of suspected Moroccan nationalists.[2]

Provoked by these revelations, Mauriac made a dramatic entry into the debate in January 1953. He published an explosive editorial in *Le Figaro*, 'La Vocation des Chrétiens dans l'Union française', in

---

[1] For example, see 'Le Bourreau de soi-même' from September 1947 (MP 443-445), and 'La Dure vérité' from October 1950 (MP 447-448).
[2] Jean Lacouture, *François Mauriac*, II, p. 253.

which he called on the Christian community in France and the colonies to resist what he notoriously termed 'ce racisme né du lucre et de la peur' infecting life in Morocco (MP 453). This phrase, a clear attack on Morocco's French community and its entrenched economic interests, caused particular controversy among the newspaper's readership, which remained largely untroubled by the colonial project being carried out in its name. As Lacouture observes,

> Qu'un membre de l'Académie française, catholique notoire, grand bourgeois, éditorialiste du *Figaro*, puisse évoquer des "crimes" et parler du "racisme" à propos du Maroc, de cet empire chérifien que la bonne conscience française tenait pour le chef-d'œuvre de la colonisation [...] il y avait là de quoi stupéfier un monde de bonnes âmes pieuses et nanties, la clientèle du *Figaro*.[3]

Mauriac also started to engage in militant activities, becoming the first president of the Association France-Maghreb, founded by Barrat in June 1953 to promote understanding and cooperation between the people of France and North Africa.[4] By this time, he had come to be seen increasingly as a troublemaker by the political establishment for his criticism of the regime in place in Morocco. At the end of this month, he was publicly attacked for his stance on the French protectorate by Marshall Juin, one of the most senior military figures in Morocco, during Juin's inaugural address to the Académie Française. Mauriac's response to Juin in his editorial column would allow him to restate his condemnation of the situation in Morocco:

> Par cette agression publique contre un confrère qui depuis vingt ans siège dans l'enceinte où il vient de pénétrer, le maréchal Juin est sans aucun doute inconscient d'avoir comblé le plus ardent désir de ces puissances économiques qui, protégées contre le fisc, tiennent le Maroc en leur pouvoir et dont nous nous sommes permis de déranger le jeu (MP 462).

As the 1950s progressed, and the problems in the French colonies worsened, Mauriac emerged as a major critic of the governments of the Fourth Republic. In particular, he was one of the first metropolitan

---

[3] *François Mauriac*, II, p. 257.
[4] On Mauriac's activities during this period, see Lacouture, *François Mauriac*, II, pp. 276-285.

intellectuals to denounce the use of torture by the police and army in Algeria, in January 1955.

Mauriac's activities during this period also had some significant practical consequences. His increasingly radical political positions are reflected in important shifts in position in the journalistic field. His outspokenness over Morocco caused tensions with both *La Table ronde* and *Le Figaro*, where he had been a major editorialist since 1934, but where he was now proving to be a financial liability: subscriptions and advertising revenue were both being adversely affected by his interventions. Although he remained with the newspaper officially until 1954, he began scaling down his contributions during the summer of 1953. As he put it in the *Nouveaux mémoires intérieurs*, 'je coûtais trop cher au journal' (OA 820). This led to one of the most crucial moments in his career, which proved decisive in confirming his position as a key figure of the intellectual field in the 1950s.

His silence at *Le Figaro* was noticed by the two young editors of *L'Express*, Jean-Jacques Servan-Schreiber and Françoise Giroud, who had launched the innovative, left-of-centre news weekly in May 1953. Mauriac was approached by Servan-Schreiber to write for the journal and he accepted, publishing two articles in November and December 1953. He joined *L'Express* on a contractual basis in March 1954, bringing from *La Table ronde* the *Bloc-notes* column he had begun in 1952 as a way of contributing regularly to the review, and whose diary-like format allowed him to range widely over various subjects: culture, faith, and above all, politics. The *Bloc-notes* would be his main contribution to *L'Express*, appearing every week on the back page until his departure in 1961.[5]

Joining *L'Express* was significant for Mauriac in a number of ways, as we shall see both in this chapter and the next. The journal had been founded with the intention of promoting the reformist political and economic agenda being put forward by Pierre Mendès France, the leader of the Parti Radical. Mendès France was one of the few politicians at the time prepared to point out the link between economic growth, modernisation and decolonisation, arguing that the

---

[5] In what follows, I use the term *Bloc-notes* to refer to the work as a whole, as published in five volumes between 1959 and 1971 by Flammarion, and in a new edition by Le Seuil in 1993. Individual columns or fragments will be referred to as 'Bloc-notes'.

costly colonial wars being fought in Indochina and North Africa were hampering the country's own development, and that relinquishing the empire might be necessary if France were to become a modern, and modernised, nation.[6] Throughout the 1950s, *L'Express* played an important role in mediating and disseminating the agenda of modernisation to a wider audience, opening its pages to a range of government advisors and academics. Moreover, the journal was striking for the way in which it not only supported this agenda, but embodied it in its very fabric: its tabloid style and bold use of cover photographs was a conscious imitation of the American news weekly *Time*, and brought a new look to French newsstands dominated by broadsheet newspapers.

   Although the partnership between Mauriac and the radical modernisers at *L'Express* is perhaps unlikely at first sight, not least because of the dramatic age gap of some forty years which separated them, the growing hostility to colonialism which he shared with his editors provided the common ground allowing him to collaborate with them. At the same time, the acknowledgement of Mauriac's status and prestige by Servan-Schreiber and Giroud meant he became a key element in their campaigns for reform. Having recognised the impact he could have as a voice of contestation, they set out to exploit and capitalise on it as much as possible. I shall discuss later how they manage the intervention in which he denounces the practice of torture in 1955, for example. Likewise, as an integral part of what had effectively become the unofficial journal of the Parti Radical, Mauriac became actively involved in the campaign for the legislative elections of January 1956, which *L'Express* hoped – in vain, as it turned out – would see victory for the 'Front républicain' coalition led by Mendès France. Mauriac made a radio election broadcast in December 1955, and it is claimed that his support for Mendès France brought with it a million Catholic votes.[7] Indeed, his collaboration with, not to say exploitation by, *L'Express* will play a central role in allowing him to assert himself as one of the major intellectuals of the period.

---

[6] See, for example, 'La France peut supporter la vérité', *L'Express*, 16 May 1953, p. 6, the interview given by Mendès France to mark the first issue of the news weekly, and which signalled its links with the politician. I return to these issues in chapter 5.
[7] See Françoise Giroud, *Profession journaliste* (Paris: Le Livre de Poche, 2003), p. 101. For the text of Mauriac's radio address, see *D'un bloc-notes à l'autre*, pp. 262-264.

This chapter examines Mauriac's motivations for his combative return to the political domain in 1953. It also investigates the forms his involvement takes, that is to say the way in which he illustrates and performs the function of committed intellectual and moral consciousness. It will emerge that the nature of his performance, and its effectiveness, depends not just on him, but also on the context in which it takes place. In other words, his involvement, and his status as intellectual more generally, are shaped in significant ways by the changed cultural context in which he operates in the 1950s, as much as by the evolution of his own position. For in the post-war period, the status of the intellectual seemed to enter a new phase. This evolution is operated by intellectuals themselves, in particular through the successful imposition of the Sartrean paradigm of the 'total' intellectual intervening on all fronts; but it is fostered too by broader cultural shifts, and the rapid evolution of mass culture especially, which responds to newly dominant intellectual figures by transforming them into what today we would term 'media stars'. We will see how Mauriac himself is caught up in, and indeed exemplifies, these processes during the 1950s, and that his time at *L'Express* is a determining factor in this.

The Nobel Prize and Mauriac's ethical shock
Mauriac's re-emergence as a critical voice in 1953 can be attributed to a variety of factors. Mauriac himself is in no doubt that religious faith is his principle motivation: writing in September 1953, he observes that 'ma vocation est politique dans la stricte mesure où elle est religieuse' (BN I 97). Indeed, the title of his first article on Morocco, 'La Vocation des Chrétiens dans l'Union française', makes clear that his position is an explicitly Christian one. On the one hand, the article is a call for Christians to resist and condemn the oppression being carried out there; on the other, it is a call to judge the events according to a Christian moral framework, and denounce the injustices being perpetrated by a country which lays claim to a Christian heritage while so obviously disregarding the teachings and example of Christ in its treatment of others.

In various articles and speeches during this period, we find repeated references to Christ as the emblematic figure of torture and victimhood. Speaking at a conference in November 1954, for example, Mauriac makes a provocative comparison between the repressive French colonial authorities and Christ's executioners, and highlights the hypocrisy of a nation which pays homage to the exemplary suffering of Christ, and yet continues to inflict similar suffering on others:

> Je suis obsédé quant à moi par toutes les croix qui n'ont cessé d'être dressées après le Christ, par cette chrétienté aveugle et sourde qui, dans les pauvres corps qu'elle soumettait à la question, n'a jamais reconnu Celui dont, le jour du Vendredi Saint, elle baise si dévotement les pieds et les mains percées.[8]

This hypocrisy is made all the more unacceptable for Mauriac given that the policies in Morocco were being implemented in the name of governments dominated by the Christian Democrats of the MRP. Mauriac becomes increasingly disenchanted by a party which, while it claimed to be informed by Christian principles, seemed in practice all too willing to ignore them.

Mauriac's understanding of his role in terms of a specifically Christian vocation has been highlighted by various observers, both Mauriac specialists and historians of the period more generally. Bernard Cocula, for example, argues that the articles of the *Bloc-notes* bear witness to Mauriac's broad Christian mission: 'toute la vie de Mauriac ayant été marquée par l'Evangile, c'est dans l'Evangile et dans sa fidélité au Christ qu'il faut chercher les raisons profondes de l'engagement mauriacien'.[9] Similarly, the historian Etienne Fouilloux remarks that 'ses interventions répétées, les premières surtout, sont le cri d'une foi blessée'.[10] Nathan Bracher, on the other hand, suggests Mauriac's motivations also have a political or ideological dimension. He argues that the events in North Africa interrogate 'the writer's keen sense of national identity'.[11] As Bracher points out, a sense of France's fundamental grandeur is a consistent element of Mauriac's world view. It underpins the patriotic rallying cry of *Le Cahier noir*,

---

[8] François Mauriac, *L'imitation des bourreaux de Jésus-Christ*, ed. by Alain de la Morandais (Paris: Desclée de Brouwer, 1984), p. 17.

[9] Bernard Cocula, *Mauriac: Le 'Bloc-notes'* (Bordeaux: L'Esprit du Temps, 1995), p. 33.

[10] Etienne Fouilloux, 'Intellectuels catholiques et guerre d'Algérie', in Jean-Pierre Rioux and Jean-François Sirinelli (eds), *La Guerre d'Algérie et les intellectuels*, *Cahiers de l'Institut d'Histoire du Temps Présent*, 10 (1988), p. 66.

[11] Nathan Bracher, 'Mauriac and Decolonisation: Civilisation, History and National Identity', *Contemporary French Civilisation*, 18 (1994), 167-187.

and informs his support for the war in Indochina. Like de Gaulle, Mauriac has – to borrow the former's famous expression – 'une certaine idée de la France',[12] a vision of the country as the epitome of the civilised and civilising nation. However, the bloody repression of the colonised people in the Maghreb, Bracher argues, forces Mauriac to acknowledge the extent to which this vision of France has been betrayed.[13] If the problem of decolonisation demands his full attention in the wake of the revelations from Casablanca, it is in large part because he realises that France itself has become implicated in crimes perpetrated until then only by others. Condemning colonial violence, and the dominant order which permits it, is the first step in bringing the country back into line, and restoring the faith of those who look to France as a model of enlightenment and liberty. Articulating this idea himself in 1957, Mauriac suggests that 'notre vocation est de rendre la France ressemblante à cette image qui survit dans le cœur des hommes libres du monde entier' (BN I 512).

However, in considering Mauriac's re-emergence as a critical voice, we must also take into account another motivation, one which has been rather overlooked in previous discussions of his return to the political domain. Little attention has been paid to Mauriac's understanding of his own situation during this period. We are often left with the sense that Mauriac is a simple witness to events, and that his intervention is an expression of outrage from a secure moral position. In characterising the *Bloc-notes* as an 'oraison', for example, and identifying what she terms its 'rhétorique de sermonnaire et de moraliste', Monique Gosselin readily evokes an image of Mauriac as a prophetic voice of conscience speaking down to the assembled crowd from the physically and morally superior position of the pulpit or orator's platform.[14] Yet while he certainly plays this role in the 1950s, reminding his readers of troubling events and demanding they confront them, I would argue that he does so with an increasingly acute awareness of his own position in the world. It seems that he is driven to intervene in the period not just by the nature of the events themselves, the violence of oppression being carried out in North Africa, but also because they oblige him to interrogate his own

---

[12] Charles de Gaulle, *Mémoires de guerre*, 3 vols (Paris: Plon, 1954-59), I, p. 1.

[13] Bracher, 'Mauriac and Decolonisation', p. 169.

[14] Monique Gosselin, 'Le *Bloc-notes* de 1953 à 1961: une oraison publique', *Cahiers François Mauriac*, 17 (1990), p. 59.

situation in a new way; and a crucial factor in this *prise de conscience* is the conjunction of the ceremony in Stockholm to receive the Nobel Prize, and the repression of the riots in Casablanca. The importance of this conjunction for Mauriac is suggested by the frequency with which he returns to it during the period. Writing to Georges Duhamel in 1953, for example, he describes the unfolding of events in Stockholm:

> A ma descente d'avion à Stockholm, dans la voiture qui m'amenait à l'ambassade, j'avais appris qu'on avait tiré sur la foule à Casablanca, qu'il y avait des morts et j'en ai ressenti, devant les étrangers, une honte et une douleur que j'oubliais dans l'émotion des cérémonies qui suivirent. Mais au milieu de tous ces honneurs, qui me tombaient sur la tête, je ne cessais de prier pour que je trouve à mon retour une occasion de les faire servir.[15]

The collision between the two events, and its role in triggering Mauriac's *volte face* over the colonial enterprise, deserve closer scrutiny.

As his comments here suggest, Mauriac identifies the significance of the Nobel Prize as a moment of recognition. The award of the Prize confirms and makes tangible a status established through his success as a novelist; but this moment of recognition is also transformative. It simultaneously endows the recipient with a new status and a new authority, which derive precisely from being a Nobel laureate, an individual acknowledged for his contribution not just to his own culture, but to that of the world as a whole. Its award is an acknowledgement of the universal value of Mauriac's work as an insight into human life. In its citation, the jury singles out 'l'analyse pénétrante de l'âme et l'intensité artistique avec laquelle il a interprété, dans la forme du roman, la vie humaine'.[16] It confirms in doing so his ability to comment on and judge human actions and human frailties, and his legitimacy as a voice of moral authority. At the same time, and as Mauriac's remark indicates, receiving the Nobel Prize not only brings with it renewed power as a figure of moral authority, but also a simultaneous awareness of the need to put that power to use, to 'faire servir' the honours which had been bestowed on him.

---

[15] François Mauriac, Georges Duhamel, *Correspondance (1919-1966)*, ed. by Jean-Jacques Hueber (Paris: Klincksieck, 1997), p. 229.
[16] Cit. in Jean Lacouture, *François Mauriac*, II, p. 242.

More specifically, Mauriac's sudden sense of responsibility derives from the conjunction of the prize-giving in Stockholm and the violent repression in Casablanca. It is this which provokes him into action. As he puts it in 1955,

> Une rencontre me frappa: je recevais le prix Nobel le jour et presque à l'heure où, à Casablanca, une foule misérable tombait dans le traquenard qui lui avait été tendu. A mon retour, un dossier irréfutable m'était apporté comme une réponse à ma secrète prière au milieu des fastes de Stockholm: qu'il me fût permis de rendre à la mer ce trop bel anneau que la fortune me passait au doigt. Désormais je fus engagé. (BN I 303)

The abrupt collision of the two events stands as a totemic moment for Mauriac. It seems he is shocked by the juxtaposition of a ceremony which, in its recognition of great artistic talents, is also a moment when Western civilisation congratulates itself for having produced such talents, and the messy violence which that same civilisation is forced to use in order to impose what it would see as its enlightened values on less fortunate and yet surprisingly recalcitrant peoples. The confrontation of the two crystallises the troubling nature of the socio-cultural order he inhabits, and affords him a glimpse of the tensions within it.

The Nobel Prize is a curious phenomenon. For all its claims to universalism, rewarding work which offers insights into that phenomenon known as 'human nature' – a notion shared and recognised, it implies, across the cultures of the globe – it remains the product of a specific socio-cultural order, as one of Western liberal democracy's highest honours. Indeed, it is a striking symptom of this system's basic contradictions. The prize is funded by the legacy of an individual who made his fortune in the arms industry, one of capitalism's most profitable and necessary enterprises, and devoted that fortune to the recognition of achievements made in those realms of investigation whose common characteristic is their disinterestedness, their disavowal of worldly and financial gain in favour of the purest of intellectual pursuits (the furthering of human knowledge and understanding). As such, it expresses the contradictions of a society which, while it is driven by the urge for capital accumulation – predicated inevitably on the exploitation and suffering of others, whether in the factory or in the colonies – must at the same time find ways at best of justifying that urge (claiming it to be a moral duty sanctioned by God), or assuaging the guilt it provokes (carrying out philanthropic acts), at worst making sure it remains hidden beneath the masks of civilisation and sophistication.

In other words, the moment when Mauriac is recognised by the dominant order for his contribution to its cultural wealth is also the point at which he is made aware of the problematic nature of that order. In many ways, Mauriac's response is a radical one: he sets out to put its most eminent prize to work, to 'jet[er] mon prix Nobel dans cette bagarre terrible' (LV 314), in the hope of provoking change within it. His crisis of confidence in a socio-cultural order with which he had for the most part been comfortable until then will also provoke a broader interrogation of the nature of society, the role culture plays within it, and his own role as a writer.

During the latter half of 1952, French radio broadcast a series of interviews with Mauriac by the Algerian-born writer Jean Amrouche. While for the most part their focus is Mauriac's work as a novelist, the conversation in the final interview, broadcast in January 1953 after his return from Stockholm, takes a noticeably more political turn. Mauriac here reflects for the first time on his changing political position. Not only does he draw attention to the scandal of what he terms 'l'injustice établie', but as he does so, he acknowledges his own growing sense of obligation to speak out: 'plus que jamais je sens ma responsabilité et je voudrais, dans les dernières années, [...] de plus en plus mettre l'accent sur ce côté de mes préoccupations' (SR 308). Reflecting on what appears to be the fundamental incompatibility between justice and the established social and political order, Mauriac concludes that the time has come to favour justice over order: 'je crois [...] que lorsque l'injustice surabonde, il ne s'agit plus de penser à l'ordre, il faut penser à la justice' (SR 308). As Amrouche remarks with evident surprise, Mauriac has suddenly placed himself in a startlingly radical position. To prefer justice to order is to call for nothing less than revolution: 'mais, cher François Mauriac, voici une position bien extrémiste, et proprement révolutionnaire que la vôtre! Préférer en toute circonstance la justice à l'ordre. Voyez où cela peut entraîner!' (SR 309).

Accompanying this *prise de conscience* of the injustice inherent in the dominant order is an increasingly acute sense of his own place within it, one which is defined in two important ways.

Firstly, various comments in the *Bloc-notes* bear witness to a growing class consciousness on Mauriac's part, an awareness of – and sudden unease with – his privileged position as a member of the bourgeoisie, the fraction of society which he describes in 1955 as 'les nantis à qui, dès le début, tout est donné d'avance' (BN I 301). Moreover, his sensitivity to that privilege, and the way in which its price has been paid by others, is strikingly reinforced by his regular contact with young Moroccans through his involvement with the Association France-Maghreb. In a 'Bloc-notes' from May 1953, for example, Mauriac talks of his reactions when faced with a group of Moroccans who had joined a pilgrimage to Chartres: 'ces garçons se savent condamnés d'avance, ils ont renoncé à tout bonheur temporel, ils n'ont pas d'avenir, nous l'avons détruit. Sentiment intolérable d'appartenir à la race qui opprime' (BN I 75). For Mauriac to meet the victims of his society's so-called 'civilising mission' is a troubling event, one which leaves him with a strong feeling of his own guilt and complicity with its acts of oppression. He signals this by the use of a 'nous' which also serves to implicate the reader of his column. Indeed, we can say that his encounters with those he suddenly recognises as the oppressed other of colonisation – the 'ils' confronted with the colonising 'nous' – and the questions they raise about his understanding of the world, produce in Mauriac what might be termed an 'ethical shock'.

The interrogative moment he recounts here, and the reaction it produces, can be usefully considered through the lens of Lévinasian ethics, and Lévinas' focus on the role played by the other in forming the self's moral consciousness. For Lévinas, the presence of the other, and the other's recognition by the self, should work to limit the self's otherwise rampant freedom. Unfettered, the self's freedom is expressed in the desire to reduce whatever is other or alien to itself to the level of the same. The world is there simply to provide for, and be enjoyed by, the self. Moral consciousness comes into being, for Lévinas, when the devouring impulse is restrained, and this happens when the self's assumption of its own sovereignty is disrupted by the eruption of the other into its sphere of consciousness. In being faced with the other – and the face is accorded an important role in Lévinas' discussion of the inter-subjective encounter – the self must learn to acknowledge its sanctity and its irreducibility, and the subsequent limits placed on its own freedom. As Lévinas puts it, 'accueillir autrui, c'est mettre ma liberté en question'.[17] In recognising and responding to the presence of the other, the self must acknowledge its absolute difference or alterity.

In many ways, Mauriac's reaction to his encounters with the young Moroccans is an exemplary illustration of this coming to consciousness in the other's presence. His feelings of guilt and responsibility are the signs of a consciousness being called to account, and this is triggered precisely by the sudden and dramatic eruption of the other before him, whether at the more abstract level of the conjunction of the events of Stockholm and Casablanca, or at the concrete level of the inter-subjective contact during the pilgrimage to Chartres, when Mauriac must meet the eye of the young Moroccans. As Lévinas evocatively puts it, 'le visage me rappelle à mes obligations et me juge'.[18] If Mauriac has a moral obligation to respond to this summons, he does so in a way which is itself morally and ethically inflected. I shall be discussing in more detail later, for example, how his article on torture in 1955 itself attempts to provoke an 'ethical shock' in the readers of the *Bloc-notes* similar to that which triggers the reawakening of his own moral and political consciousness.

It is Mauriac's recognition of his own responsibility – in terms of a sense both of culpability and of moral obligation – which can be seen to distinguish his writing on decolonisation from his earlier work. Indeed, we can trace a clear evolution in his position from the articles of the early 1930s onwards. The first pieces, and those from his time at *L'Écho de Paris* especially, are marked by a sense of solipsism: the significance of events in the world around him is judged, it seems, by their impact on the artist's soul. In the 'avertissement' to *Journal* of 1934, which draws together articles from the previous two years, Mauriac observes that 'il arrive qu'une maladie ou une simple lecture prenne autant de valeur qu'une révolution: c'est bien leur retentissement dans notre vie intérieure qui mesure l'importance des événements' (OC XI 4). His articles on the Spanish Civil War, meanwhile, if they reflect Mauriac's increased engagement with what

---

[17] Emmanuel Lévinas, *Totalité et Infini: essai sur l'extériorité* (Paris: Le Livre de Poche, coll. "Biblio", 1996), p. 217. Although Lévinas accords an important to role to the face in his discussion of the encounter between self and other, its status in his work remains problematic. See Colin Davis, *Lévinas: An Introduction* (Cambridge: Polity Press, 1996), p. 46.

[18] Lévinas, *Totalité et Infini*, p. 237.

we could term 'la vie extérieure', display a distinct air of moral superiority. In 'Le démon de l'Espagne', for example, Mauriac attacks the passivity of the cinema audience, 'la foule engourdie et repue', before the interrogative gaze of the victims of Franco's aggression as they look out from the newsreels (MP 85). The sense of history awakened in him by the conflict in Spain is not yet matched by a recognition of his own position, and therefore responsibility, in that history.

Furthermore, when that moment of recognition does come, it means acknowledging not just the privilege which derives from being a member of the dominant fraction of society, but also the significance of the function he performs in that society as a contributor to its cultural heritage and wealth. This is the second key insight afforded by his *prise de conscience*. In the wake of the Nobel Prize, Mauriac is led to question both the dominant socio-cultural order, and the more specific issue of his status as a writer within that order, to consider what it means to occupy such a position. In other words, he finds himself addressing precisely the issues which Sartre had succeeded in imposing on the field in the years following the Liberation, as he tackles the question of the writer's role in society and his commitment.

In the previous chapter, I discussed Mauriac's initial hostility to Sartre's conception of the committed writer, and his call for literature to be harnessed for political ends. Yet the Nobel Prize and its aftermath bring with them various ironies. Firstly, as his political consciousness sharpens and he becomes increasingly critical of the world in which he lives, Mauriac begins to provide an illustration of the committed writer defined by Sartre: 'je dirai qu'un écrivain est engagé lorsqu'il tâche à prendre la conscience la plus lucide et la plus entière d'être embarqué', Sartre writes in *Qu'est-ce que la littérature?*[19] Sartre argues that writers must be aware of their 'situation' in the world, alert both to the nature of society and to their position within it. Sartre sees this awareness as essential for further action, for with it comes the knowledge that words can have performative force, and that what the writer says can bring about change in the world. Conversely, without that knowledge, their performative force is lost: 'l'écrivain "engagé" sait que la parole est

---

[19] Jean-Paul Sartre, *Situations, II* (Paris: Gallimard, 1948), p. 124.

action: il sait que dévoiler c'est changer et qu'on ne peut dévoiler
qu'en projetant de changer'.[20] The task of 'dévoilement', the need to
unmask the world for his readers and to ask them to confront its true
nature, will be central to Mauriac's activities as a journalist
throughout the 1950s.

A second irony is the sudden appearance of Sartrean language
in Mauriac's own discussion of the role of the writer. As we have
seen, the first signs of this are already apparent in his conversations
with Amrouche, and his expression of a sense of responsibility (SR
308). It emerges even more explicitly a few months later in an article
entitled 'L'engagement de l'écrivain', as he asserts the writer's
obligation to confront and engage with the events unfolding around
him:

> De nombreux écrivains se jugent eux-mêmes invités par
> vocation à ne se mêler que de l'éternel. Je l'ai cru moi-même à
> certaines époques. Mais notre génération a payé cher cette
> connaissance que nous sommes tous engagés, que nous sommes
> tous embarqués dans la même tragique aventure, tous solidaires,
> tous responsables. (MP 457)

It seems that the Sartrean vocabulary of responsibility and
commitment have provided Mauriac with the most effective way of
articulating his evolving perception of the role of the writer.

That the award of the Nobel Prize triggers some sort of crisis
in Mauriac's understanding of the writer and his function in society is
signalled by a further conjunction: not only does the Nobel Prize
provoke Mauriac into embarking on a long period as an outspoken and
controversial journalist, but his investment in it also coincides with a
striking artistic silence, one which will last for fourteen years.
Following the publication of *Le Sagouin* and *Galigaï* in 1952 and
L'Agneau in 1954 – all of which Mauriac had begun writing either
during the war or in the immediate post-war period – there was no
more fiction until *Un adolescent d'autrefois* of 1968. This silence
should not simply be taken as a sign that Mauriac's literary inspiration
had finally disappeared, after having waned gradually since the mid-
1930s. Rather, his decision to stop writing fiction can be traced to
other factors, a clue to which lies in one of the most striking and

---

[20] Sartre, *Situations, II*, p. 73.

dominant themes of the *Bloc-notes* in the months which follow his return from Stockholm.

Mauriac's sudden crisis of confidence in the socio-cultural order, and his politicised sense of his own place within it, provokes a disillusioned and surprisingly radical cultural critique. Repeatedly during the mid-1950s, as Nathan Bracher has noted, he offers an analysis of culture and society whose tone is worthy of Marx or Foucault.[21] Mauriac returns insistently to the idea that our apparently 'civilised' society, one we deem appropriate to impose on others, is nothing but a sham, a thin veneer masking violence and corruption. 'Toute civilisation repose sur une horreur cachée: prostitution, traite des femmes, police des mœurs, maisons de correction, geôles pour les fous et les idiots, toutes les tortures', he writes in 1955 (BN I 240). Not only that, but a clear causal link can be established between 'civilisation' and violence, one he finds clarified in Henry James' accounts of Victorian high society. Civilised society depends on violence, Mauriac tells us as he reflects on James' portrait of the English aristocracy, with its castles, hunts and maids. It is built on acts of repression and exclusion: 'toute civilisation exquise repose sur l'esclavage. Sinon, elle ne serait pas exquise'. The wealth and refinement of a privileged few is predicated on social injustice, on 'de bas salaires et le refus de toute législation sociale' (BN I 139). Mauriac's analysis here takes on an almost Nietzschean dimension: his portrait of the privileged minority reminds us of the Superman who delights in his sublime nature, one predicated on the wilful oppression of inferior classes or races.

Moreover, Mauriac's reflection goes further in drawing out the troubling place of art and culture in this social order. We have seen how Mauriac was disconcerted by the collision of two events which captured the contradictions of Western civilisation. His unease is echoed in the columns of the subsequent months and years, which return frequently to the problematic status of culture and its place in society – and thus, by extension, to the equally problematic status of

---

[21] While my analysis here coincides with that of Bracher, his concern is more with the issues Mauriac's comments raise about French national identity than with the place of art and culture in a morally compromised society, which is the focus of the present chapter. See Bracher, 'Mauriac and Decolonisation', and *Through The Past Darkly: History and Memory in François Mauriac's 'Bloc-notes'* (Washington, D.C.: The Catholic University of America Press, 2004), ch. 3.

those who contribute to or participate in it. We are made increasingly aware of the way in which culture is problematised by the acts of violence perpetrated by an apparently 'civilised' society, one which sees in art and culture the clearest evidence of its refinement and sophistication.

Two issues in particular emerge from his reflections. Firstly, the repeated juxtaposition of violence and culture forces us to question the validity of art and culture in the context of barbarity, to consider the legitimacy of cultural pursuits and other *divertissements* when we are faced with evidence of violence and repression. Having been confronted by this problem in Stockholm, Mauriac confronts it again three years later, when he learns that torture is being used by French police in Algeria. In the 'Bloc-notes' of 15 January 1955, he recounts a visit from the lawyer Pierre Stibbe, who informs him of the systematic use of torture in Algeria. In doing so, Mauriac becomes one of the first journalists to break the news in France. Towards the end of the article, Mauriac dwells on his reactions following Stibbe's departure. Left alone in his appartment, his initial move, almost a reflex action, is to choose a record. 'Me voici seul. J'ouvre distraitement l'album des disques de Mozart, les Sonates pour piano interprétées par Gieseking, que J. m'a rapporté de New York. J'en choisis un… Mais non: l'horreur de ce que j'ai entendu emplit encore la pièce' (BN I 241). Striking here are the details he foregrounds in his brief self-portrait. He conjures an impression of a cultivated figure who is an admirer not just of Mozart, but of a particular interpretation of his music, 'les Sonates pour piano interprétées par Gieseking'. Yet such extreme refinement sits uneasily, seems almost vulgar, in the wake of what he has just heard. Culture is suddenly a tasteless pursuit in the face of more urgent matters. 'Cette musique du ciel n'est pas pour moi. Je suis comme un homme qui a pris part, sans le vouloir, à un crime et qui hésite à aller se livrer' (BN I 241).

Secondly, Mauriac becomes alert to the way in which art and culture have been compromised by the established social order. In June 1953, he reflects on a party at the British Embassy, the highlight of which is a ballet performed in the gardens. The excessive elegance of the event reminds him of the France of the *ancien régime*: 'Versailles fut une perfection dans cet ordre: le décor sublime inventé pour masquer la misère et le désespoir permanent des deux tiers de l'espèce humaine' (BN I 78). Culture begins to appear as a distraction to Mauriac, a *divertissement* in the Pascalian sense, used by society to mask and suppress the brutality on which it is founded, and which serves to keep it in place. Suddenly, it seems that culture has lost its innocence for Mauriac. Each time he comes into contact with it – whether it be the ballet performed at the Embassy, or the Mozart sonatas he reaches for after Stibbe's visit – he is reminded of what it hides. It has become an index not of man's refinement so much as of his violence, as Mauriac sees in it evidence of the unjust social order which seems to be a precondition of its existence. The Mauriac of the mid-1950s would doubtless subscribe to Walter Benjamin's famous remark that 'there is no cultural document that is not at the same time a record of barbarism'.[22]

If this is true, of course, then it must apply not only to the art and culture which surround Mauriac, but also to his own artistic output. Like the ballet or the recording of the Mozart sonata, Mauriac's fiction can be seen as symptomatic of a socio-cultural order whose 'advanced' state is signalled by the fact that certain of its members can devote themselves to 'unproductive' activities (in an economic sense) such as literary or artistic creation, thanks to the 'productive' effort of the labouring majority. At the same time, his *œuvre* helps to distract attention from the fundamental inequalities on which the system depends in order for it to exist and function as it does. In raising questions about the function and value of culture in society, Mauriac inevitably invites us to interrogate the legitimacy of his own work as an artist.

Indeed, in a 'Bloc-notes' from October 1955, we find Mauriac engaging in a startling auto-critique, as the newly committed journalist takes to task his earlier incarnation as a novelist. He begins by pointing out the irony that one of the key themes of his fictional work is what he terms 'la férocité des hommes' – that is to say, precisely the problem which preoccupies the journalist caught up in the debate over decolonisation. Yet if man's ferocity was of interest to the novelist, it was above all because of the role it played in the aesthetic success of his work: 'que m'importait la férocité des hommes, si je la peignais?' (BN I 301). The violence which, for the committed writer, calls into question the very possibility and validity of culture was, for the

---

[22] Walter Benjamin, 'Eduard Fuchs, Collector and Historian', in *One-Way Street and other writings*, trans. by Edmund Jephcott and Kingsley Shorter (London: Verso, 1997), p. 359.

novelist, merely a pleasing aesthetic effect. Furthermore, Mauriac implies here that writing for purely aesthetic ends, simply for the purposes of artistic creation, is a problematic – not to say morally irresponsible – gesture. 'Ecrire était toute ma vie', he observes (BN I 301). Absorbed in the business of artistic creation, he suggests, and concerned with writing as an end in itself, the writer loses sight of its political potential, the possibilities it offers for intervention in the world. In this analysis, Mauriac can be seen to align himself once more with the Sartre of *Qu'est-ce que la littérature?*, for whom prose is a tool with which the writer can help bring about change in the world.[23]

The ethical shock triggered by the Nobel Prize, therefore, gives birth to a radical Mauriac, a Mauriac whose revolutionary call to place justice before order startles Jean Amrouche in 1952, as we have seen (SR 309). His denunciation of the colonial order in Morocco and the use of torture in Algeria reaffirm the break with the established order first signalled by his response to the Spanish Civil War in the late 1930s. This is certainly how Jean-Jacques Servan-Schreiber chooses to represent Mauriac's trajectory when he looks back over the period in 1959: 'François Mauriac, un jour de 1953, eut la très rare courage de quitter la place qu'il occupait dans la société dirigeante, avec le confort moral et matériel qu'il en recueillait légitimement, pour venir lutter avec nous contre l'ordre établi'.[24] For Servan-Schreiber, Mauriac's collaboration with *L'Express* is an unambiguous signal that he has joined the forces of radicalism on the political Left. Indeed, such is the apparent clarity of his position that in 1954, Sartre can consider approaching him to contribute to a special number of *Les Temps modernes* on the Left in France.[25]

However, the nature of Mauriac's position in the years following the Nobel Prize needs closer scrutiny, for it is rather more complex than Servan-Schreiber suggests. On the one hand, as Servan-Schreiber's comments correctly imply, the impact of Mauriac's return to the political domain lies in the unexpected nature of his position, in the disjunction between the stance he adopts and his perceived place in the social order. His stance would seem to resist the dispositions

---

[23] See Jean-Paul Sartre, *Situations, II*, pp. 63-75.
[24] Jean-Jacques Servan-Schreiber, 'Réponse à François Mauriac', *L'Express*, 13 August 1959, p. 3.
[25] 'Mauriac vu par Sartre, propos recueillis par Jean Touzot', p. 46.

which might have guided his trajectory in a more conventional direction. For Servan-Schreiber, indeed, Mauriac's validity as an intellectual would appear to stem precisely from his ability and willingness to break with the conventions of his class and the expectations associated with his social position, a willingness which signals and guarantees his status as a free-thinking and independent mind. On the other hand, it is clear that Mauriac's radicalism has its limits, which are paradoxically defined by some of the motivations which initially provoke him into action. Both his faith and his sense of national identity curb his radical reflex, and stop him from adopting the truly revolutionary or 'extremist' position which Amrouche identified as the logical outcome of his initial reaction to the situation in North Africa, and his call to privilege justice over order.

While Mauriac may be critical of the existing political order, he continues to believe in the fundamental grandeur of France and the role it can play as a beacon of civilisation in the world. Writing to his brother Pierre Mauriac in February 1953, for example, he suggests that his own engagement in the North African debate can help restore Moroccan faith in France:

> Notre action, mais surtout *ma présence*, a des conséquences que tout ce qui n'est pas colon reconnaît: dans l'Islam entier des garçons arabes, parlant français, nourris de culture française, se tournent de nouveau vers la France avec une immense espérance. (LV 314, Mauriac's emphasis)

He remains convinced that the future of the colonies lies in their remaining within the orbit of a guiding and protective mother country.

Likewise, while he criticises the colonialist exploitation of Africa, he will often express his support and admiration for the work of Christian missionaries in their conversion of indigenous peoples, and talk willingly of the white man's 'vocation' on the continent.[26] This investment in the myth of French grandeur and in the 'civilising' mission remains incompatible with a truly radical perception of French colonialism. Mauriac's position is thus marked by the compromise which distinguishes what Paul Clay Sorum terms anti-colonialism from the more radical anti-imperialism of figures such as

---

[26] See 'La vocation de l'homme blanc' (1960), in *Paroles perdues et retrouvées*, ed. by Keith Goesch (Paris: Grasset, 1986), pp. 270-281.

Sartre: while critical of the colonial regimes in existing form, anti-colonialists remained sympathetic to the notion of a 'civilising mission', and the idea that France should continue to have a guiding role in the future of its former colonies.[27]

In other words, the positions he adopts in the 1950s replicate once more the contradictions and oscillations which mark his choices and trajectory throughout his career. His desire to align himself with the autonomous pole of the literary field in the 1920s, or his rebellious reaction when confronted by the politics of the Académie Française in the 1930s, are echoed in his break with the Right and the right-wing press and his critique of the dominant order in the 1950s. Yet at the same time he cannot disavow that order entirely, and this is indicated by the position he adopts in the journalistic field as a columnist at *L'Express*. For while Servan-Schreiber is certainly right to suggest that in joining *L'Express*, Mauriac is joining the forces of radicalism, it is also the case that the radicalism represented by the news weekly is of a certain sort.

The radicalism of *L'Express* is defined in terms of its enthusiastic support for Pierre Mendès France, the most dynamic representative of the non-Communist Left in France during the 1950s. The Left of what became known as *mendésisme* was one which, while it still believed in the necessity and effectiveness of state intervention – Mendès France was a keen promoter of Keynesian economics, and one of the figures responsible for its import into France – nevertheless accepted the basic premise of a capitalist, market economy. Thus, in promoting Mendès France and calling for the implementation of his economic reforms, *L'Express* is concerned not to call into question the existing economic and social order, but to interrogate its current configurations, which it sees as responsible for hampering growth, modernisation and future prosperity. As such, the position held by *L'Express* in the journalistic field is that of the radical or avant-garde fringe of the established socio-economic order.[28]

This position also represents the limits of Mauriac's 'espace des possibles', to borrow Bourdieu's term, the range of possible positions he can hold in the field.[29] *L'Express* will prove to be the

---

[27] Paul Clay Sorum, *Intellectuals and Decolonisation in France* (Chapel Hill: University of North Carolina Press, 1977), p. 16.
[28] I develop these points further in chapter 5.
[29] See Pierre Bourdieu, *Les Règles de l'art*, pp. 384-385.

most radical position Mauriac can take up in the post-war journalistic field, the furthest left he can go. This is confirmed, moreover, by the fact that while Sartre can think about inviting Mauriac to contribute to *Les Temps modernes* in 1954, Mauriac not only declines the invitation, but Sartre himself also recognises that it was appropriate for him to do so: 'quand le numéro s'est fait, sa place n'y était plus, parce que c'étaient uniquement des gens proprement de gauche qui y écrivaient'.[30] In many respects, Mauriac's move to *L'Express* in 1954 reproduces the position he adopts in the Académie Française during the 1930s. If he acts as a critical or rebellious voice, he nevertheless chooses to remain within, and fundamentally loyal to, the established order.

At the same time, Mauriac's collaboration with *L'Express* will have various unforeseen consequences for him as it unfolds over seven years, owing mainly to the news weekly's forceful political agenda and its innovative nature. *L'Express* set out to play a key role in shaping the economic and political agenda for the country in the 1950s, and would quickly establish itself as the companion of the new generation of dynamic middle class men and women – exemplified by its two young editors – whose goal it was to revitalise and modernise the country; but the news weekly also illustrated some of the broader shifts affecting the socio-cultural sphere at the time. Central to the formal and technical innovation of the news weekly was a sensitivity to presentation and an ability skilfully to exploit what Barthes terms the 'rhetoric' of the image.[31] During the 1950s, *L'Express* would play a significant role in the 'dawning of image culture', as Kristin Ross puts it.[32] One of the corollaries of this would be the confirmation of Mauriac as a recognised and respected intellectual figure. The remainder of this chapter examines some of the ways in which Mauriac performs the function of the intellectual. It will reveal too how *L'Express* comes to play a determining role in ensuring the effectiveness of that performance.

---

[30] 'Mauriac vu par Sartre', p. 46.
[31] Roland Barthes, 'Rhétorique de l'image' (1961), in *L'obvie et l'obtus* (Paris: Seuil, coll. "Points", 1982), pp. 25-42.
[32] Kristin Ross, *Fast Cars, Clean Bodies: Decolonisation and the Reordering of French Culture* (Cambridge, MA.: The M.I.T. Press, 1995), p. 12.

The intellectual in action

Writing to Mauriac in April 1955 after his split with *Le Figaro* over the Moroccan crisis, the newspaper's editor Pierre Brisson observes that 'vous sentez bien vous-même depuis la crise marocaine le changement profond qui s'est opéré en vous, le caractère d'apostolat qu'a pris votre action à vos propres yeux' (LV 440). Brisson's choice of words here, his description of Mauriac's actions as 'apostolic', captures the impression we often have of the intellectual's activity as in some sense prophetic, or charged with other-worldly energy. Intellectuals are seemingly endowed with a vision or understanding of the world which others lack; they speak with clarity and truth about what to others appears opaque, or what others have set out wilfully to obscure. As Bourdieu puts it, writers and intellectuals

> Détiennent un pouvoir spécifique, le pouvoir proprement symbolique de faire voir et de faire croire, de porter au jour, à l'état explicite, objective, des expériences plus ou moins confuses, floues, informulées, informulables, du monde naturel et du monde social, et, par là, de les faire exister.[33]

They seem to intervene in the world from a different plane, their voice taking on a timeless or universal quality as they talk about the world in unfamiliar ways, ways which reveal what others fail to see. When they erupt into the political field, they set out to measure the world against a universally recognised set of values – liberty, justice, equality – and find the world wanting, denouncing those responsible as they do so.

Indeed, this denunciatory gesture provides a key to understanding how the intellectual functions in the political field. I discussed briefly in the introduction how the impact of the intellectual's intervention derives from the attempt to impose the particular values of the intellectual field as universal values, values against which the rest of the social sphere, and especially the political field – the field of power, where judgements and decisions are made which have real moral, social and cultural consequences – should be measured. The intellectual's ability to act in this way, making incursions into the political field in order to impose their values on it,

---

[33] Pierre Bourdieu, 'Le champ intellectuel: un monde à part', in *Choses dites* (Paris: Editions de Minuit, 1987), p. 174.

can be traced to the autonomy which the intellectual field has obtained within the broader field of power. This was a gradual process, whose completion was signalled for Bourdieu by Zola's 'J'accuse!' of 1898, the founding act of the modern intellectual tradition. The moment when the intellectual erupts into the political domain is also the sign that the intellectual field has reached maturity, that its autonomy is secure:

> Le "J'accuse" est l'aboutissement et l'accomplissement du processus collectif d'émancipation qui s'est progressivement accompli dans le champ de production culturelle: en tant que rupture prophétique avec l'ordre établi, il réaffirme, contre toutes les raisons d'État, l'irréductibilité des valeurs de vérité et de justice, et, du même coup, l'indépendance des gardiens de ces valeurs par rapport aux normes de la politique [...] et aux contraintes de la vie économique.[34]

Henceforth, it is the intellectuals' very autonomy, their dislocation from the political sphere, which authorises and legitimises their intervention in that sphere, their right to speak of political matters. To put it another way, the intellectual comes to be seen as an individual whose independence and disinterestedness gives him the ability and willingness to speak the truth; and the truth of what he says is guaranteed precisely by his status as an intellectual.[35]

Mauriac's activities in the 1950s, and his reflections on them, illustrate clearly this perception of the role of the intellectual, and

---

[34] Pierre Bourdieu, *Les Règles de l'art*, p. 216.

[35] The circularity of this logic (intellectuals speak the truth because they are intellectuals) is arguably central to what Bourdieu would term the 'magical' properties of intellectuals and other 'charismatic' members of the fields of cultural production (writers, religious prophets, fashion designers), properties invested in them by society in a moment of 'croyance collective'. For Bourdieu, collective belief is better understood as a collective act of 'misrecognition': bewitched by the creative power or commanding voice of a charismatic individual, society fails to recognise the structural conditions which permit the emergence of such individuals, seeing them not as the products of a social organisation at a particular moment, but as exceptional beings whose genius transcends the particular and the historical. It continues to invest in the myth of the creative talent or free-thinking spirit, what Bourdieu terms the 'créateur incréé', whose appearance has nothing to do with social or historical processes. See Pierre Bourdieu, 'La production de la croyance', *Actes de la recherche en sciences sociales*, 13 (1977), 3-43, and *Questions de sociologie* (Paris: Editions de Minuit, 1984), pp. 207-221.

clarify the way in which he is constructed – and constructs himself –
as a voice of truth and a moral arbiter. In his critique of the socio-
cultural order, Mauriac joins the minority who are prepared to
challenge the 'official history' or accepted understanding of events.
He shows himself to be fully conscious of his role in the political
arena, writing in 1956 that 'mon rôle à moi est de déranger
l'inteprétation officielle des événements' (BN I 321). He recognises
that he has the power to challenge authority and unmask the true face
of the world, a power which arises from his unassailable position in
the cultural realm: 'je suis peut-être le seul aujourd'hui à pouvoir dire
ce que je crois être vrai sans me soucier d'aucune consigne' (BN I
320). At the same time, he willingly lays claim to the position of
political outsider, or political innocent. We see this early in 1953, for
example, when he reflects on the reactions provoked by his articles on
the Moroccan situation:

> Je découvre à des signes souvent imperceptibles que mes articles
> du *Figaro* troublent des intérêts puissants. [...] On me glisse à
> l'oreille: "Il y a de grands intérêts en jeu..." Je manque de sérieux,
> je ne sais pas de quoi je parle. "Vous êtes un enfant au fond!"
> Oui, peut-être. (BN I 49)

In accepting his designation as a child, he neutralises the insult and
invites his readers to recognise it as an asset. To be a child in the
realm of politics, perhaps, is to speak of the world as one finds it, to
see the world through eyes untainted by corruption.

If Mauriac's initial interventions in the Moroccan crisis have
the impact they do, it is due in no small part to the disjunction
between his position in the journalistic field as an editorialist at *Le
Figaro* and his *prises de position*, between what he says and where he
says it. It comes as a shock to find someone denouncing the colonial
enterprise in Morocco on the front page of a newspaper which largely
reflected Establishment opinion, and which had a wide readership
among the colonial population of North Africa. Clear evidence that
Mauriac largely succeeds in his task of troubling received opinion,
and of confronting his readers with an alternative vision of the world,
is to be found in the letters he receives from the newspaper's readers,
and which he puts on display in a 'Bloc-notes' column in April 1953
(BN I 61-62).

However, while this disjunction ensures that Mauriac's articles make an impact in the short term, his position at *Le Figaro* ultimately proves to be untenable, as we have seen. If Mauriac is to intervene in the debate over North Africa, he needs to find a more appropriate position in the field from which to speak his mind. The impact of his collaboration with *L'Express* stems not from the gap between Mauriac and the platform from which he speaks, but from the position of that platform in the journalistic and political fields: such is Mauriac's political evolution in the early 1950s that he has enough common ground to collaborate with a left-of-centre news weekly, and to do so for seven years. Not only that, but he is to be found sharing the columns of the journal with Camus and Sartre among others. As Françoise Giroud puts it, reflecting on the startling nature of his move,

> Cela a été superbe, le spectacle de ce vieux monsieur cousu d'honneurs, enroulé de toutes les bandelettes avec lesquelles l'*establishment* attache les siens, quittant l'honorable *Figaro* pour rejoindre le journal quasi inconnu de deux rebelles qui ne pouvaient même pas lui payer ce qu'il était en situation d'exiger.[36]

Mauriac's collaboration with *L'Express* will play a key role in confirming and asserting his status as an intellectual. His prestige when he joins the news weekly is already beyond doubt, as Giroud's comment reminds us; but his relationship with the journal will be notable in particular for the way in which it puts that prestige to use. Mauriac is a valuable resource for the team at *L'Express*, one of their most useful assets in the battle to bring about change in France. At the same time, mobilising Mauriac also involves mediating him to their audience, and asserting a certain image of Mauriac as intellectual.

We have a clear sense of this when we consider the very first 'Bloc-notes' published by *L'Express*, on 10 April 1954, and which introduces Mauriac to the readers of the magazine. His piece is accompanied by a photograph in the central column of three, showing a meditative and sombre Mauriac, his eyes half-closed as he reflects on the world.[37] The portrait is a potent one, loaded with motifs (wisdom, reflection, spirituality) which invite us to recognise the

---

[36] Françoise Giroud, *Si je mens...* (Paris: Stock, 1972), p. 146.
[37] *L'Express*, 10 April 1954, p. 15. Problems of copyright prevent me from reproducing the page here.

writer as a voice of moral authority. The message is clarified by the strap line which accompanies the column, and which presents Mauriac as a powerful and authoritative figure: 'le grand écrivain catholique commente librement et avec le courage que l'on sait les événements de l'actualité littéraire et politique'. This comment carries two implications especially. Firstly, reference is made to the accepted idea of intellectuals as free and therefore trustworthy agents, 'librement' reminding us that he is not bound by any partisan interests. Secondly, there is an appeal to common knowledge ('avec le courage que l'on sait') which makes Mauriac's status as free-thinking commentator a given and undisputed fact.

It is noticeable too that Mauriac plays a willing part in shaping his image. An initial indication of this can be found in his first article for *L'Express*, a piece published in November 1953 on the candidates for the forthcoming Presidential elections, and famous for an irreverent remark he makes about Joseph Laniel: 'il faut rendre justice à M. Joseph Laniel: en voilà un qui ne trompe pas son monde! Ce président massif, on discerne du premier coup d'œil ce qu'il incarne: il y a du lingot dans cet homme-là' (BN I 104). With comments such as this, Mauriac asserts himself as a satirical voice, an outsider critical of the political establishment, who can exploit his novelist's skill to grasp an individual's defining characteristic.

The first 'Bloc-notes' column published in *L'Express* is particularly important for establishing the form his subsequent interventions will take. It is made all the more significant by the fact that Mauriac is also writing for a new audience, one which is much larger and more broadly based than that of *La Table ronde*. While his new readership may have been unfamiliar with the *Bloc-notes* in its previous incarnation, it would nevertheless have some sense of what to expect of Mauriac as a writer. We can see how the first column guides its readers' expectations by setting down the basic structure of the *Bloc-notes* (a series of dated, diary-like entries on a variety of subjects), and at the same time responds to or echoes them in the themes it introduces and the tone it adopts.

The first entry in the column is striking in this respect. The dateline signals that it is written at Malagar, his country house in Gascony, and a place of retreat from the pace of life in Paris. Indeed, the theme of escape is articulated in the opening lines: 'je n'ai pu attendre Pâques. Je suis venu ici me terrer et me taire. Le printemps n'est pas là encore et je m'en moque. C'est le silence que je cherche' (BN I 113). Thus, on their first encounter with Mauriac, the readers of *L'Express* find the committed journalist talking of a desire to disengage from the events in which he is caught up, and to find the space to think and reflect. The reader is plunged straight into the drama of commitment, and the tension between action and reflection at its heart. Throughout the *Bloc-notes*, Mauriac will map this tension on to an opposition between city and country, Paris and Malagar. To return to Malagar, which he does each Spring and Autumn, is to leave behind what he calls 'la mécanique parisienne' (BN I 264) and insert himself once more into the slower temporality of rural life. At Malagar, he can reflect more clearly on the world and grasp the nature of the events unfolding around him. The first column plays out this process for us as it unfolds over time. Ten days after his first entry, for example, we find him noting his meditation on two texts by the philosopher Alain, and he returns again to themes familiar from the articles of 1953: 'méditant sur ces textes, je me pose la question: D'où vient ce calme dont nous bénéficions, cette tranquillité de l'ordre qui constitue la loi et les prophètes pour la société bourgeoise, si injuste que soit cet ordre?' (BN I 122). His comments once more take on a prophetic edge as he exposes the truth of his society, and lays claim to his status as a timeless voice of wisdom: 'sans la détruire, nous avons rendu la misère supportable puisqu'elle est supportée. Telle est la grande victoire de l'ordre' (BN I 122).

Yet at the same time, there is also a clear sense of self-dramatisation in this column. In effect, as it unfolds, we find Mauriac staging the intellectual at work. The reader becomes privy to the processes of reading and reflection on which Mauriac's interpretation of the world is based. As he paints an image of himself thinking and reading, Mauriac reinforces our sense of the intellectual as a singular individual endowed with the capacity to move beyond surface phenomena and recognise their deeper significance. He reminds us too of his ability and willingess to speak his mind, and the power which this gives him as a result: 'je ne m'en étais jamais avisé: il n'est rien de si rare qu'un homme qui pense tout haut – ni de si redouté' (BN I 114). Moreover, we can also see how he fulfils his readers' expectations in other ways, by displaying what Barthes might term his *mauriacité*.[38] Woven into the column is a series of typically Mauriacian themes, which will recur frequently in later articles: scenes of Gascon life which recall the faintly disturbing atmosphere familiar from his novels ('J'entends pour la première fois le coucou, mais aussi les cris d'enfant assassiné du cochon qu'on égorge', BN I 114); or an evocation of a church service which reminds us both that Mauriac is a leading Catholic voice, and that he is nonetheless unafraid to criticise the Church:

> Mauvaise messe. Une de ces messes dialoguées dont je ne discute pas les bienfaits mais d'où toute prière individuelle se trouve pratiquement bannie, comme s'il y avait désormais une suspicion jetée sur le recueillement, sur le rapport personnel avec Dieu. (BN I 115)

Overall, the three different aspects of this first article (Mauriac's own text, the accompanying editorial paratext, and the photograph which illustrates and reinforces both), work together to establish and assert the impression for his new audience of Mauriac as an important and authoritative intellectual figure.

Perhaps the most significant example of the way in which Mauriac is mobilised by *L'Express* occurs a few months later, in January 1955, when Mauriac breaks the news that torture is being practised by French forces in Algeria. If the use of torture quickly became a subject of controversy in the Algerian War, it was not only because it was in clear contradiction to France's image as the country in which the Declaration of the Rights of Man was made, but also because it was a deeply troubling echo of the practices only recently inflicted on the French themselves by the Nazis during the Second World War. Mauriac readily invokes this memory in his article, referring to the French methods of internment and interrogation as belonging to 'l'école de Himmler' (BN I 240); and at the same time, writing in *France-Observateur*, Claude Bourdet describes the French forces as 'votre Gestapo d'Algérie'.[39] Along with Bourdet, Mauriac was one of the first writers to denounce the use of torture in Algeria,

---

[38] Cf. Roland Barthes, *Mythologies* (Paris: Seuil, coll. "Points", 1972), p. 210.

[39] *France-Observateur*, 13 January 1955. Work on the use of torture in the Algerian War is extensive. See in particular Pierre Vidal-Naquet, *La Torture dans la République (1954-1962)* (Paris: Editions de Minuit, 1972) and Benjamin Stora, *La Gangrène et l'oubli* (Paris: La Découverte, 1991).

as Jean-François Sirinelli notes.[40] His article is therefore particularly important in terms of the impact it must make. The dramatic developments in France's colony require an equally dramatic response on the part of those who are charged with acting as the country's moral consciousness. In what ways, then, does Mauriac play his role?

The power of the article itself is immediately apparent when we encounter it in volume form (BN I 237-241). Mauriac's piece stages a dialogue between himself and the militant lawyer Pierre Stibbe, who has visited the writer in the hope of encouraging him to speak out about the use of torture. It is a dramatic encounter, as Stibbe makes a direct appeal to Mauriac to use his status and position in order to draw attention to the problem: 'vous seul pouvez parler... Vous seul' (BN I 237). We see how Mauriac's initial reluctance to become involved is gradually overcome, and he acknowledges his duty to intervene. However, before considering the article in greater detail, we need also to examine a second, and hitherto overlooked factor contributing to its potential performative force: namely, the context in which it was originally received by its readers.

Reading Mauriac's article today in its most readily available volume form is different from doing so in its original setting on the last page of the news weekly. Firstly, what was a piece of journalism embedded in a particular moment has become a historical and cultural document, whose significance is signalled by its republication in Seuil's prestigious 'Points' series. Our own historical distance with respect to the events of the War means that the original shock and controversy provoked by the emerging evidence of torture has leached away. Secondly, we must take into account fundamental differences between the two types of print media. The techniques of design and layout which journals and magazines exploit mean that our response to the text can be inflected in various ways; and as I suggested earlier, this is especially true in the case of *L'Express*, which since its launch had shown itself sensitive to the importance of design, using its own new look (tabloid size, cover photographs, banner headlines) to signal its equally new vision of the future.[41] The news magazine's design

---

[40] Jean-François Sirinelli, 'Mauriac, un intellectuel engagé', in *François Mauriac entre la Gauche et la Droite*, ed. by André Séailles (Paris: Klincksieck, 1995), pp. 145-158.

[41] I develop these points further in the next chapter.

literacy is seen to its full effect in its presentation of Mauriac and his article, as it sets out to maximise the impact of his intervention.

Mauriac's article is announced on the front page of *L'Express*, which is dominated by a photographic portrait of the writer. Off-set to the right against a dark background, his face is half-lit as he stares broodingly in the direction of the lens, his eye thus catching that of the reader picking up the magazine. The hands clasped in front of his chin give him a judgemental pose. This position of judgement is confirmed by the headline which overlays the photo in the top left hand corner and which announces, in white block capitals on a red background, 'Mauriac accuse'.[42] The headline is an obvious reference to another famous intervention over an act of injustice, and serves to underline Mauriac's place in the tradition of engaged intellectuals – to the point of implying that Mauriac is no less than the contemporary Zola.[43] Indeed, as we consider the glowering figure about to launch into a sulphurous denunciation, it seems that the verb 'accuser' takes on a performative force: the mere fact that it is Mauriac who speaks will be sufficient to bring about change. Finally, the photograph is accompanied by a quotation from Montaigne's *Essais*, 'je hais cruellement la cruauté, et par nature et par jugement, comme l'extrême de tous les vices', which will also reappear as an epigraph to the article itself. While in the first instance, this serves to confirm the general tone and mood of the cover composition through its commentary on cruelty and hatred, its invocation of Montaigne also provides a second reference point for Mauriac's activity as it reminds us not just of the intellectual's militant activity, but also of his more reflective role as thinker and philosopher. At the same time, though, the cover also serves skilfully to provoke the curiosity of the reader. If the captions encourage a certain reading of the photograph (Mauriac as angry and accusatory), they leave us sufficiently curious to discover who is being accused, and about what.

---

[42] Technical problems prevent me from reproducing the cover here.

[43] The echo would doubtless have appealed to Mauriac all the more since, as both Malcolm Scott and Nathan Bracher have underlined, the Dreyfus Affair serves as a crucial reference point for his engagement with, and understanding of, French history and politics. See Scott, 'Mauriac and the Raising of Dreyfus', in John Flower and Bernard Swift (eds), *François Mauriac: Visions and Reappraisals* (Oxford: Berg, 1989), pp. 133-146, and Bracher, *Through The Past Darkly*, ch. 2.

The article itself, entitled 'La Question', is to be found as usual on the back page of *L'Express*.[44] When we turn to it, we can see how the cover prefigures various themes of the piece in a complex and sophisticated way, something signalled immediately by the ambiguity of the title. The noun 'la question' can refer both to torture and to a more general form of interrogation or questioning. That Mauriac wants to keep both the narrower and broader meanings in play is indicated by the theme of accusation introduced by the headline on the front page, and confirmed by several striking features of the article itself. Firstly, as we read his text, we realise that it is not about torture as such, but about Mauriac's discovery of and reaction to the news, his initial reluctance to become involved, and his realisation that he must speak out about it. Secondly, the passage is overtly literary in style. Its dialogue form gives it a theatrical quality, stichomythic exchanges ('– Il faudrait des preuves. On n'a jamais de preuves. – Moi, j'ai vu.') combining with brief interjections in the present tense ('je soupire', 'je l'observe') to create a strong sense of pace and tension.

The encounter between Mauriac and Stibbe unfolds in what we might call three 'acts'. In the first, we see how Mauriac's resistance and his interrogation of Stibbe's story allows details about the practice of torture to accumulate as Stibbe puts forward his evidence in an effort to convince the writer:

> Ils n'ont pas renoncé aux coups de nerf de bœuf, vous savez! Mais la baignoire, [...] mais le courant électrique sous les aisselles et entre les jambes, mais l'eau souillée introduite par un tuyau dans la bouche jusqu'à ce que le patient s'évanouisse...

In the second, we see Mauriac's frustration and his denunciation of the order which allows such things to happen: 'Ils admettent que toute civilisation repose sur une horreur cachée. [...] Malheur à qui ose en parler ouvertement!' In the third, following Stibbe's departure, we see Mauriac recognise the nature of his own position, in terms both of his guilt and of his responsibility: 'je suis comme un homme qui a pris part, sans le vouloir, à un crime et qui hésite à aller se livrer'.

We might say, in other words, that the passage stages the gradual process of *dévoilement* which Mauriac undergoes as he listens to Stibbe's account of events in Algeria. It plays out the coming to

---

[44] *L'Express*, 15 January 1955, p. 15.

consciousness necessary for political action as Mauriac overcomes his weariness ('que de fois l'aurai-je entendu ce "vous seul"!') and realises he must continue his campaign. The opening moment of the scene underlines this. Dominated by the thematics of the look, it is a reminder of the meetings with young Arabs in 1953 which, as we saw earlier, made concrete to Mauriac the abstract roles of colonised and coloniser and strengthened his moral consciousness as a result. Stibbe's appeal to Mauriac is reinforced by his look, 'le regard de ceux qui ont vu de leurs yeux, qui ne peuvent plus penser à rien d'autre'. Yet Mauriac's first acknowledgement of this look is elliptical: he acknowledges it precisely as he turns away, unable to support it and its summons ('je détourne la tête'). Indeed, Stibbe's clear look of witness is in ironic contrast to the surreptitious look Mauriac gives in return ('je l'observe à la dérobée'). He makes a vain attempt to justify his resistance, blaming a lack of hard evidence ('à quoi bon, puisque "ça" ne laisse pas de traces!'), and expressing incredulity at Stibbe's description of torture ('ce n'est pas possible, dis-je').

At this point, we see the effectiveness of the dialogue form as Mauriac exploits the various ironies it allows. The discussion begins to take the form of an interrogation, as Mauriac poses a series of questions about why torture is being practised, and the legal situation surrounding it. However, as he questions the lawyer, he finds his own position interrogated as evidence of malpractice mounts up. He is startled to find that suspects are taken before the judge without a defence lawyer: 'sans avocat? Je croyais que la présence de l'avocat était exigée par la loi'. The questions he asks reflect the received opinions of the majority, opinions of which he is quickly disabused: 'la police a donc le droit de détenir un individu plus de vingt-quatre heures sans le déférer au magistrat? On m'avait pourtant dit...' Mauriac finds himself confronted by a central truth: the extent to which the system of justice – understood as the hallmark of any civilised society – has been corrupted. Indeed, Stibbe's evocation of one suspect's feeling of guilt after having revealed the identity of his comrades encourages the reader to draw a parallel between the cynical abuse of the law by the French authorities and the tortured Arabs' sense of honour and adherence to a strict moral code: 'il était fou de désespoir et de honte: "je suis déshonoré, gémissait-il, je les ai livrés..."'.

After Stibbe has painted a graphic picture of the situation in Algeria, attention shifts to Mauriac's reaction. Familiar preoccupations of the period resurface as he reiterates his critique of the so-called 'civilised' world, and expresses his anger at the betrayal of France: 'nous sommes cette France qui a proclamé les droits de l'homme à la face d'une Europe enivrée'. A new response to the colonised Other must be found instead of force, a response based on France's philosophy, its culture, its spirituality: 'ce n'est pas par la force, c'est par son message humain que la France reste conquérante'. Yet part of the frustration of his outburst stems from his doubt over the effectiveness of such outbursts, since the majority of people would rather ignore what is being carried out in their name: 'ils s'irritent au contraire de ce qu'on les oblige à voir ce qu'ils sont résolus à ignorer'. His reluctance persists as Stibbe leaves, a final appeal for action met with a half-hearted, almost dismissive 'oui... oui...'

As the closing scene of the final 'act' focuses on Mauriac, alone after Stibbe's departure, we see the first of a further series of ironies. His initial reaction is to behave like those he has just denounced, as he distractedly reaches for a record. He too will be guilty of ignoring the situation, and will do so by turning to the pleasures and escapism afforded by culture; but it is the jolt of reaching for music after what he has heard, the clash of violence and culture, which finally provokes in him a sense of his own guilt. The resistance shown by others cannot be an excuse for his own inaction. As the article closes, we see a haunted figure 'qui hésite à aller se livrer'. He must overcome his hesitation and accept his responsibility as both accomplice and witness; he must speak as Stibbe desired, and write a text which will reveal the truth about events in Algeria.

These closing moments clarify the peculiar power of the text. For it becomes clear at this point that the text he will choose to write in order to break the news of torture must be the very text we have been reading. He writes a text which focuses not on torture as such, but on the meeting which convinced him to speak out about it. He writes a text which tells the story of that text's own prehistory, of the encounter and events which gave rise to it. Indeed, we can see Mauriac's reiteration of Stibbe's story, and his depiction of its impact upon him, as a *mise en abyme* of committed writing and its performative potential. It is because he hears Stibbe's account of violence and corruption that Mauriac will write the text we read. He also hopes this text will provoke the reader in a similar way, both by repeating the story of torture and its gruesome details, and by recounting and demonstrating the effect of that story on him; by staging for us his own *dévoilement*, and encouraging us to follow his example as he does so. The questions posed by the front cover begin to be answered. It becomes clear that Mauriac is denouncing not only the practice of torture but also those who allow it to be practised, the majority of French people who choose to look away as he was tempted to do. The look with which Stibbe confronted him at the start of their meeting, and which he could not tolerate, is the one with which he now interrogates the reader.

Mauriac's article, therefore, mobilises the aesthetic in the service of the ethical. It employs sophisticated artistic techniques in order to question our right to the refinement and escapism of art and culture in the face of violence, and provoke those who read it into action. As he would say in response to a reader's letter in the weeks following the publication of his article, 'il n'y a qu'un moyen de faire cesser le crime, c'est que l'opinion publique intervienne avec force et c'est à quoi nous nous employons'.[45] At the same time, the article is an exemplary illustration of Benjamin's assertion that cultural documents are also records of barbarism, brutally honest in the way it carries the scars of the violence which permits it: we are not allowed to forget that this artful and sophisticated text has its roots in violence, that it bears witness to, and is a product of, the torture being practised in Algeria. As it documents acts of brutality committed against members of another culture, it opens up a disturbing perspective: that the glorious emergence of Western culture through time, exemplified by the Great Men of the literary tradition introduced to native children in the schools of the Empire, has entailed the less-than-glorious suppression of other cultures, and continues to do so.

Yet in a final twist, as Mauriac opens up this perspective, and reminds us of the logic of power at work in the colonialist project, he unwittingly articulates the inevitable limits of his own commitment, limits which are reflected in both his own response to the cultural other, and in the anti-colonialist position he adopts. For, as I discussed earlier, while Mauriac may situate himself on the radical margins of the political domain during the first years of the *Bloc-notes*, he

---

[45] *L'Express*, 26 February 1955, p. 2.

nevertheless remains a cultural insider. He continues to recognise the validity and importance of the cultural order of which he is part. I want to conclude the current section by exploring further the implications of this position. I have argued that one of the motivations for his engagement is the need for a more enlightened response to the other of colonisation, one which is non-violent above all. However, I would also suggest that the response he proposes can itself be seen to involve a form of violence.

Mauriac's intervention over the practice of torture invites us to consider not only the value and roots of culture, but also the intersubjective dynamic involved in the colonial relationship, that between the colonial self and the colonised other. The nature of the relationship is articulated by the acts of torture practised by the French authorities; it is inscribed on Arab bodies by the weapons they wield. To adopt again the perspective offered by Lévinasian ethics, colonialism is clearly a situation in which the absolute alterity of the other has not been respected.

Lévinas argues that with the self's recognition of the other's alterity comes peaceful co-existence. The relationship between the two 'se maintient sans violence – dans la paix avec cette altérité absolue. La "résistance" de l'Autre [...] a une structure positive: éthique'.[46] A peaceful and therefore ethical relationship establishes a divide between self and other, a limit in the form of the other's resistance to the self and its desire to draw on, or 'live from' the world. Inversely, therefore, violence is inevitable when the self ignores the other's alterity, when the presence of the other fails to trigger the self's moral consciousness. This is a situation illustrated, it could be said, by the actions of the colonial self, which aims simply to appropriate the colonised, to 'live from' them and their labour in the way that it 'lives from' the energies provided by food, air, light and so on. Torture is required, it seems, when the colonised other refuses to acquiesce, when it finally resists being absorbed by the self in this way. As Pierre Vidal-Naquet points out, 'les victimes ne sont pas un petit groupe en quelque sorte spécialisé de malfaiteurs ou de "suspects", mais la masse même de la population dans la mesure où elle ne se laisse pas docilement encadrer par l'appareil colonial'.[47] In

---

[46] Emmanuel Lévinas, *Totalité et Infini*, p. 215.
[47] Pierre Vidal-Naquet, *La Torture dans la République*, p. 17.

short, attempts to bridge the gap which exists between self and other, to reduce the other to the same as the colonial powers want to do, cannot help but result in violence.

In his denunciation of torture, as we have seen, Mauriac recognises that violence simply is not the way to approach the situation. Rather, he says, 'c'est par son message humain que la France reste conquérante' (BN I 241); but Mauriac here is betrayed by his metaphor. His characterisation of France as 'conquérante', triumphant as it spreads its message, signals the problematic nature of his own response: for if Mauriac is involved in an encounter with the colonised other, it is very much on his own terms, as befits his continuing belief in France's 'mission civilisatrice'. The Arabs he meets appeal to him above all because they have received a French education and have been drawn into French culture: 'dans l'Islam entier des garçons arabes, parlant français, nourris de culture française, se tournent de nouveau vers la France avec une immense espérance' (LV 314). Similarly, if at the time he can preach reconciliation and co-operation between Christianity and Islam,[48] it is because he is reassured to find that Islam has many elements in common with his own faith: 'j'ignorais par exemple la place que la Vierge Marie occupe dans la spiritualité musulmane...', he writes in a letter to Georges Duhamel.[49] To identify a common ground in this way, to make the other familiar, is to make it what Lévinas terms 'intelligible', and so neutralise and subsume it: 'l'intelligibilité, le fait même de la représentation, est la possibilité pour l'Autre de se déterminer par le Même, sans déterminer le Même, sans introduire d'altérité en lui'.[50] In short, Mauriac's own response of assimilation, however well-intentioned, is itself a kind of violence in the way it erases the identity of the other. As we consider it alongside the violence of torture, we realise that we face a stark choice in our dealings with the other: either we recognise the other's absolute alterity, or we reduce the other to the same – we choose either peace or violence. There is no half-way measure. The compromise which the anti-colonialist position seems to offer, enlightened reform which

---

[48] See for example, 'Pour une nouvelle alliance entre la France et l'Islam' (MP 454-455), published in March 1953.

[49] François Mauriac, Georges Duhamel, *Correspondance (1919-1966)*, p. 230.

[50] Emmanuel Lévinas, *Totalité et Infini*, p. 129.

nevertheless recognises some role for a (former) colonial power, emerges as an illusory one.

Nevertheless, it would be churlish to suggest that this problem invalidates an intervention which was fundamentally sincere. Mauriac's bold and courageous stance over the events in North Africa, and his denunciation of the political and moral corruption which underpinned them, won him widespread respect. As one young Frenchman observed, responding in 1957 to Françoise Giroud's survey of the post-war generation which she had snappily labelled the *Nouvelle Vague*, 'j'admire aujourd'hui Mauriac pour son courage politique et humain (qui semble "inutile" et "utopique" pour un homme qui n'avait pas besoin de faire cela)'.[51] But it was precisely because Mauriac did not need to intervene that he felt obliged to do so. His recurrent questioning of culture and its role in society is nothing less than an examination of his own *raison d'être*, and brings to the surface fundamental and uncomfortable tensions. With our historical distance, as we admire the power and sophistication of his articles, it is all too easy to forget that they often have their roots in violence, and to overlook what Mauriac himself realised in a way which was both powerful and poignant. Above all, perhaps, the preoccupations he expresses in the first years of the *Bloc-notes*, and the questions he raises, provide a response to his concern that political journalism is inevitably ephemeral, that 'rien ne s'évapore aussi vite qu'un écrit politique et ne devient si rapidement incompréhensible' (NLV 296). For while the political events and issues he reflects on may themselves be transitory, they serve to highlight profounder concerns, ethical issues which cut through history and remain with us today. Mauriac's analyses remind us again not only that the ethical should inform the political, but also that the two spheres are held apart with disturbing regularity.

The success and failure of committed writing
One crucial aspect of Mauriac's incisive denunciation of torture – arguably, in fact, its most significant – remains to be addressed, as the issues it raises are those I go on to explore further in the next chapter. While 'La Question' retains its relevance for the modern-day reader through the persistent moral and ethical issues it raises, what counted

---

[51] Françoise Giroud, *La Nouvelle Vague* (Paris: Gallimard, 1958), p. 132.

in the short term was its political effect. Hence, I have argued, the way the article is packaged by *L'Express* in order to maximise its impact. To consider the success of the article as an intervention in the debate over decolonisation – attempting to gauge whether its rhetorical intention is matched by its performative force – is to shift from an ethical to a historical perspective. Reconsidering 'La Question' from this angle also reminds us that decolonisation is not an isolated event or problem, but part of a complex series of changes affecting France in the 1950s and 60s, changes in which Mauriac is caught up because of his status as an intellectual and his participation in *L'Express*.

Mauriac's article presents us with something of a paradox. On the one hand, it does indeed appear to be an apparently successful intervention. As Mauriac observed later in the same year, 'il a suffi d'un seul de mes articles sur les méthodes policières en Algérie pour qu'elles aient été fort adoucies pendant trois ou quatre mois' (BN I 311). Pierre Vidal-Naquet, in his account of the use of torture during the Algerian War, highlights the role played by Mauriac's article in contemporary parliamentary debates, and points out that it led directly to two measures being taken by the authorities. Firstly, police officers suspected of using torture were returned to France, and secondly, a commission of enquiry into the use of torture was set up under Roger Wuillaume.[52] Yet as Mauriac himself implies, the effects of the article were short-lived. Indeed, one of the conclusions of Wuillaume's enquiry was to recommend that torture be permitted under certain restricted circumstances;[53] and the practice of torture certainly continued unabated for the remainder of the war, despite a concerted campaign by press and intellectuals alike. Thus, what the brief and isolated success of 'La Question' serves to do more than anything, perhaps, is highlight the general *failure* of such interventions, and focus attention as well on a central question raised by Vidal-Naquet: 'comment la torture a-t-elle pu subsister de pair avec la dénonciation qui en a été faite dans une partie de la presse, et notamment dans les journaux considérés comme "sérieux"?'[54] – newspapers, that is to say, such as *L'Express*, which placed themselves at the forefront of the campaign against torture.

---

[52] Pierre Vidal-Naquet, *La Torture dans la République*, pp. 25-26.
[53] Vidal-Naquet, *La Torture dans la République*, p. 28.
[54] *La Torture dans la République*, p. 21.

The answer to this question is complex; but ironically, the issue of *L'Express* which promotes Mauriac's successful intervention provides some of the most graphic clues to its solution – graphic here in a literal sense in fact. The original setting of 'La Question' reveals how an important contemporary tension is displayed in the page layout of the news weekly. The only piece of editorial material on the last page, Mauriac's article occupies just over half the space. The lower half is dominated by two advertisements. One, the larger of the two, is for Perrier mineral water; a second, smaller one on its left, is for a Parisian shop specialising in fur coats. In other words, at the same time as Mauriac is calling his readers to account and denouncing those who want to ignore the injustice in Algeria, advertisements for products designed to appeal to their sophisticated lifestyles are trying to distract them. His readers are being tempted to avert their eyes – literally and also figuratively.

In attempting to answer the problem he poses, Vidal-Naquet argues that if their interventions fail, the fault lies not so much with the intellectuals themselves as with the apathy of their readers. However 'enlightened' or receptive a readership appears to be, 'il manquera toujours à beaucoup ce qui est nécessaire pour la protestation comme pour la révolte: *la disponibilité*'. Readers are repeatedly distracted, 'sollicité[s] par bien d'autres émissions'.[55] Their attention is caught by other events, other narratives. One of these in particular is especially potent and appealing – and told most passionately by the magazine which is simultaneously trying to encourage their protests.

The advertisements which frame another gloomy episode of the distasteful narrative of decolonisation are pointers to, and invitations to participate in, the second story dominating *L'Express* at the time: that of the rejuvenation and prosperity that come with the much-needed modernisation of France. In the face of these conflicting messages, the readers show themselves to be all too willing to respond to the latter, and to avert their eyes from the former – to turn away, in other words, from Mauriac's gaze. In 1957, the magazine published yet another victim's account of the experience of torture; and at the same time, it launched its survey into the new generation it had labelled the *Nouvelle Vague*, an attempt to understand and define the

---

[55] *La Torture dans la République*, p. 21. Vidal-Naquet's emphasis.

mood of the era. The *Nouvelle Vague* survey provoked 15,000 responses, the account of torture virtually none.[56] The next chapter sets out to explore more closely this narrative of modernisation, the role played by *L'Express* in promoting it, and the consequences it has for Mauriac and his trajectory.

---

[56] Serge Siritzky and Françoise Roth, *Le Roman de 'L'Express', 1953-1978* (Paris: Atelier Marcel Jullian, 1979), p. 152.

Chapter Four

Commitment and Commodification

In his discussion of the various fields of cultural production, Pierre Bourdieu suggests that every writer has a 'lieu naturel', by which he means that they find a place in a publishing house or newspaper which most closely matches their own values, agenda, or socio-cultural profile. Finding this site is essential for their success, for 'les producteurs ou les produits qui ne sont pas à leur place – qui sont, comme on dit, "déplacés" – sont plus ou moins condamnés à l'échec'.[1] As we have seen at various points, it is unsurprising to find Mauriac writing for right-wing newspapers such as *L'Écho de Paris* or *Le Figaro* for much of his career. He shared with them a broadly similar conservative perspective which was rooted in and reflected the worldview of a traditional, patrician, bourgeois constituency. During his time at *Le Figaro*, Mauriac's articles coincided by and large with the viewpoint of both the paper and its readers. This is true in the immediate post-war period, for example, when he became involved in a polemical debate with the Communists, and adopted a strongly patriotic stance which included expressions of support for the French government's colonialist policies in Indochina.

However, as we saw in the previous chapter, his compatibility with the newspaper and its constituency was tested and then disrupted by his sudden *prise de conscience* over the problem of decolonisation, and his espousal of a more liberal, anti-colonial standpoint. His forthright expression of views such as these in the columns of a newspaper which, like its readers, was in broad agreement with the colonialist project, created a widening rift with the editorial board, and made his departure inevitable. A more appropriate site was required if

---

[1] Pierre Bourdieu, *Les Règles de l'art*, p. 276.

he was to continue to make known his views on the situation in North Africa. In the context of the debate over colonisation at least, *L'Express* had become a far more natural home for Mauriac than the Right-wing press.

Yet intriguingly, Mauriac's collaboration with the news weekly seems in several other respects to be highly unusual, an infringement of the unwritten laws of the journalistic field, and so apparently at risk from the failure Bourdieu predicts. The sense that Mauriac might have 'misplaced' himself in moving to *L'Express* is captured nowhere more vividly than in a photograph taken in 1954, soon after his arrival at the news weekly. The photo (reproduced on the cover of this book) shows Mauriac sitting at a desk, pen in hand over what might be a contract. He is flanked by the magazine's two editors, Jean-Jacques Servan-Schreiber and Françoise Giroud.

Two things in this image strike us immediately: the first is the pronounced difference in age between the columnist and his editors, a gap of nearly two generations, since Mauriac was approaching seventy at the time, while they were in their mid-thirties. The second is a difference in dress which reflects this dramatic age gap, though what catches our eye is not so much Mauriac's dark, formal suit, as the look of the other two: while Giroud, in her pale and simple dress, is the epitome of contemporary style, Servan-Schreiber has his jacket off and his sleeves rolled up – a neat echo of his determination metaphorically to roll up his sleeves and get on with the business of reinvigorating France.

Giroud, born in 1916, had already established her credentials as a voice of change thanks to the vision of modern woman which she had begun to articulate during her time at *Elle* magazine, launched in conjunction with Hélène Lazareff in 1946. Servan-Schreiber, born in 1924, had established similar credentials at *Le Monde*, where he had begun his career as a journalist in the years following the Liberation. He was also a member of the powerful Servan-Schreiber family which, through its interests and connections in the related domains of politics, administration, business and the print media (it published the respected business newspaper *Les Échos*, as a weekly supplement to which *L'Express* first appeared), played an influential role at the political and economic avant-garde in post-war France.[2]

It is by working with two people who embodied the dynamism of a new generation that Mauriac seemed to have strayed some way from his 'lieu naturel'. To quote again Giroud's reaction to Mauriac's arrival at *L'Express*, 'cela a été superbe, le spectacle de ce vieux monsieur cousu d'honneurs, enroulé de toutes les bandelettes avec lesquelles l'*establishment* attache les siens, quittant l'honorable *Figaro* pour rejoindre le journal quasi inconnu de deux rebelles'.[3] Her impression is shared by Mauriac. Looking back on his time at *L'Express* in the *Nouveaux mémoires intérieurs*, he recognises that it brought together 'des esprits que tout aurait dû séparer, et que tout sépara d'ailleurs, après peu d'années' (OA 821).

Given the surprise they both express here, then, what conditions allowed for the collaboration over a period of seven years between an ageing, essentially conservative writer, and a youthful, then-radical, left-wing news weekly? Moreover, what motivated Servan-Schreiber and Giroud actively to pursue Mauriac, and secure his participation in *L'Express*? This chapter explores the complex relationship between Mauriac and *L'Express* and examines both why, however briefly, it can be his natural site and why divorce between the two nevertheless proved inevitable. For by 1961, Mauriac's place was no longer with a magazine which promoted what he saw as the tawdry and degraded culture of what had become known as the *Nouvelle Vague*, and he switched the *Bloc-notes* to the *Figaro littéraire*.

The chapter argues in particular that Mauriac's collaboration with *L'Express* is crucial to his development as an intellectual – or more accurately, to the consolidation of his status as an intellectual. Indeed, it suggests that in passing through the hands of the news weekly, Mauriac is not just confirmed as an important intellectual figure, but is turned into what today would be called a 'media star'. He takes his place in an expanding star system being fed, and fuelled,

---

[2] On the role played by the Servan-Schreiber family in helping to shape the agenda for change in the 1950s and 60s, see Luc Boltanski, *Les Cadres: la formation d'un groupe social* (Paris: Editions de Minuit, 1982), pp. 164-170. For a biographical account of Jean-Jacques Servan-Schreiber's life, see Jean Bothorel, *Celui qui voulait tout changer: les années JJSS* (Paris: Robert Laffont, 2005). On Françoise Giroud, see her two books *Se je mens...* and *Profession journaliste*.
[3] Françoise Giroud, *Si je mens...*, p. 146.

by a burgeoning mass media. Linking this to contemporary trends in French culture, it argues that the story of Mauriac's relationship with *L'Express* is an example of what Kristin Ross has called the 'reordering' of French culture in the 1950s and 60s,[4] a series of seismic shifts which *L'Express* helped to trigger. Underlying both these issues is the nature of *L'Express* itself, the agenda it pursues and the ideology it articulates. In order to grasp them fully, therefore, we must consider in more detail the news weekly, its ethos and its evolution over the first few years of its life.

Between commitment and commercialism: the first years of *L'Express*

Desire alone on the part of Sevan-Schreiber would not have been sufficient to secure Mauriac's involvement in the magazine. Common ground was also required, and it proved to be quite extensive during the initial years of their collaboration. Mauriac shared with the magazine not only concern over the question of decolonisation, but also a more general dissatisfaction with the Fourth Republic. Established after the Liberation, the Fourth Republic was dogged by instability, the consequence of a parliamentary system which saw a series of coalition governments toppled and replaced. Progress on some of the key issues facing France at the time, such as its relationship with the colonies, or cooperation in Europe, was slow and haphazard. Moreover, the country's economy has been struggling since the Liberation, and although signs of growth were beginning to emerge, the general feeling among the French population in the early 1950s was that living standards had been in decline for some time.[5] Nevertheless, both Mauriac and Servan-Schreiber recognised that Pierre Mendès France, leader of the centre-left Parti Radical, had the vision and intelligence to tackle such problems, or 'remettre le vieux pays à flot', as Mauriac puts it (BN I 176).

The broad agreement which forms this shared platform, however, belied crucial differences between Mauriac and *L'Express*, differences which would ultimately lead to the split between the two.

---

[4] Kristin Ross, *Fast Cars, Clean Bodies: Decolonisation and the Reordering of French Culture.*

[5] Serge Serror, '*L'Express* et l'opinion publique' (unpublished mémoire de DEA, Université de Paris, 1960), p. 10. See also Jean-Pierre Rioux, *La France de la Quatrième République*, 2 vols (Paris: Seuil, coll. "Points", 1983), II, pp. 248-249.

They can be traced to the fact that each invested the situation facing the country with different meanings, and has a different understanding of what its future should be. Where Mauriac's response was informed by a poetic idealism, that of *L'Express* was based on political pragmatism. As we saw in chapter four, Mauriac relates the colonial conflict and its violence to an idealistic or symbolic 'certaine idée de la France'. He hopes to see the country's tarnished grandeur restored by a more enlightened form of relationship with the colonies. Similarly, prefiguring his portrayal of de Gaulle, he begins to cast Mendès France as an epic hero, who captures his imagination as he battles against the mediocre men around him in the name of France (BN I 250).

For *L'Express*, on the other hand, decolonisation was part of an entirely different paradigm. What concerned the journalists was not so much an abstract sense of France's 'grandeur', but its present and future development. As Ross puts it, they were

> Anxious to leave the crises of the *après-guerre* period and decolonisation behind them, to consecrate [sic] their efforts on the economic renovation of their country, and to benefit from the general improvement in the standard of living that followed from it.[6]

They saw decolonisation as a component of a comprehensive political and economic agenda. It was an essential part of the process of modernisation required by the country in the post-war years. Françoise Giroud would later observe that *L'Express* 'demandait alors qu'on ne situe pas le bonheur et l'avenir de la France dans la conservation de son empire coloniale. Mais que l'on trace et que l'on prenne les vrais moyens de pouvoir'.[7] *L'Express* saw the colonies as a relic of the country's imperial past, which hampered its move into the future. Colonisation was simply incompatible with modernisation. Where, then, *did* the future reside? How was modernity to be defined, and modernisation achieved?

L'Express was in no doubt that the best solution to France's problems lay in the left-of-centre agenda being put forward by Mendès France. The close links between the news weekly and the

---

[6] Ross, *Fast Cars, Clean Bodies*, p. 144.
[7] Giroud, *Si je mens...*, p. 196.

leader of the Parti Radical were forged early on, and signalled by the long interview published in its first issue, in which Mendès France set out his plans for reform.[8] Indeed, during the 1950s, it became the unofficial organ of Mendès France and the Parti Radical, the main platform from which its leader addressed the voters. *L'Express* was a key component of what became known as the *nébuleuse mendésiste*, a network of academics, intellectuals and – crucially – journalists working to disseminate and promote the Mendès France programme as widely as possible. Mendès France's interviewer in that first issue, for example, was Simon Nora, one of the politician's closest advisors, who had also been involved in setting up the news weekly. While the largest number of *mendésistes* was to be found at *L'Express* – Jean Daniel and Maurice Duverger among those teaming up with Giroud and Servan-Schreiber – support was also voiced in other progressive journals such as *Esprit* and *Témoignage Chrétien*.[9] Such was the news weekly's commitment to Mendès France that, in October 1955, and despite the financial risks involved, it turned itself into a daily paper in order to support more effectively the Parti Radical campaign during the run-up to the legislative elections in January 1956, only reverting to its weekly format the following March.[10]

Mendès France was one of the key thinkers on the economy in post-war French politics, having been involved in drawing up the first economic plans after the Liberation. An early advocate of Keynsian economics, he argued that state intervention, in the form of productive investment, was essential to ensure a strong industrial and manufacturing base. At the same time, and significantly for *L'Express*, as we shall see, he recognised the importance of enterprise, and the need to ensure a strong market economy: efficiency and productivity were to be stimulated and improved by opening up the French market to foreign competition. Giroud is quick to underline this when she says that Mendès France 'était planificateur, mais partisan résolu de l'économie de marché'.[11] What this also meant, as Mendès France and

---

[8] 'La France peut supporter la vérité', *L'Express*, 16 May 1953, p. 7.

[9] For further discussion of the emergence and role of the *nébuleuse mendésiste*, see Patrick Rotman, 'La diaspora mendésiste', *Pouvoirs*, 27 (1983), 5-20. See also Boltanski, *Les Cadres*, pp. 164-167.

[10] 'L'entreprise a beau perdre 20 millions par mois, seul compte à ses yeux l'objectif politique qu'il s'est fixé: en gagnant les élections de juin 1956, remettre PMF au pouvoir.' Siritzky and Roth, *Le Roman de 'L'Express'*, p. 85.

[11] Giroud, *Si je mens...*, p. 186.

the other modernisers in the government ministries realised, was that recovery and growth could not come from the supply-side alone, but depended heavily on the demand-side as well: modernisation would be predicated not just on the consolidation and expansion of the industrial and manufacturing base, but on the *consumption* of that output. Indeed, growth could and would become increasingly demand driven: expansion in post-war France, as in the other European capitalist economies, would take the form specifically of consumer capitalism, the high mass consumption which W. W. Rostow would identify in 1960 as the final stage of economic development under capitalism.[12]

For this to occur, of course, depends in turn on the presence of willing consumers. However, one of the key problems facing the governments of the Fourth Republic was precisely the *lack* of such a consumer culture. As Richard Vinen points out, while it had certainly existed on the Parisian boulevards since the end of the nineteenth century, the attitude of the French as a whole towards the pleasures of consumerism remained rather different: the country, he writes, was 'dominated by a culture of self-sufficiency, utilitarianism and meanness';[13] and as Susan Weiner puts it, the Fourth Republic had to 'encourage the French to do away with their traditionally parsimonious ways and become consumers'.[14] In other words, if economic take-off were to be achieved, it would require nothing less than the wholesale re-education of the French, and the creation of a consumer society. The emergence of this *société de consommation* would, of course, become one of the most significant narratives of the France of the 1950s and 60s, and would come to have huge ramifications at all levels of French society – political, cultural, psychological. It was also a story in which *L'Express* was a central protagonist.

Particularly striking is the way in which this story unfolded on different fronts simultaneously. The most obvious was direct government intervention at the economic level: throughout the 1950s, various governments engaged in attempts to stimulate the market and

---

[12] Walt W. Rostow, *The Stages of Economic Growth: a Non-Communist Manifesto* (Cambridge: Cambridge University Press, 1960)

[13] Richard Vinen, *France 1934-1970* (London: Macmillan, 1996), p. 121.

[14] Susan Weiner, 'The *Consommatrice* of the 1950s and Elsa Triolet's *Roses à crédit*', *French Cultural Studies*, 17 (1995), 123-144 (p. 124).

encourage spending. Between 1952 and 1954, for example, price freezes were combined with wage increases.[15] These efforts met with some success: between 1950 and 1957, consumption of goods increased by 40%.[16] At the same time as the French were finding more goods in the shops, and more money in their pockets to spend on them, they were also being offered visions of the new life they could lead with them. The mass media – which, as the launch of *L'Express* itself testified, was a sector undergoing rapid expansion – played a crucial part in disseminating and articulating the changes affecting the country and those who lived there, and this was true of *L'Express* especially.

L'Express is both intriguing and important because its support for Mendès France and his ideas went beyond a series of favourable editorials. Convinced that he was the only politician capable of carrying out the necessary reforms, it displayed more or less absolute commitment both to the possibility of bringing Mendès France to power and to the rebirth of France along the lines he was suggesting. Giroud makes clear that 'dans ses implications politiques – et l'imbrication est constante – l'économie a été la raison d'être de *L'Express*'.[17] The journalists at *L'Express*, she says, were 'un groupe de gens qui voulaient de toutes leurs forces faire "décoller" la France',[18] a group intent on helping to redefine France, and define the modernity it would experience. The news weekly can be seen to play a full and complex part both in promoting the tenets of liberal economics and in re-educating the French as the system required.

---

[15] Richard Kuisel, *Capitalism and the State in Modern France* (Cambridge: Cambridge University Press, 1981), p. 268.

[16] Jean-Pierre Rioux, *La France de la Quatrième République*, II, p. 240. The extent to which the French proved themselves willing converts to the consumerist cause is the central drama of this narrative of education. In many ways, the birth of the *société de consommation* stands as a traumatic event, responses to which began to be articulated almost immediately – in the work of Henri Lefebvre, Edgar Morin and Jean Baudrillard among others – but from which, arguably, the French have still yet properly to recover.

[17] Giroud, *Si je mens...*, p. 153.

[18] *Si je mens...*, p. 138. As Kristin Ross notes, in evoking France's 'take-off' here, Giroud may well be referring to the final stage of Rostow's theory of capitalist economic growth, the transition from a traditional economy to one based on high mass consumption. See Ross, *Fast Cars, Clean Bodies*, p. 222, n. 32, and Rostow, *The Stages of Economic Growth*, ch. 2.

Indeed, in the way it sets out to promote a clear agenda, rooted firmly in an economic and political philosophy, *L'Express* of the 1950s could be said to have something in common with Sartre's *Temps modernes*, launched a few years previously in 1945. Both journals demonstrate a similar ethos in their belief that it is through dynamic intervention, the persuasiveness of writing, and the pooling of ideas and resources that change can be brought about. The complementarity of the two journals at the time is suggested by the way *L'Express*, throughout the 1950s, repeatedly plays host to leading figures of *Les Temps modernes*, including Sartre and Merleau-Ponty; and following the Soviet invasion of Hungary in 1956, Sartre chose the news weekly to announce his split with the Communist Party.[19]

More precisely, *L'Express* of the 1950s can be described as bringing the serious analysis of the specialist press – that found in journals such as *Les Temps modernes* – to a wider audience, or what might today be called the mass market.[20] In the early years especially, the news weekly carried a number of items on the economy, giving summaries of official government audits, or using strip cartoons to explain the principles of industrial reconversion. It also explored other issues likely to be of concern to forward-thinking French citizens, whether it be nuclear power, urban renewal, or economic cooperation in Europe. These issues were usually discussed in the section entitled *La marche des idées*, which was designed to 'apporter à nos lecteurs des documents qu'ils ne peuvent trouver ailleurs [...] et la synthèse des ouvrages importants dont ils doivent connaître le contenu'.[21] Such documents were frequently published as 'dossiers' within the magazine itself, numbered separately and clearly intended to be detached and kept as a sort of reference library of modern life.

For Giroud, the innovative nature of *L'Express* lay in the way it mediated between a form of 'think tank' working to define and shape France's future, and the general public:

---

[19] *L'Express*, 9 November 1956, pp. 14-15.

[20] From an initial level of 35,000 copies at its launch in 1953, the circulation of the magazine grew steadily: after two years, 150,000 copies a week were being printed and 115,000 sold, making it the second most popular news weekly after *Le Canard enchaîné*. It was regularly outselling its natural rival, *France-Observateur* (the first news weekly, launched in 1950), by two or three to one. Data from Serror, '*L'Express* et l'opinion publique', pp. 14-15 and Table 5, p. 81.

[21] *L'Express*, 12 October 1956, p. 13.

> C'était une aventure assez originale en ceci qu'elle réunissait une poignée de véritables journalistes [...] c'est-à-dire des gens capables de mettre des idées en forme de façon qu'elles soient claires et frappantes, de les simplifier, de les diffuser, et une poignée de hauts fonctionnaires, d'universitaires, de chefs d'entreprise, d'hommes politiques, capables de nous livrer [...] les véritables éléments d'appréciation et d'analyse qui fondaient nos positions.[22]

In short, the magazine 'était le premier à allier ce qu'on pourrait appeler une doctrine [...] à la technique journalistique pour la rendre vivante et sensible'[23]. One of the most obvious manifestations of this new journalistic practice, as I discussed briefly in chapter three, was the format adopted by the magazine. Its own deliberately modern design, modelled on the American news weeklies, embodied the modernity being advocated by its contributors. The brevity and clarity of the articles setting out the agenda were reflected in typography and layout which were themselves clear and uncluttered. As Servan-Schreiber remarks, 'le fond de la pensée est neuf, la forme doit l'être aussi. Dès le départ, je demande, avec Françoise, le respect d'une règle: pas de "tourne"! Les articles doivent se lire d'une traite sur la même page'.[24] Giroud similarly highlights the innovative nature of *L'Express*, and the importance of form in articulating and communicating the break with the past it represents: 'le tout était de réussir la traduction journalistique [...] de ce renouvellement. Du format au sommaire, en passant par la technique d'écriture, les sélections, l'emploi des légendes, l'unité typographique, nous avons inventé'.[25] Not content simply to discuss and define modernity in its pages, the news weekly also intended to display modernity through its formal innovation.

If *L'Express* resembled *Les Temps modernes* in its general ethos and spirit of *engagement*, it remained radically different in one very important way. For while it may have brought the rigorous

---

[22] Giroud, *Si je mens...*, p. 152.
[23] Giroud, *Si je mens...*, p. 187.
[24] Jean-Jacques Servan-Schreiber, *Passions* (Paris: Fixot, 1991), p. 214.
[25] Giroud, *Si je mens...*, p. 161. Strictly speaking, her claim is not entirely accurate. *France-Observateur* was exploiting a similar template at the time, albeit with less commercial success. Nevertheless, what is interesting is less the accuracy of Giroud's claim, than what is at stake for her in making it – namely, the need once again to stress the innovative, cutting-edge nature of the magazine.

analysis of specialist and academic reviews such as *Les Temps modernes* to the mass market – could even, perhaps, be characterised as *Les Temps modernes* with advertisements – it is precisely the presence of advertisements, the news weekly's relationship to the market, which made the difference. Whereas the whole philosophy of Sartre's journal was reflected in the way it stood aloof from the market, that of *L'Express* was reflected in the fact that it was prepared to embrace it. The magazine's relationship to the market is a crucial factor both in its overall development during the 1950s, and in its involvement with Mauriac in particular, as we see it caught between two opposing logics – one of commitment, the other of commercialisation.

This important tension arises because *L'Express* is a committed journal arguably committed to one task especially: namely, promoting the consumer society on which the success of the new agenda depends, and helping to usher the French towards the market. Its commitment to the reformist agenda of Mendès France emerges not only in its weighty political and economic analyses, but also in the seemingly unrelated, apolitical areas of the magazine – areas, in fact, where we can see the theoretical ideas being translated into the more recognisable terms of everyday life.

One of the most important examples of this is *Madame Express*. The magazine introduced a section devoted to women's interests, entitled *une page au féminin*, in 1954. In November 1958, this expanded to some eight pages, and became *Madame Express*, 'supplément pratique'. The development of such a section is another example of the magazine's innovation, for it was unheard of at the time in the mainstream political press.[26] It took place in response to the fact that *L'Express* counted a large number of women amongst its readers (at 36%, by far the largest among the *journaux d'opinion*[27]). Thus, in addressing and responding to its female audience, the magazine once more reinforced its status as a messenger of change, promoting and shaping the revolutions underway: the image offered by the supplement was that of the newly dynamic career woman, epitomised by Giroud herself, and one which its readers, coming from

---

[26] Serror, '*L'Express* et l'opinion publique', p. 27.
[27] Serror, '*L'Express* et l'opinion publique', p. 24.

a predominantly middle- or lower middle-class background, would recognise, or to which they would aspire.

At the same time, however, the emergence of a section aimed at the female readership can also be understood as a pragmatic response to the key role women were beginning to have in building a consumer society. The editors themselves make this point in the introduction which accompanies the first *page au feminine*, pointing out that '83% des achats sont effectués par les femmes'.[28] It made perfect sense to target women and encourage them further into the market – encourage them to consume more, in other words, if consumption was one of the keys to modernisation. Consequently, it is no surprise to find the pages of *Madame Express* dominated by guides to the latest fashions and accessories, which aim to make consumption easier for busy women and prevent it simply becoming another chore for those preoccupied with having to 'tenir une maison, élever des enfants, s'habiller'.[29]

As this last quotation suggests, an interesting message is to be found in the pages of *Madame Express*. The supplement is above all a space where Giroud can put forward her vision of the modern woman, a vision which inevitably defined itself in relation to the one Simone de Beauvoir had begun to articulate in the 1940s. Giroud's was rather less radical, or more pragmatic, than that of Beauvoir, of whom she was deeply critical. She considered Beauvoir to be out of touch with the preoccupations of real women, and the reality of their everyday lives.[30] Consequently, the vision of the modern woman which comes into focus in *Madame Express* is a complex, not to say problematic one.

The world of *Madame Express* is certainly one of dynamic, active women, exemplified by Giroud herself; but that dynamism appears unproblematic as long as it does not affect their place within the established bourgeois framework. Modernity, at least as far as *Madame Express* is concerned, does not seem to involve any profound

---

[28] *L'Express*, 10 April 1954, p. 10. On the part played by women in establishing the consumer society in France, and the role played by the mass media in stimulating their participation and fuelling their desires through its representation of modern domesticity, see Weiner, 'The *Consommatrice* of the 1950s', and Ross, *Fast Cars, Clean Bodies*, ch. 2.

[29] *L'Express*, 10 April 1954, p. 10.

[30] On Giroud's attitude to, and relationship with, Beauvoir, see Ross, *Fast Cars, Clean Bodies*, pp. 68-69.

change in women's roles. Rather, it is more about making those roles easier to play. It is not about liberating women from the domestic environment, so much as making that environment, and women's exploitation of it, more efficient: the supplement promotes the merits of new appliances making life easier in the kitchen, or suggests activities for children during school holidays. Above all, modernity is about changing styles, fashion and look – about something which can and must be bought. *Madame Express* works assiduously to oil the wheels of the market. It acts as an intermediary between consumers and producers, and educates both in the market's complex mechanisms. It sets up consumer tests which expose products to the rigours of competition, and alerts producers to the need to recognise the desires, and power, of the consumer: 'nous signalerons aux industriels, aux commerçants [...] les améliorations que les femmes souhaitent, les suggestions qu'elles font pour que leur vie quotidienne matérielle soit simplifiée'.[31] The ideology of free market economics is articulated in even the most innocent of consumer tests as the magazine works to stimulate competition.[32]

L'Express, of course, is a far from disinterested player in this. Its best interests lie in ensuring that the circulation of goods is maintained, not only because it stands to gain further profit from increased advertising, but also – and more fundamentally – because its own future depends on that continued circulation. If, as Giroud asserts, economics is the *raison d'être* of *L'Express*, then this is not only because it is central to the ideas which the news weekly is trying to promote, but also because, like the goods whose advertisements it carries, the news weekly is itself a commodity. Its survival depends on it being bought and read; it must carve out a place in the market and fend off its competitors. Indeed, it proves to be exemplary in this respect. It offers a textbook case of business success as it achieves sustained growth despite an initial capital of $20,000, which Giroud

---

[31] *L'Express*, 10 April 1954, p. 10.

[32] 'Régulièrement, une petite équipe mettra à l'épreuve les produits nouveaux [...] qui sont proposés aux consommateurs. Toutes les femmes savent qu'il est impossible de juger vraiment une crème, un aspirateur ou un tissu avant de l'avoir essayé. Ce sont ces essais que nous nous proposons de faire le plus scrupuleusement possible, tant à l'égard de nos lecteurs qu'à celui des fabricants. Nous sommes, d'ailleurs, persuadés que si ceux-ci veulent bien admettre que nos observations seront fondées sur l'expérience de l'usager, ils pourront en bénéficier.' *L'Express*, 17 November 1955, p. 7.

describes as 'dérisoire'.[33] Such success is achieved because it operates precisely according to the modern, efficient practices being advocated within its own pages by people such as Mendès France and Alfred Sauvy: as an alert business should, it exploits gaps in the market and capitalises on opportunities, such as the chance to expand its readership amongst women. The fact that *L'Express* succeeds as a commodity is itself part of the point: the magazine is not simply promoting the new agenda, but proving its validity as it does so.

The magazine's status as a commodity can be seen to have an important bearing on its evolution in the 1950s and 60s. Central to this evolution is its need to resolve the tension between the two conflicting logics at work within it, between commitment on the one hand, and commercialism on the other. Both Giroud and Servan-Schreiber show themselves to be aware of the problematic relationship between the two, of the way in which commercial interests can interfere with the purity of motive associated with commitment. As Giroud puts it, 'la direction d'une entreprise de presse est difficile, parce qu'elle exige que celui qui prend les décisions d'ordre commercial sente précisément la nature particulièrement du "produit" journal'.[34] Her sensitivity is reflected in Servan-Schreiber's efforts to ensure the financial independence of the magazine and so protect it from outside interference.

Equally, however, the tension between commitment and commercialism had important consequences for the news weekly's relationship with Mauriac. It makes his passage through *L'Express* a transformative one, bringing to bear pressures which shape his development as an intellectual in new ways. Indeed, the significance of these pressures lies in the fact that they seem not just to confirm his status as an intellectual, but to make him into something else, something more than that: during his time at *L'Express*, Mauriac acquires what we could call a 'star quality'. Furthermore, the resolution of the tension between commitment and commercialism in the 1960s is the key to a general paradigm shift within *L'Express*, in which Mauriac himself becomes embroiled, and which provokes his departure.

---

[33] Giroud, *Si je mens...*, p. 148.
[34] Giroud, *Si je mens...*, p. 164.

'La vieille poule aux œufs d'or': Mauriac and the intellectual as media star

We saw earlier that one of Servan-Schreiber's first moves was to establish *L'Express* as the voice of an authoritative 'think tank', which provided the magazine with its weighty analytical content. It is striking that this move was accompanied by an explicit claim to the truth when, in his first editorial, he states that 'il faut dire la vérité telle que nous la voyons'.[35] The presence of a 'think tank' reinforces this claim by acting as a sign and guarantor of the journal's honesty and integrity, and by confirming the impression that the news weekly is a voice to be listened to. In other words, the 'think tank' has both a serious analytical purpose and a rhetorical function, as it appeals to our understanding of academics and intellectuals as disinterested individuals who are willing to disavow short-term interests and profits in favour of the greater good. Indeed, Giroud chooses to describe Mauriac's own participation in just these terms. His collaboration was motivated not by vulgar ambition, she argues, but by a desire to see France reborn: 'il ne s'agissait pas d'aider à satisfaire des ambitions vulgaires, mais de mettre Mendès France et ses idées au pouvoir, en action, pour le meilleur de la France'.[36]

Mauriac's involvement works slightly differently to that of the magazine's 'think tank', however, for it is not based on the possession of any particular political or economic knowledge or expertise. Rather, he brings with him the power of personality, an aura which confers a greater moral authority: 'l'arrivée du prix Nobel va renforcer l'influence du journal'.[37] The very fact that he agrees to join forces

---

[35] *L'Express*, 16 May 1953, p. 7.

[36] Giroud, *Si je mens...*, p. 151. Further evidence of the *savant*'s fabled disinterestedness is expressed nicely in Giroud's remark that Mauriac was prepared to join *L'Express* even though its founders 'ne pouvaient même pas lui payer ce qu'il était en situation d'exiger' (ibid., p. 146). The correspondence between Mauriac and Servan-Schreiber gives an indication of their financial arrangements: on joining *L'Express* in 1954, Mauriac agreed terms of 100,000 *anciens francs* a month (letter from Jean-Jacques Servan-Schreiber to François Mauriac, 26 March 1954, Bibliothèque Littéraire Jacques-Doucet, fonds Mauriac). To put this in context, Servan-Schreiber, writing to Pierre Mendès France in June of the same year, mentions that the total cost of producing an issue of *L'Express* was 2.5 million *anciens francs* (letter deposited at the Institut Pierre Mendès France, Paris). Details of Mauriac's contract with *Le Figaro* and *Le Figaro littéraire* remain elusive, making it difficult to judge precisely what financial sacrifice he made in joining *L'Express*.

[37] Siritzky and Roth, *Le Roman de 'L'Express'*, p. 38.

with *L'Express* confirms that the news weekly is something to be taken seriously. Mauriac is of strategic interest for *L'Express*. If Servan-Schreiber is attracted to him, it is because he recognises in him a source of what Bourdieu calls 'capital symbolique'. Bourdieu uses this term to refer to the prestige and status acquired over time by an individual within the social order, as a result of not just their activities, talents or abilities, but also the recognition of those abilities by those around them as valuable or useful. Crucially, too, that capital has its greatest value when it is endowed by those in society with the greatest ability (status and power) to do so. As Bourdieu puts it,

> Le capital symbolique, c'est n'importe quelle propriété (n'importe quelle espèce de capital, physique, économique, culturel, social) lorsqu'elle est perçue par des agents sociaux dont les catégories de perception sont telles qu'ils sont en mesure de la connaître (de l'apercevoir) et de la reconnaître, de lui accorder valeur.[38]

Symbolic capital brings with it authority and respect, and as such is essential for any agent intending to intervene successfully in the world.

By the time he joins *L'Express* in 1954, Mauriac has of course, through his activities as an outspoken columnist and his fame as a novelist, acquired a sizeable amount of capital, which the news weekly can co-opt as it intervenes in debate. Writing to the author after the French army's defeat at Dien Bien Phu in May 1954, Servan-Schreiber articulates clearly his perception of Mauriac's ability to influence opinion simply by dint of being Mauriac: 'je crois que, *plus que tout autre*, vous pouvez sonner l'alarme jusqu'au fond des cœurs'.[39] Overall, Giroud makes the news weekly's strategy clear when she argues that

> Quand on fait un journal, c'est-à-dire quelque chose qui doit être frappant dans l'instant et pas rétrospectivement, qui peut être en avant d'un pas mais pas de cinq, il vaut mieux, en effet, y donner la parole à des gens qui ont une certaine "force de frappe".[40]

---

[38] Pierre Bourdieu, *Raisons pratiques* (Paris: Seuil, coll. "Points", 1994), p. 116.
[39] Letter from Jean-Jacques Servan-Schreiber to François Mauriac, 8 May 1954, Bibliothèque Littéraire Jacques-Doucet, fonds Mauriac, v°. My emphasis.
[40] Giroud, *Si je mens...*, p. 180.

Likewise, the magazine's powerful presentation of 'La Question' shows the skill with which that symbolic capital can be exploited, and the 'force de frappe' unleashed. However, examples such as this also help to make clear that Mauriac's relationship with *L'Express* is more complicated than a simple process of appropriation on the part of the magazine.

Mauriac's relationship with *L'Express* is transformative for two related reasons. Firstly, it reconfirms his status as an important intellectual figure. Mauriac certainly arrives at *L'Express* with the symbolic capital he has accrued over the previous decades. Indeed, it is the precondition for his involvement with the news weekly. However, the value of that capital, and his status, are enhanced precisely by virtue of the fact that he is pursued by *L'Express* and recognised by it as a significant intellectual figure. His importance as a free-thinking voice of moral conscience is confirmed by the magazine's desire, its efforts to secure his collaboration: the photograph showing Mauriac with Servan-Schreiber and Giroud, smiling proudly at having got their man, captures the moment of what Bourdieu terms *reconnaissance*, the point at which the value of symbolic capital is recognised and reendowed. Secondly, this moment of recognition has particular signifiance because it takes place between generations. As such, it marks an essential stage in his consecration as an intellectual. Just as the publication of Sartre's article in 1939 indicated that Mauriac would struggle to find a place in the new literary order which was beginning to emerge, so too the fact that he is identified by a new generation as a figure of moral authority serves to confirm his importance as an intellectual.

The religious connotations of consecration are entirely appropriate to the process of *reconnaissance*, which marks the elevation by the community of an individual to an unassailable position of authority, a position which seems almost natural or immutable. The extent to which those around him had internalised this sense of Mauriac's rightful place in the pantheon of great minds can be gauged from Servan-Schreiber's letters to him at the time, which are striking for their tone of respect, and even awe. Somewhat tentatively inviting Mauriac to participate in the routine of editorial committees, for example, Servan-Schreiber writes, 'nous souhaitons vivement que vous acceptiez de guider notre action – littéraire et politique – en participant à des réunions régulières d'orientation'.[41] It is as if those around him recognise there is something qualitatively different about Mauriac, something which sets him apart.

We can say, then, that Mauriac's collaboration with *L'Express* is perhaps a question not so much of his development as an intellectual, as of the development of his status as an intellectual. It shows too how a change in the latter may affect the former. Moving to *L'Express* does not necessarily bring any objective change in Mauriac's ability to intervene or to formulate convincing interventions: he remains the same polemical editorialist. But what it can been seen to change is the *perception* of those interventions and the individual making them. His consecration by *L'Express* offers a good example of what Bourdieu calls a 'rite d'institution', a symbolic act which brings about changes in reality, above all by investing certain individuals with the power to make change, and this chiefly through the way it alters perception of those individuals.[42] In the case of Mauriac, this is reflected both in the attitudes manifested by those around him, particularly by his editors, and in how Mauriac himself acts. Supported by *L'Express*, he can afford to adopt increasingly critical positions, can break the news of torture being practised in Algeria, and so on. Moreover, perceptions of Mauriac are undoubtedly shaped by the way in which he is constructed as an intellectual by the magazine. As we saw in chapter three, *L'Express* plays an active role in reinforcing our impression of Mauriac as an intellectual through the way it presents him in its pages. This is the second key feature of the news weekly's relationship with the writer, and I want now to return to it in order to consider further some of its implications and consequences.

One of the most noticeable aspects of Mauriac's involvement with *L'Express* is that it leads to a proliferation of images of him. Images of Mauriac circulate in ways and volumes they had not previously as he is given wide exposure by the magazine. *L'Express* was distinctive in its use of a single, dominant photograph, usually three-quarter size, on the front cover, a layout it borrowed from *Time* magazine in America. Mauriac appears on the cover three times

---

[41] Letter from Jean-Jacques Servan-Schreiber to François Mauriac, 26 March 1954, Bibliothèque Littéraire Jacques-Doucet, fonds Mauriac, v°.

[42] Pierre Bourdieu, 'Les rites d'institution', in *Langage et pouvoir symbolique* (Paris: Seuil, coll. "Points", 2001), pp. 175-186.

during his collaboration with the magazine, twice on his own – including the edition of 15 January 1955, in which 'La Question' is published – and once in the company of Jean-Paul Sartre. Distinctive too is the nature of these photographs: they are often heavily codified, set up and taken in ways which show sensitivity to what Barthes would call the 'rhetoric' of the image, its ability to connote or imply certain things.[43] I discussed in the previous chapter how the portrait used on the cover of *L'Express* to introduce the article on torture connotes what we might term *intellectualité*: a sober setting provides the backdrop for Mauriac's judgemental and sombre gaze, which searches to meet that of the reader. We have seen too how the photograph's motifs or connotations echo those to be found in the image accompanying the first *Bloc-notes* column published by *L'Express* in April 1954. In both cases, the images exploit a certain combination of settings and poses (the solitary figure caught in a moment of contemplation) to generate a vivid sense of the intellectual as an individual whose isolation or distance from the world is vital for his clear-sighted analysis of it.

I would suggest that Mauriac's sudden exposure, and exposure through a series of images in particular, is not just striking in itself, but also revealing of a more general trend at work in post-war French culture. The post-war period is a time when the phenomenon of the intellectual evolves in important ways. With the emergence of figures such as Sartre, Beauvoir and Camus, and their rise to prominence in the years following the Liberation, the public profile of the intellectual undergoes a dramatic transformation. Intellectuals break through into popular consciousness and capture the public's attention in a new way. This is a consequence of three things in particular: firstly, what they were saying. While Beauvoir was engaged in a radical critique of the role of women in society, Sartre was articulating a new and controversial philosophy of action. Furthermore, in his persistent intervention in political debate (which included founding the Rassemblement Démocratique Révolutionnaire with David Rousset in 1948), Sartre had come to exemplify the vision of the intellectual as politically committed individual he had set out to impose.

---

[43] Roland Barthes, 'Rhétorique de l'image', in *L'obvie et l'obtus*, pp. 25-42.

The second reason why the profile of the intellectual evolves in the post-war years lies in the way several of them were living their lives. The intellectual suddenly seemed to leave the study and the writing desk for the café; or rather, was turning the café into a study, making this public space the centre of intellectual activity. Philosophy no longer seemed to belong in the classrooms of the Sorbonne and other remote academic institutions, but in the basement clubs of the Left Bank. Likewise, its practitioners appeared to have far more in common with those at the cutting edge of popular culture – actors, jazz musicians, writers – than with the traditional academic elite. The fascination in the late 1940s for the unconventional life being led in the cafés of Saint-Germain is well-known, with newspapers in both France and abroad investigating and reporting extensively on the 'existential lifestyle' inspired by Sartre's philosophy, and being lived by the fashionable Parisian youth;[44] and it is the increasing interest in intellectuals on the part of the mass media, along with the consequent exposure it affords them, which is the third key factor affecting their evolution in the post-war period.

The relationship between intellectuals and the mass media is a long-standing one, inaugurated by the publication of Zola's 'J'accuse!' on the front page of *L'Aurore*. Indeed, the emergence of intellectuals in their modern form – understood as prestigious figures from the field of cultural production who enter the political field in the name of justice, morality or some other fundamental value – is arguably linked with, not to say predicated on, the expansion of the mass media. In the first instance, this meant rapid growth in both the number of newspapers, and the circulation of those newspapers, in the late nineteenth century.[45] If the role of the intellectuals is to intervene in political debate with as much impact as possible, or to draw cases of injustice or moral failure to as many people as possible, then they are dependent on the mass media if they are to do so with any success. The significance of 'J'accuse!' lies not just in the content of the article

---

[44] See Mauricette Berne (ed.), *Sartre* (Paris: Bibliothèque nationale de France/Gallimard, 2005), pp. 114-120 and Jean-Pierre Rioux and Jean-François Sirinelli, *Histoire culturelle de la France*, vol. 4 (Paris: Seuil, coll. "Points", 2004), pp. 263-264. For first-hand accounts of the period, see Simone de Beauvoir, *La Force des choses* (Paris: Gallimard, 1963), and Boris Vian, *Manuel de St-Germain-des-Prés* (Paris: Toutain, 1950).
[45] See Pascal Ory and Jean-François Sirinelli, *Les Intellectuels en France*, pp. 45-49.

or the identity of its author, but in the fact that it exploits the newspaper as a powerful tool of communication, as the most obvious and effective way to reach a large audience.

In the sudden proliferation of images of intellectuals such as Sartre and Mauriac, however, we can see the emergence of a new situation, a result in particular of changes affecting the evolution of the mass media itself during the post-war period. Kristin Ross has characterised the 1950s and 60s in France as marking the 'dawning of image culture'.[46] By this she means the increasing dominance of the visual image in culture, as film and especially television begin to assert themselves, and the world becomes mediated through images as much as through words; but the trend towards the visual can also be found in the print media, as more and more use is made of photographic images. This is most clearly seen in the development of news magazines and photojournalism, which appeared in the United States in the inter-war years with *Time* and *Life*, and arrived in France in the years following the war in the form of *Paris-Match* (launched in 1949) and *L'Express*.

One of the consequences of this development is undoubtedly the greater exposure of intellectuals in the public eye. As they become an increasing part of public life in post-war France, not only are they talked about more and more frequently, but they are also captured by photographers who recognise their significance as part of the contemporary cultural landscape. It is during this period that some of the iconic images of intellectuals are produced, such as Henri Cartier-Bresson's portrait of Sartre on the Pont des Arts in Paris,[47] or Robert Doisneau's photograph of Beauvoir working at a table in the *Deux Magots* café on the Boulevard Saint-Germain.[48] This latter photograph is particularly interesting for the way in which it presents Beauvoir in what had become the intellectual's natural habitat. Yet it also captures the somewhat paradoxical status intellectuals had acquired: they suddenly become very present, working in a public or semi-public space, yet are presented in a way which conveys a certain distance and mystique. She sits amidst tables, but those tables are unoccupied,

---

[46] Ross, *Fast Cars, Clean Bodies*, p. 12.
[47] Reproduced in Henri Cartier-Bresson, *Tête à Tête* (London: National Portrait Gallery, 1998), plate 47.
[48] Reproduced in Julian Stallabrass (ed.), *Paris Pictured* (London: Thames and Hudson, 2002), plate 62.

Beauvoir remaining an isolated, even unapproachable figure. She appears simultaneously near and far, accessible and remote, human and superhuman.

During the post-war period, that is to say, intellectuals can be seen to take on a star-like quality. They acquire qualities possessed by the most obvious figure of mass culture, the film star. Like film stars, they succeed in breaking through into the wider popular consciousness because of their repeated exposure in the mass media, exposure which involves mediation through visual images above all. If parallels can be drawn between intellectuals and film stars, it is because at the time, the star began to emerge as an increasingly noticeable and widespread phenomenon, one which was attracting the attention of contemporary cultural commentators, and consequently becoming the subject of reflexion and theorisation.

In 1957, for example, the sociologist Edgar Morin published *Les Stars*.[49] Although concerned primarily with the cinematic star system, his definition of the film star as an Olympian – at once distanced from, yet familiar to, mere mortals – could apply equally well to intellectuals. Indeed, in *L'Esprit du temps* of 1962, Morin makes clear that the phenomenon of the star is not restricted to the world of cinema, but is to be found wherever remarkable or significant individuals are exposed to the public gaze, or mediated to the public by the mass media: 'ces olympiens ne sont pas seulement les stars de cinéma, mais aussi les champions, princes, rois, play-boys, explorateurs, artistes célèbres'.[50] In the case of Mauriac, it is striking not just that *L'Express* sets out to construct him as an Olympian figure for its readers, but also that, as we have seen, Servan-Schreiber himself relates to the writer precisely in the way Morin suggests we relate to stars. From Servan-Schreiber's correspondance comes an image of Mauriac as a demi-god who has deigned to descend and move among the mortals. Not only, we might say, does *L'Express* confirm Mauriac's status as an intellectual, but it also transforms him into a star as it does so.

This star status is problematic, however. It is indicative of the broader trends which begin to affect French culture in the post-war years, and which can themselves be understood as a side effect of the

---

[49] Edgar Morin, *Les Stars* (Paris: Seuil, coll. "Points", 1972)
[50] Edgar Morin, *L'Esprit du temps* (Paris: Grasset, 1962), p. 139.

economic changes affecting the country at the time. Moreover, these changes are not only ones which *L'Express* helps to unleash, but also ones in which it is caught up as a result of its status as a commodity. At the same time, they will also shape the developments leading to Mauriac's split with the news weekly in 1961.

Central to these shifts and developments is the role of the image. The post-war period can certainly be seen to mark the dawning of image culture, a culture in which the visual image predominates; but the notion of the 'image culture' must also be understood in another way, one which Roland Barthes was exploring at the time. In *Mythologies*, Barthes analyses a culture which is predicated increasingly on the circulation of projected images – defined as constructed or intended appearances – and which feeds off them as much as it feeds off reality. Or more precisely, as he was intent on demonstrating, it was taking those projected images *as* reality, confusing the culturally constructed with the natural.[51] In fact, this culture of appearance could undoubtedly establish itself more effectively thanks to the increased circulation of visual images, a relationship suggested by the way visual images provide a starting point for several of the analyses in *Mythologies*.[52]

Furthermore, from Barthes' examination of contemporary culture emerges not only the importance of image-as-appearance *per se*, but also its importance in the broader socio-cultural order. This is seen most clearly, appropriately enough, in his brief discussion of *L'Express* and its involvement in the Minou Drouet affair. This controversy, over a series of poems supposedly written by an eight-year-old girl, yet displaying an unusually advanced level of technical and emotional sophistication, broke in 1955. *L'Express* devoted several pages over a number of issues to the *affaire Minou Drouet*, publishing poems, interviews, and analyses of her handwriting, as specialists attempted to determine whether the works were genuine.[53] Barthes suggests that the fascination with the young girl's poetry can be attributed to the way her work overtly displays all the signs of

---

[51] Roland Barthes, *Mythologies* (Paris: Seuil, coll. "Points", 1972)
[52] The most famous being his analysis of the photograph in *Paris-Match* of a young African soldier saluting what we assume to be the French flag. See *Mythologies*, p. 201.
[53] See *L'Express*, 15 November 1955, pp. 6-7. The controversy remains unresolved to this day.

poetry, that it can be readily recognised as such: what counts above all is that it has the *appearance* of poetry. He goes on to observe that 'ce n'est pas par hasard que *L'Express* a pris en charge Minou Drouet: c'est la poésie idéale d'un univers où le *paraître* est soigneusement chiffré'.[54] Drouet's poetry is that of a world where appearance is costed with care. Barthes points here to a crucial conjunction between image and consumption, to a growing awareness of the link between image and profit. In doing so, he provides a key to understanding how the culture of the period is working. For it is surely no coincidence that the image culture dawns at the same time as consumerism is being encouraged and beginning to spread through French society; nor that several of the images Barthes analyses are those projected by an expanding range of consumer goods (detergents, cars, plastics).

The link between image and consumption was one which which *L'Express*, its finger as always on the pulse of new trends, had itself noticed. In March 1958, it published an article entitled 'Voici comment les magasins vous achètent...', in which it revealed the latest advertising techniques being developed in America and spreading to France.[55] The novelty of these techniques, the article claims, is that they work on the principle that consumers buy into an image as much as they buy a product. Manufacturers, it suggests, are increasingly aware of the fact that an attractive image is the key to a successful commodity. The period is one where goods must sell themselves, and fight off their competitors, by projecting themselves more effectively.

As Barthes' rather acerbic remarks also make clear, however, it was a lesson which *L'Express* too had clearly learned. After all, while it was a committed, campaigning journal wanting to contribute to the modernisation of France, it was also a commodity which had to find success in the market place. Its sensitivity to the image it projects can be seen to mark its thinking from the start, as it adopts a bold new style to signal the new approach being advocated in its pages; and its stylisation of Mauriac as an intellectual is simultaneously part of its self-stylisation as what Serror terms the 'journal des intellectuels'.[56]

---

[54] Barthes, *Mythologies*, p. 159. Barthes' emphasis.

[55] *L'Express*, 20 March 1958, pp. 16-17.

[56] Serror, '*L'Express* et l'opinion publique', p. 42. As Serror observed at the time, 'un journal se vend [...] autant pour ce qu'il est réellement, que pour ce qu'il paraît être'. '*L'Express* et l'opinion publique', p. 34.

Moreover, the image to which Mauriac contributes proves to be a successful and lucrative one: the magazine's sales rose continuously throughout the 1950s, its print run never dropping below 120,000 after 1955.[57] During his time at *L'Express*, that is to say, Mauriac is put to work and made to turn a profit; and he himself is quick to realise that Servan-Schreiber is interested in him not just for the symbolic capital he possesses, but also for the latent economic capital this represents.[58] As he remarks in a letter to Pierre Brisson in August 1955, referring to his relationship with Servan-Schreiber, 'je suis pour lui sa vieille poule aux œufs d'or. Mais quand il n'y aura plus d'œufs d'or!...' (LV 331). As the magazine shows itself alert to ways of maximising its assets and manipulating its resources, it once more gives a working demonstration of how an effective modern business must operate.

Here lies the significance of Mauriac's transformation into a star at the hands of *L'Express*. His collaboration with the news weekly undoubtedly results in his consecration as an intellectual, but it does so at the price of his commodification. As Morin was well aware, the star is a product of the mass media, not only in the sense that it is the mass media which offers the exposure that the star requires, but also in the sense that the mass media manufactures stars. It creates stars because it needs them to survive, living off them by packaging them well and feeding them to the public.[59] The dominance of the image is something which Mauriac must confront with increasing frequency in the 1950s and 60s. It is one facet of a new social and cultural order with which, as I will go on to explore in chapter five, he becomes increasingly uncomfortable.

The 'Nouvelle Vague' and the problem of modernity

Mauriac plays an important role in contributing to the image of *L'Express* as a committed, dynamic and campaigning journal, an image whose appeal would seem to be confirmed by the consistent growth in sales enjoyed by the magazine during the 1950s. Particularly interesting is the way in which the image seems to strike a

---

[57] Serror, '*L'Express* et l'opinion publique', Table 3, p. 50.

[58] Cf. Bourdieu, *Les Règles de l'art*, p. 235: 'le capital symbolique est un capital "économique" dénié, reconnu, donc légitime, véritable crédit, capable d'assurer, sous certaines conditions [...] des profits "économiques".'

[59] Morin, *L'Esprit du temps*, p. 131.

chord with the young: at the time of Serror's survey in 1959, 44% of the magazine's readers were below the age of 35,[60] confirming Florence Malraux's feeling on arriving at the news weekly that it was 'le journal de ma génération'.[61] Interesting too is the way in which it seems to be the image specifically which attracts them. *L'Express* becomes the magazine 'dont la seule lecture constitu[e] déjà un engagement politique'.[62] It is the magazine to be seen reading – a response perhaps appropriate to those growing up in an image culture. What is more, the news weekly's own reaction to this popularity is similarly appropriate to a journal at the forefront of such a culture.

There is a certain irony in the news weekly's success among younger readers, because it can be seen to be partly responsible for the developments which provoke Mauriac's departure. In 1957, *L'Express* launched a detailed survey of France's post-war youth, which Giroud famously labelled *La Nouvelle Vague*, and once more, the tensions and ambiguities we have traced through the creation of *Madame Express* and Mauriac's own collaboration came to the surface. For on the one hand, the survey was a serious study, which again confirmed the magazine's place at the leading edge of modernity. The team set out to exploit the latest polling techniques to provide the most complete picture of the nation's youth since 1870.[63] Yet on the other hand, the survey provided the opportunity for an extensive marketing exercise, as the magazine worked to confirm and capitalise on its image as the journal of choice for the young and forward-thinking. As Serror observes, 'on ne saurait sous-estimer la contribution de l'enquête d'octobre 1957 dans la formation de "l'image de *L'Express*"'.[64] The survey was trailed extensively from mid-summer 1957, when the project was announced, and between July and October 1957, the magazine adopted the sub-title 'le journal de la nouvelle vague'. The commercial importance of the *Nouvelle Vague* phenomenon for the magazine is also neatly summed up by the fact that it took care to copyright the slogan.[65]

---

[60] Serror, '*L'Express* et l'opinion publique', Table 2, p. 21.
[61] Siritzky and Roth, *Le Roman de 'L'Express'*, p. 142.
[62] Ibid.
[63] *Le Roman de 'L'Express'*, p. 154.
[64] Serror, '*L'Express* et l'opinion publique', p. 33.
[65] '*L'Express* et l'opinion publique', p. 34, n. 3: 'on notera que l'expression "nouvelle vague" a été déposée par *L'Express* et est protégée par la loi'.

The *Nouvelle Vague* exercise thus became a clear attempt by the news weekly to respond to market conditions and exploit its success in a particular area of the market. That it does so is an indication of the increasing importance of image in determining the direction of the magazine. At the same time, the magazine's definition and promotion of the *Nouvelle Vague* also proved to be a key turning point in its relationship with Mauriac, becoming a focus for the tensions which would lead to his departure in April 1961.

As a slogan, *La Nouvelle Vague* serves to define not only the rising generation of twenty- and thirty-somethings typified by Giroud and Servan-Schreiber themselves, but also the cultural practices of that generation, and its film and fiction in particular. As Lynn Higgins points out, the new generation identified by Giroud 'included the majority of the *Nouveaux Romanciers* and all of the *Nouvelle Vague* film-makers'.[66] Indeed, there is a striking coincidence between the ability for Giroud clearly to identify and label the new social group, and the appearance of the visibly new cultural practices which reflect that group, including the first films by the 'new wave' of directors such as Godard and Truffaut.[67] As Higgins observes, there are obvious similarities between the dominant themes of the novels and films on the one hand, and the attitudes and opinions expressed by the generation itself on the other.[68] This means above all a sense of alienation, and a suspicion of the established order which echoes the tone of the original *prise de position* taken by *L'Express*. The period of the final years of the 1950s can therefore be seen to mark an important stage in the development of the new bourgeois order, the point at which it starts being represented and mediated by a range of cultural practices.[69] Unsurprisingly, *L'Express*, as its self-appointed spokesman, readily played a role in consolidating this developing social and cultural identity. In 1958, it established a prize for fiction, 'le prix de la Nouvelle Vague', won by Christiane Rochefort's *Le*

---

[66] Lynn Higgins, *New Novel, New Wave, New Politics* (Lincoln, Ne.: University of Nebraska Press, 1996), p. 6.

[67] Godard released his first full-length film, *A bout de souffle*, in 1959. Truffaut was a founder of the *Cahiers du cinéma*, the forum in which the new filmmakers defined their cinematic agenda.

[68] Higgins, *New Novel, New Wave, New Politics*, p. 19 and n. 1.

[69] Arguably a second important stage comes in the mid-1960s, when the new order becomes the subject of a series of satirical portraits in novels such as Georges Perec's *Les Choses* (1965), and Beauvoir's *Les Belles Images* (1966).

Repos du guerrier, and it was a keen supporter of the new cinema, publishing pre-release stills from Resnais' *Hiroshima mon amour* in 1959, for example.[70]

At the same time as the new mood became more clearly defined and reflected by the representations to be found in the films and books of the period, so too Mauriac's awareness that there was some sort of shift or reordering under way began to grow. In short, if the modern spirit embodied by *L'Express* saw Mauriac being exploited in certain ways, the first real challenge to him came when that modernity took on a concrete form, and it began to be articulated in the cultural practices with which he found himself increasingly confronted.

Mauriac's attitude is initially one of ironic superiority. In December 1957, he publishes an article on Philippe Sollers, who had just published his first novel, *Le Défi*. Entitled 'Une goutte de la vague', it begins 'voici ma contribution personnelle à la "Nouvelle Vague"' (BN I 551). However, his mood quickly turns into real anger. Two things especially disturb him. Firstly, he is disconcerted by increasingly overt images of sexuality, which begin to figure more prominently both in the arts and in everyday street decor. As he says in 1958, 'l'érotisme coule à pleins bords aujourd'hui. Il crie, il hurle dans toutes les rues, par mille affiches. Chaque salle de cinéma lui est dédiée' (BN II 182).

His sense of the role played by cinema in fuelling this new mood provokes a striking and bitter 'Bloc-notes' in 1959. He relates how, having resolved to see one of the films of the *Nouvelle Vague* 'dont on nous rebat les oreilles' (BN II 301), he goes into a restaurant for lunch beforehand, where his attention is seized by the spectacle of a couple at the table in front of him: 'déjà, seul à ma table, [...] j'étais dans un film'. Mauriac creates the impression of a sexually charged atmosphere, suggesting an affair or liaison between 'cette blonde, belle et fanée qui [...] décortiquait des crevettes avec une avidité hideuse, sous l'œil froid d'un Don Juan fatigué lui aussi' (BN II 302).

The effectiveness of the passage lies in Mauriac's ironic and knowing use of cinematic terms and filmic descriptive techniques as he evokes the scene. Having suggested that cinema has the power to influence our modes of perception – le cinéma accoutume notre œil à

---

[70] *L'Express*, 30 April 1959, pp. 38-39.

voir partout une figuration autour d'un couple en gros plan (BN II
302) – he illustrates this in his own description of the incident. The
couple dominates the foreground of the scene and the cinematic eye
zooms in to linger on a series of small and significant details. Physical
actions and gestures accumulate to give the sense of sexual tension
between the two: the 'avidity' with which she eats, suggesting desire
displaced, his cold eye and pallor, her throat and laugh, 'un rire
scandalisé et complaisant' (BN II 302). This sense of tension and
claustrophobia is increased by the describing eye cutting back and
forth between them, switching from the woman devouring her prawns
to the man's eye as it observes her. His thumbnail sketch rapidly
establishes an overpowering mood of malaise and degradation, not
least in Mauriac himself.

A further degree of complexity is added to this brief passage
by the way it also focuses on his reaction to the scene as spectator,
recreating the position of cinema-goer as voyeur: 'ce qui allait suivre
était inscrit en clair. Je pouvais me passer de sous-titres'. His response
is one of almost physical repulsion, and he flees the 'horreur' at the
earliest opportunity: 'je réglai en hâte l'addition, donnai au taxi
l'adresse de mon appartement désert' (BN II 302). The scene presents
him with the human relationship reduced to the bare bones of the basic
sexual transaction. Here, in the world of the new order, this
transaction would seem to be the default mode of interaction with
others, one from which it appears to be increasingly difficult to escape
other than by shutting out the world entirely – once in the sanctuary of
his flat, he wants to 's'étendre, fermer les yeux' (BN II 303).

The second problem troubling Mauriac is linked in various
ways to the first. In December 1960, he publishes two 'Bloc-notes'
which he terms his 'examen de conscience' (BN II 517). In these, he
sets out what he sees as the reasons for his increasingly tense
relationship with *L'Express*. For the first time in these articles, he
identifies the *Nouvelle Vague* explicity as a problem. He criticises
what he calls the split personality of *L'Express*, divided between the
serious political and economic analysis of the first pages, and a latter
half dominated by *Madame Express*, where 'on pénètre dans un autre
monde très "féminisé", voué au mythe de la Nouvelle Vague' (BN II

518).[71] He singles out in particular an ironic article by 'une de ces dames de *L'Express*' (BN II 519) on the young Spanish princess Fabiola after her wedding to the Belgian king, and which treated her 'd'un peu haut, gentiment, bien sûr, en "petite fille modèle"'. He takes offence above all at 'le complexe de supériorité d'une romancière de la Nouvelle Vague devant une jeune fille espagnole qui croit ce que Thérèse d'Avila a cru et qui a peut-être rêvé d'imiter sa vie' (BN II 519).

There are two clear issues involved here, which help to crystallise the emerging differences between Mauriac and his colleagues. Firstly, the stance of critical irony adopted by the author of the article in question, the novelist Christine de Rivoyre, is itself significant. What is at stake in her critique, seemingly, are changing conceptions of the role of women and the notion of femininity – conceptions which the magazine hoped to shape in the same way that it wanted to help bring about economic and social renewal. The attitudes of the enterprising, independent and career-minded women at *L'Express*, exemplified by Françoise Giroud and reflected in the pages of *Madame Express*, are at odds with the traditional model of passive femininity which the princess seems to embody for them. Rivoyre is looking at her from across a gap which the magazine itself helped to widen, one which Mauriac himself had already recognised some three years earlier in fact. In an interview with Madeleine Chapsal, he points out that 'la conception de la femme a changé, les femmes ont changé: la femme d'aujourd'hui est autre'.[72]

The particular cause of Mauriac's anger though, and the second issue raised by the disagreement, is Rivoyre's apparent disdain for the princess's religious beliefs. Her attitude reflects what had become an increasingly dominant theme in the magazine, and one which Mauriac was quick to detect: the persistent questioning of religious authority. In January 1960, for example, *L'Express* published a newly-discovered critique of Christianity by Jean Jaurès. For

---

[71] As I argued earlier, however, the content of *Madame Express* (its role in educating both consumers and manufacturers in the mechanisms of the market, for example) and indeed its very presence in the magazine can both be traced to the political and economic thinking Mauriac considers a hallmark of the 'proper' *Express*.

[72] 'Le métier d'écrivain', *L'Express*, 5 April 1957, repr. in Madeleine Chapsal, *Envoyez la petite musique* (Paris: Le Livre de Poche, 1984), p. 19. Though how radical their notion of women's 'liberation' really is, as I suggested in my discussion of *Madame Express* above, remains open to question.

Mauriac, 'ce qui m'inquiète le plus dans le texte de Jaurès [...], ce n'est certes pas son contenu, c'est la place importante qu'il occupe dans ce numéro' (BN II 368). Moreover, he found confirmation of the magazine's increasingly anti-clerical position in the same issue, as Servan-Schreiber published a satirical cariacture of a priest by the radical left-wing cartoonist Siné. Indeed, in the face of repeated pleas from the Catholic Establishment for him to leave the magazine, Mauriac justifies his continued collaboration by suggesting that his role is to 'faire entendre une certaine parole là où elle n'est presque jamais entendue' (BN II 516).

However, the strained relations between Mauriac and *L'Express* could not withstand a famous attack by Servan-Schreiber on de Gaulle in an editorial in April 1961: criticising what he saw as de Gaulle's mercenary approach to the negotiations with the FLN over Algerian independence, he dismissed the President as a 'marchand de tapis'.[73] Servan-Schreiber had been hostile towards de Gaulle since his return to power in June 1958, following the attempted coup in Algeria which had precipitated the demise of the Fourth Republic. Like many people at the time, he had been suspicious of the circumstances in which it took place, and in particular of de Gaulle's possible links with the generals in Algiers who had staged the coup. He was also troubled by the concentration of so much power in the hands of one man, a consequence of the new constitution of the Fifth Republic which de Gaulle himself had drawn up, and which gave sweeping powers to the President.[74]

For Mauriac, on the other hand, the return of de Gaulle was a providential moment. He saw him as the only man capable of leading France out of the quagmire of decolonisation, and gave him his full support, the enthusiastic tone of the *Bloc-notes* often in direct contradiction with the main editorial line of *L'Express*. Servan-Schreiber's provocative treatment of de Gaulle was an insult too far for Mauriac, and he abruptly ended his column. Usefully for him, this final disagreement coincided with a visit by de Gaulle to the South West, one of many regional trips he made during his presidency.

---

[73] 'Un homme dans l'espace', *L'Express*, 13 April 1961, p. 5.
[74] On the crisis which leads to de Gaulle's return, and the uncertainty over his relationship to the plotters in Algeria, see Rioux, *La France de la Quatrième République*, II, pp. 154-163. See also Robert Gildea, *France Since 1945* (Oxford: Oxford University Press, 1996), pp. 43-45.

Mauriac was among those waiting to meet him at Langon, near his country house at Malagar, and told him in person of his decision to leave the news weekly.

Nevertheless, while the immediate cause of Mauriac's departure may have been political – clashing opinions over de Gaulle and his policies – it has its roots in more fundamental differences at an ideological level. As Mauriac says in his *examen de conscience*, 'nos divergences politiques ne sont pas graves. Ce qui est grave, c'est la contradiction entre deux esprits' (BN II 517); the contradiction, that is to say, between old and new orders. As the new order incarnated by Servan-Schreiber and Giroud begins to assert itself, Mauriac finds key tenets of his ideology being challenged: that of the old bourgeois order into which Mauriac himself had been quickly inserted, with its clearly demarcated gender roles, its taboos on sexuality, and the religious discourses which help to keep these in place. There is thus a certain symbolism in Mauriac's departure from *L'Express*. It serves as a tangible sign that the new order was displacing the old, and that the old order and its values were being increasingly challenged, something which Mauriac would begin to feel and articulate with growing concern as the 1960s progressed.

Yet it is also true that Mauriac may in any case have found himself leaving *L'Express* for other reasons not long afterwards: by the mid-1960s, the intellectual figures it had courted during the 1950s, and whose place in the cultural firmament it had helped to consolidate, had all but disappeared from its pages. In 1964, *L'Express* underwent a radical redesign and realignment in the market as it finally resolved the long-running tension between the conflicting demands of commitment and commercialism in favour of the latter. For if the image or style of a product is what determines its success, then ultimately it will also determine its substance. After all, *Madame Express* had been telling manufacturers since its inception that a commodity needs to be modified when it no longer meets the requirements or desires of its consumers. It is striking, and highly appropriate, that *L'Express* should heed its own advice in the early 1960s.

During the 1950s, as we have seen, political commitment was central not only to the journal's activities, but also to the image which took shape around it. The news weekly offered those who bought it a sort of *engagement* by proxy. However, it is when commitment is commodified in this way, when it is translated into circulation figures, that it is most at risk. With the end of the Algerian war in 1962, *L'Express* finds its sales falling rapidly. The management team blames this on the journal's vigorous campaigning during the war, when it had been seen as 'le journal de la guerre d'Algérie'. With the war over, 'les Français n'ont plus qu'une envie: oublier ce cauchemar. Ils ont donc tendence à vouloir oublier aussi *L'Express*'.[75] The image of the committed journal which had contributed to the success of *L'Express* now proves to be a financial liability. The solution is a radical one, Servan-Schreiber abandoning the tabloid-size format and replacing it with a smaller, squarer, glossier magazine. The *journal d'opinion* which had shaped debate during the 1950s gave way to a *journal d'information*, which presented itself as an efficient and neutral purveyor of news and current affairs.

However, if the reinvention was successful in halting the slide in sales figures, it also had its price, as commitment was finally eclipsed by commercialism. There was now literally no room for the often provocative columns and analyses provided by the writers and intellectuals who had populated its pages in the 1950s. As Kristin Ross observes, 'had Sartre wanted to write for *L'Express* after 1964, he could not have. Its new format [...] featured short, unsigned news chunks in a standardised, accessible style'.[76] The journal had decided to address one audience in particular, an audience which was also the prime target of the advertisements it carried with increased prominence in its pages – namely, the newly-emerging social group of young and relatively wealthy middle-class workers known as 'cadres'. These engineers, managers and other 'technocrats' were in the process of creating the modern France Servan-Schreiber had been calling for during the 1950s. As the next generation of the middle-classes asserted itself and rose to power, the journal which had accompanied it during its formative years, and had profiled it in 1957, established itself as its companion and guide. Indeed, the distance travelled by *L'Express* since the 1950s was crystallised when its long-term rival *France-Observateur* itself underwent a redesign in the same year, re-emerging as *Le Nouvel Observateur*. While the format it adopted was similar to that of *L'Express*, its political position was clearly different.

---

[75] Siritzky and Roth, *Le Roman de 'L'Express'*, p. 253.
[76] Ross, *Fast Cars, Clean Bodies*, p. 69.

Where *L'Express* had shifted to the centre, if not centre-right, its rival remained anchored firmly on the left, something signalled in its first issue by declarations of support not just from Sartre, but also – in an ironic echo of the first issue of *L'Express* in 1953 – Pierre Mendès France.[77]

By 1961, then, it had become clear that *L'Express* was no longer Mauriac's natural site. The radical, modernising agenda which had, against expectations, made their collaboration possible in the first place, finally drove them apart. The various ways in which this agenda expresses itself – whether it be the development of *Madame Express*, or the magazine's preoccupation with the *Nouvelle Vague* – bring to the surface their basic ideological incompatibilities. The gap between old and new orders, which had been masked by Servan-Schreiber's pursuit of Mauriac's symbolic capital, finally proved impossible to ignore. Mauriac had to look elsewhere for his 'lieu naturel'. In October 1961, after a break of six months, Mauriac's column reappeared in the pages of *Le Figaro littéraire*, the literary supplement published by the newspaper which had for many years been his most appropriate home. The last years of the *Bloc-notes* are the subject of the concluding chapter.

---

[77] For further discussion of the reinvention of *L'Express* in 1964 as the 'journal des cadres', see Edward Welch, 'Commitment, commercialism and the dawning of image culture: the early years of *L'Express*', *Web Journal of French Media Studies*, 4 (2001) (http://wjfms.ncl.ac.uk/express.htm). On the phenomenon of the 'cadre' in post-war France more generally, see Boltanski, *Les Cadres*.

Chapter Five

Abdication and Alienation

If we can date the beginning of Mauriac's career as an intellectual to spring 1937, when he published his articles in support of the Republican cause, and signed the petition 'pour le peuple basque', so too we can date its decline to summer 1958, and the return to power of Charles de Gaulle. Other actors in the field at the time were in no doubt that Mauriac's position and role had changed following de Gaulle's return. Sartre, for one, was disappointed by the way in which Mauriac became a willing and enthusiastic supporter of the new President: 'on lisait un article gaulliste de Mauriac: ça n'amusait plus. Ce qui intéressait, c'était Mauriac lui-même sans qu'il obéît à des principes gaullistes. C'était avant'.[1] Reviewing *Mémoires politiques* in 1967, by which time Mauriac had acquired a notorious reputation as de Gaulle's chief hagiographer, Michel Winock expressed a similar opinion. Mauriac could no longer be considered a political analyst, and had instead become a partisan and an ideologue: 'son effusion gaulliste déborde de sincérité, mais son aménité pour la politique du Général, sa promptitude à la défendre, en font davantage un capitaine de la garde qu'un analyste politique'.[2]

For both Sartre and Winock, Mauriac was guilty of relinquishing his responsibilities as an intellectual. In siding with de Gaulle, he had abandoned the critical independence in relation to the field of power which was by now well established as the defining feature of the intellectual's role in the social order. As Winock puts it, 'cette lucidité, cet esprit critique, qui ne font pas défaut à ceux qu'on baptise "gaullistes de gauche", il nous semblait que Mauriac les avait

---

[1] 'Mauriac vu par Sartre, propos recueillis par Jean Touzot', p. 46.
[2] Michel Winock, 'Mauriac politique', *Esprit*, December 1967, 1004-1014 (p. 1006).

abdiqués'.[3] Indeed, for some, Mauriac's shift in position was little short of a betrayal. Writing in *France-Observateur* in 1959, the journalist Claude Bourdet recounted his efforts to persuade Mauriac to remain on the critical margins, where he could serve as an important and influential counterweight to the new regime:

> Parce que Mauriac a beaucoup d'influence, parce que son appoint dans notre lutte serait important, je cherchais, l'autre semaine, à le ramener sur la ligne de bataille de la démocratie, qu'il abandonne ces temps-ci trop souvent, voulant à tout prix justifier de Gaulle.[4]

Bourdet's comments confirm the status that Mauriac had acquired by the end of the 1950s. They also indicate the seriousness with which his change of allegiance was viewed: Mauriac was giving his support to an individual who many perceived to be a threat to national sovereignty and the Republican tradition.

The early years of de Gaulle's Fifth Republic were defined by its struggle to assert its legitimacy, a legitimacy challenged from the start by many intellectuals. As I discussed briefly in the previous chapter, there were concerns over the way in which de Gaulle had come to power in June 1958, and his links with the rebellious generals in Algeria. There were fears too that the Gaullist regime itself may have dictatorial leanings, or at least pave the way for a more hard-line (i.e. fascist) regime in the short- to medium-term. Writing in *L'Express* in May 1958, Sartre argued that

> Lorsque le Général de Gaulle se déclare prêt à assumer les pouvoirs de la République il a déjà reçu l'investiture prétorienne, la seule qui compte à ses yeux. Les officiers et les civils européens [in Algeria] l'ont désigné pour exercer au nom des colons une dictature inconditionnée sur les indigènes métropolitains.[5]

Hostility towards the regime was reinforced when it became clear that, far from moving towards the solution promised by de Gaulle, the Algerian problem was worsening: not only was military

---

[3] Winock, 'Mauriac politique', p. 1005.
[4] Claude Bourdet, 'Mauriac, l'action politique et nous', *France-Observateur*, 16 July 1959, p. 5.
[5] Jean-Paul Sartre, 'Le Prétendant', *L'Express*, 22 May 1958, pp. 8-9 (p. 8).

action intensifying in Algeria as the French army attempted to gain as strong a position as possible before the start of negotiations, but political violence and repression increased on the mainland as the state took action against suspected FLN activists and sympathisers. September 1960 saw the trial of the *porteurs de valise* of the *réseau Jeanson*, a network organised by the Sartrean philosopher Francis Jeanson, who had been charged with undertaking fundraising activities for the FLN. The first day of the trial was marked by the publication of the 'Déclaration sur le droit à l'insoumission dans la guerre d'Algérie', the 'Manifeste des 121' in support of those refusing to fight in Algeria, signed by academics, writers and filmmakers. Word spread of the increasing and indiscriminate arrest and torture of Algerian immigrants by the police; and the regime's policy of repression was made shockingly clear on the infamous night of 17 October 1961, when the violent suppression in Paris of a peaceful demonstration by the Algerian community against the imposition of an evening curfew led to dozens of deaths, the exact number of which has still yet to be established.[6]

For Mauriac, however, de Gaulle represented not a threat, but the promise of salvation. He saw in him an individual who had the ability single-handedly to lead the country out of its problems, problems for which the political parties of the Fourth Republic were largely responsible in Mauriac's eyes. Mauriac had always been suspicious of parliamentary politics, much preferring to invest his faith in a charismatic and singular leader who could take responsibility for the nation's fortunes. As he notes in 1960, reflecting on de Gaulle's appeal,

> Je crois naïvement qu'il faut quelqu'un pour penser une politique et pour la mener à sa fin, quelqu'un, c'est-à-dire un homme différent de tous les autres, et dont les différences, déjà frappantes au départ lorsqu'il s'agit d'un homme exceptionnel, auront été accrues chez de Gaulle par l'étrangeté du destin, par la mission historique assumée à une certaine heure et superbement accomplie, et enfin par le retour au pouvoir dans une conjoncture dramatique et qui dure encore. (BN II 494)

---

[6] On 17 October 1961, see Jean-Luc Einaudi, *La Bataille de Paris: le 17 octobre 1961* (Paris: Seuil, 1991).

De Gaulle's distinctive authority derives from the conjunction of a great individual and a moment of historical crisis, a conjunction which has propelled him into the realm of legend. He stands as a providential figure for Mauriac, called upon to save his country a second time after the disaster of 1940.

By February 1961, still at *L'Express*, but in increasingly antagonistic mood, Mauriac was happy to recognise and acknowledge his new role as Gaullist partisan:

> Dès que de Gaulle fut là de nouveau, ramené non pas par un coup d'Etat militaire, pour empêcher au contraire ce coup d'Etat militaire, et parce qu'entre la République et les commandos parachutistes il ne restait plus, à la lettre, que les intellectuels de gauche, c'est-à-dire politiquement personne, à partir de ce moment-là, j'ai pensé [...] que de Gaulle seul gardait une chance de mettre fin à cette guerre, notre douleur et notre honte. Dès lors, je l'ai suivi, avec des hauts et des bas dans mon espérance mais non dans ma fidélité. (BN III 25-26)

Significantly, Mauriac's expression of support in this article comes in the context of a broader discussion of the relationship between the intellectual community and the Gaullist regime, triggered by the publication in *Les Lettres nouvelles* of a declaration of solidarity by international intellectuals in support of the signatories of the 'Manifeste des 121'. Mauriac is dismissive of claims made about the 'persecution' of French intellectuals in the aftermath of the Jeanson trial, and of perceived threats to the freedom of speech in France:

> J'invite nos intellectuals persécutés à rassurer eux-mêmes leurs confrères italiens, allemands, finlandais et suisses sur le sort qui leur a été réservé. Le seul, à ma connaissance qui ait fait quelques jours de prison politique, en a été tiré par le garde des Sceaux en personne. Le plus puni de tous aura été Jean-Paul Sartre, très fâché qu'on ne l'ait pas poursuivi' (BN III 25).

Mauriac's sarcastic tone, and his condescending use of the possessive pronoun in referring to 'nos intellectuels persécutés', both indicate the growing distance between Mauriac and the radical intellectual community with which he had been in alignment only a few years previously. This distance becomes all the clearer as the article unfolds.

As befits the journal-like style of the *Bloc-notes*, Mauriac's article is composed of two entries written over a weekend, the reflection begun on the first day being pursed into the second. In this second entry, we find him unequivocally breaking ranks with his erstwhile allies, and turning to attack them in startling ways. He questions their right to intervene on the grounds that intellectuals are divorced from the realities of political action: 'les écrivains décident de tout dans l'absolu. Arrêter la guerre d'Algérie, c'est pour le penseur une opération de la pensée' (BN III 27). It is easy for intellectuals to pass judgement, he suggests, when they operate in a realm of abstraction, and are free from the responsibilities and pragmatism which govern political decisions.

Such attitudes mark a dramatic shift in Mauriac's position, as he attempts to dismiss a role which he himself had considered of vital importance only a few years previously. In 1956, for example, we find him criticising precisely the reactionary position he had now come to adopt:

> Les intellectuels! Quelle basse envie se soulage dans ce vocable devenu une injure, qui, du temps de Dreyfus, servait déjà à ameuter les foules furieuses et qui, hier encore, pour les S. S. et pour les chemises noires, désignait le premier ennemi. C'est encore l'intelligence et l'usage de l'intelligence qu'il s'agit aujourd'hui de disqualifier. (BN I 357)

At the height of his campaign against the practice of torture, he underlines the pressing need for intellectuals in society, those who attempt to silence them a threat to democracy. Yet Mauriac is now himself guilty of questioning and disqualifying 'l'usage de l'intelligence' as he responds to criticism of the Gaullist regime.

De Gaulle's arrival in 1958 therefore brings with it Mauriac's return to the Establishment fold. The shift in his political position is confirmed by a corresponding change of position in the journalistic field in 1961. Following his split with *L'Express* in April 1961, and a hiatus of six months, the *Bloc-notes* was re-launched in *Le Figaro littéraire* in October of that year. The move restored the necessary homology between his political position and his position in the field, which had been disrupted by his differences with the news weekly. Indeed, only a month after the column's first appearance in *Le Figaro littéraire*, Mauriac finally made clear his break with the Left: 'mais je cède à une sombre paresse, je n'ai plus envie de me mêler à vous, hommes de gauche' (BN III 74). The choice of *Le Figaro littéraire* as the new home of the *Bloc-notes* is significant. Although Mauriac had ceased to write for *Le Figaro* following his departure from the editorial board in 1954, he had continued to publish in the newspaper's literary supplement throughout his time at *L'Express*. He studiously avoided current affairs, however, contributing the articles which made up *Mémoires intérieurs* (1959), the first of two volumes of autobiography and literary reflection.

Taking his political column to *Le Figaro littéraire* rather than *Le Figaro* itself was an indication that Mauriac was beginning to distance himself from mainstream political debate and the politically active interlocutors with whom he had engaged since the early 1950s. For Michel Winock, the move to *Le Figaro littéraire* meant that Mauriac more or less disappeared from the political landscape: 'il passait d'ailleurs dans un autre journal, ou plutôt il y revenait, qui n'était pas de nos lectures familières. Pour des milliers de fidèles qui l'avaient lu pendant des années, Mauriac n'existait plus'.[7] Those involved in shaping political debate were unlikely to form the readership of a conservative newspaper's literary supplement. Mauriac himself was fully aware of this. Reflecting at the time on his audience at *Le Figaro littéraire*, and comparing it to the youthful readership he had known at *L'Express*, he notes, somewhat laconically, that it is 'un public très intéressant, mais c'est autre chose. Beaucoup plus de dames'.[8] Entering the calmer waters of *Le Figaro littéraire* would allow Mauriac to develop his favourite themes in peace.[9]

Mauriac's evolution in the late 1950s can be seen as a shift from a position of paradox to one of orthodoxy. Where once Mauriac had been intent on challenging and inflecting government policies, and speaking out against the *doxa*, or received opinion, he increasingly seemed content to reflect and consolidate them.[10] If Mauriac's allegiance to de Gaulle provoked particular hostility on the Left, it is because he began to adopt positions which were in clear

---

[7] Winock, 'Mauriac politique', p. 1005.

[8] François Mauriac, *Les Paroles restent*, ed. by Keith Goesch (Paris: Gallimard, 1985), p. 200.

[9] For an overview of Mauriac's role at *Le Figaro littéraire*, see Claire Blandin, 'François Mauriac, "pierre angulaire" du *Figaro littéraire*?', *Revue des lettres modernes*, série François Mauriac, 6 (Caen: Minard, 2003), 39-59.

[10] On paradox as speaking against the *doxa*, see Roland Barthes, 'La division des langages', in *Le Bruissement de la langue* (Paris: Seuil, coll. "Points", 1984), pp. 119-133.

contradiction to the attitudes he had expressed only a few years before. His reaction to the on-going problems of torture and repression in both Algeria and France is the most obvious example of this.

Despite clear evidence that the practice of torture was continuing – and indeed intensifying – under the new regime, Mauriac became steadily more reluctant to confront the issue in the *Bloc-notes*. While his hesitancy can undoubtedly be understood in terms of a desire not to compromise the regime with ill-judged words, particularly when he felt a solution to the crisis was close, it led to what were perceived at the time to be problematic silences and shifts in opinion. Following the publication of *La Gangrène* in 1959, which tells of the torture suffered by Algerian students in Paris, and which was seized by the authorities, Mauriac returns to the question after what he admits is a year of silence on the matter. When he does so, it is to argue that torture is an inevitable consequence of the sort of conflict in which the army is caught up:

> Si depuis un an je me tais, ce n'est pas, comme certains me le laissent entendre, parce que je suis désormais "du côté de la manche". Il est pourtant vrai que j'ai acquis une certitude: la gangrène est une infection qui ne se traite pas à part; il faut remonter à la cause. Un temps de terrorisme et de contre-terrorisme est un temps de torture: rien ne prévaut contre cette loi. Le général de Gaulle s'efforce de détruire la cause. Lui seul en a le pouvoir.[11]

Mauriac's claim that torture was an unavoidable part of the conflict was highlighted by Claude Bourdet as a sign of his betrayal. For Bourdet, writing the following week in *France-Observateur*, Mauriac was guilty of trying to explain away what previously he had condemned to such effect: 'pourquoi vous *battiez-vous* (alors que vos forces étiez si faibles) contre des crimes que vous *expliquez* aujourd'hui (alors que votre influence est si grande)?'[12] Mauriac had adopted the position of the pragmatist who sees torture as an unfortunate but unavoidable part of a process which will nevertheless produce the desired conclusion. His belief in de Gaulle's ability to

---

[11] François Mauriac, *D'un bloc-notes à l'autre*, p. 514.
[12] Claude Bourdet, 'Mauriac et le gaullisme', *France-Observateur*, 2 July 1959, p. 5. Bourdet's emphasis.

bring about a solution to the conflict appeared to outweigh the moral and ethical problems raised by the practice of torture.

Mauriac rejected Bourdet's criticism in his next column. He argued that Bourdet had been selective in his quotation from the first article, having chosen to highlight Mauriac's comment about the inevitability of torture without mentioning the rest of his analysis, and in particular his assertion that de Gaulle was setting out to deal with the root cause of the problem (BN II 277-278). Nevertheless, evidence in support of Bourdet's argument did begin to accumulate over time. When Mauriac lets pass without comment the events of 17 October 1961, for example, he finds himself forced to defend his silence in a later 'Bloc-notes': 'si je me suis tu, ce n'est ni par politique, ni par timidité, mais parce que je ne veux rien avancer que ce que je crois juste. Ce que j'ai à dire sur ce sujet sinistre, je le dirai' (BN III 67). When he does discuss the subject, however, he seems more concerned to deflect blame from de Gaulle than to condemn the atrocities themselves, suggesting somewhat curiously that de Gaulle could hardly be held responsible for the deaths since he had no control over the police:

> Pour l'armée, le général de Gaulle lui appartient, il a pu agir sur elle. Il joue la partie avec elle, et non contre elle. En revanche, la police lui demeure étrangère. La police relève de l'Intérieur. Pour lui, il la subit comme nous tous. (BN III 73)

It is hard to imagine Mauriac's readership at the *Figaro littéraire* being reassured by such an analysis.

By the end of 1961, Mauriac's reputation as one of de Gaulle's chief supporters, not to say apologists, was firmly established. The dominant theme of the *Bloc-notes* during the 1960s is Mauriac's consistent, some would say excessive, support for de Gaulle. As Malcolm Scott puts it, his chief role seems to become that of 'Gaullist myth-maker',[13] a role exemplified in 1964 by the publication of a portrait entitled simply *De Gaulle*. Mauriac sees in de Gaulle the man of destiny who embodies his own vision of France, and who will restore its grandeur. Writing in 1962, Mauriac argues that 'il incarne la France de l'histoire; il donne une réalité charnelle à ce qui n'était qu'une idée. Tant qu'il respire, qu'il conçoit, qu'il agit,

---

[13] Malcolm Scott, *Mauriac: The Politics of a Novelist*, p. 115.

cette France a l'air d'exister' (BN III 133). He promotes him as one of the great figures of French history, individuals who single-handedly keep alive the spirit of France: 'cet homme est entré dans la compagnie des héros et des saints qui, à travers le temps et ses malheurs, ont maintenu la France vivante' (BN III 462). Mauriac is generous in his comparisons, drawing parallels with Charlemagne (BN IV 408), Joan of Arc (BN III 462), and even Christ (BN III 544). In his recent book, Scott paints a less monochrome picture, and suggests that Mauriac's support for de Gaulle during the 1960s was not unconditional: 'le soutien de Mauriac ne s'offrait aucunement comme un chèque en blanc'.[14] He points out that Mauriac was ready to disagree with the President over various issues, such as de Gaulle's friendly approaches to Germany, or his desire to make France a nuclear power.[15] Nevertheless, Mauriac's broad support of de Gaulle and his regime was beyond doubt. It was no longer his intention to challenge Official History, to 'déranger l'interprétation officielle des événements' (BN I 321), as he put it in 1956, but to play his part in writing it.

Although Mauriac's activities as Gaullist myth-maker plays a central part in this, not least for the sheer volume of writing it generates, perhaps equally significant is the more passive position he adopts as consumer and interpreter of Gaullist myths. In the *Bloc-notes* of the 1960s, Mauriac responds enthusiastically to the spectacle of the Gaullist regime. Like *L'Express* in the 1950s, the Gaullist regime recognised early on the growing power and importance of the image in modern society, understood both in terms of visual images, and of a particular look or style (the former, of course, being the most effective means of conveying the latter). As it sought to establish itself, it seized on the advantages offered by the relatively new technology of television, which had taken hold in France only in the latter half of the 1950s. Raymond Kuhn points out that television 'fitted in perfectly with de Gaulle's personal vision of how France should be governed, by furnishing a direct link between the President and the people';[16] but the dramatic, stage-managed press conferences at which de Gaulle announced policy measures were inevitably exploited also for their symbolic impact. As Kuhn goes on to observe,

---

[14] Malcolm Scott, *Mauriac et de Gaulle* (Bordeaux: L'Esprit du Temps, 1999), p. 199.
[15] Scott, *Mauriac et de Gaulle*, pp. 204-208.
[16] Raymond Kuhn, *The Media in France* (London: Routledge, 1995), p. 113.

> De Gaulle used television to help propagate the myth of his self-ascribed destiny to rule France. His television appearances were as much a part of his own conscious fashioning of his place in history as immediate responses to the exigencies of the political situation.[17]

Mauriac's written myths can be seen as a response to, and a translation of, the visual images put before him as he watches the President on television. Several articles begin by noting and commenting on de Gaulle's televised appearances: 'je regarde sur mon petit écran le général de Gaulle au milieu de la foule qui le presse. Il pleut, il est tête nue' (BN II 488). Mauriac identifies the fragile strength of de Gaulle's lofty isolation ('Je m'intéresse moins d'abord à ce que dit de Gaulle qu'à son aspect physique. Comment résiste-t-il? Comment tient-il? Sa force calme rassure. Oui, il tient, il résiste. Je puis l'écouter en paix', BN II 338), or his intimate contact with the people during his regional tours ('Il sourit, serre les mains tendues, caresse des têtes d'enfants', BN II 488).

To switch from a position of paradox to one of orthodoxy, then, is also to switch from an active to a passive mode. Under de Gaulle's reign, Mauriac becomes an accepting subject. The journalist of the period does not so much act through his writing as react, fending off what he sees as unjustified and disloyal criticism of de Gaulle; and as stability and growth continue into the late 1960s, Mauriac can announce that for the first time in his life, he feels that he is well governed:

> Je l'ai dit et redit, et le redirai encore: à tort ou à raison, pour la première fois depuis que je suis attentive à la politique, et cela fait un peu plus de soixante années, je me trouve gouverné raisonnablement. (BN IV 153)

However, Mauriac's passivity during this time also needs to be understood in another sense, one which provides an intriguing counterpoint to the first. For what strikes us in the columns of the 1960s is not only Mauriac's willing acceptance of de Gaulle's rule, but also the passivity of someone caught up in, and affected by, the policies of a regime which is pursuing modernisation at an increased

---

[17] Kuhn, *The Media in France*, p. 116.

pace. As Nathan Bracher has noted, the *Bloc-notes* of the period is dominated by two parallel narratives: on the one hand, the continuing success of de Gaulle's reign; and on the other, the rapid change affecting the country as modernisation takes hold, a change which will come increasingly to preoccupy Mauriac as time goes on.[18] What Bracher fails to identify, however, but what Mauriac himself is ultimately forced to recognise, is the problematic link between these two narratives. As the 1960s progress, Mauriac must confront the fact that his growing sense of alienation in what he terms 'le monde [...] dans sa mutation accélérée' (BN III 532), is a result largely of policies pursued by the regime he otherwise celebrates.

The *Bloc-notes* offers us a commentary on contemporary life which helps us to grasp the distinctive nature of the Gaullist project as it unfolds during the 1960s, and as de Gaulle puts into action his 'certaine idée de la France'. In the early days of the Gaullist regime, Mauriac had been quick to recognise de Gaulle's political strategy. Writing in October 1958, for instance, he highlights de Gaulle's efforts to reassert France's political authority, and to reinvigorate the country's national identity:

> Restaurer l'Etat dans sa puissance souveraine, équilibrer à l'intérieur les forces antagonistes qui en avaient fait ce grand paralytique, risée des autres nations; resserrer nos liens avec les peuples d'Afrique noire, les rendre indissolubles grâce à la liberté de choix qui leur serait donnée; ramener l'armée à sa vocation' (BN II 149).

De Gaulle's political vision, his action at the political level, is something of Mauriac can wholeheartedly approve.

However, the distinctiveness of de Gaulle's reign is to be found in the forms this vision will take, and the ways in which it will be implemented. It becomes clear in particular that the restoration of the nation's status and grandeur will involve its modernisation first and foremost, political strength being reflected in economic rejuvenation. Moreover, an important innovation of the Gaullist regime is to place the task of modernisation, and the implementation of reform, in the hands of a range of specialists and experts such as

---

[18] Nathan Bracher, *Through The Past Darkly*, ch. 5.

managers, engineers and technicians, or what otherwise came to be known as 'technocrats'.

The role and influence of the technocrats began to grow in the 1950s. Their importance had been identified first by those at the political and economic avant-garde such as Jean-Jacques Servan-Schreiber, who were keen to import the new sciences of management and government being developed in the United States in particular; but it is only under the Gaullist regime that this emerging class of managers and experts was systematically put to work in the service of the state. As Delphine Dulong has demonstrated, one of the regime's most important innovations lay in the new understanding of government it brought with it: the modernisation of political practice was considered the prerequisite for the modernisation of the nation. Increasingly, government became less a question of the representation of the people than of the efficient management of them and their world.[19] This change in perspective is one of the things implied by the shift in de Gaulle's new constitution away from the legislative bodies towards the executive.

Having entered widespread usage in France in the late 1950s, the term 'technocrate' began rapidly to acquire negative connotations, used by critics to describe a situation in which anonymous state servants were perceived (accurately, as Dulong makes clear) to be acquiring more power than the elected representatives of the people. Mauriac himself recognised the evolution brought about by de Gaulle's government in the early 1960s; and as a faithful lieutenant of the regime, he was happy to defend the rise to power of what he calls in 1962 'des gens qui sont à leur affaire sans demander d'autre avis qu'aux compétences, des gens qui ont l'audace de recourir aux méthodes qui conviennent ici et maintenant, sans aucun souci d'orthodoxie, et l'efficacité est leur unique loi' (BN III 273). For him, the emergence of the technocrats is a welcome innovation, one which exemplifies the regime's dynamism and effectiveness. He jumps to their defence again three years later, dismissing the criticisms made by politicians who see in technocracy the sign of an authoritarian and arrogant government, criticisms which are doubtless a reflection of their own sense of impotence: '"gouvernement de technocrates..."

---

[19] Delphine Dulong, *Moderniser la politique: aux origines de la Cinquième République* (Paris: L'Harmattan, 1997).

J'admire que des politiciens soient parvenus à donner un sens péjoratif
à ce qui signifie un gouvernement d'hommes compétents et qui ont
pour unique loi l'efficacité' (BN IV 39). Mauriac's contempt is
signalled neatly by his own use of the pejorative term 'politiciens'.

However, Mauriac's praise and defence of technocracy in the
1960s coexists in the *Bloc-notes* with an increasingly troubled
reflection on the state and direction of the world. Indeed, the first
'Bloc-notes' written for the *Figaro littéraire* marks the appearance of
a striking motif which will recur at various points over the subsequent
years, that of the sonic booms triggered by jet fighters as they pass
above Malagar, his house deep in the Gascon countryside: 'un coup
sourd fait trembler les vitres. Les pierres tressaillent comme si elles
étaient blesses, et en vérité elles le sont' (BN III 58). These booms
acquire an emblematic power for Mauriac, as they come to symbolise
the real and physical threat posed by the invisible and increasingly
menacing forces at work in the modern world. They are a sign of what
he perceives to be the growing determination of the present to erase
the past. The threat to the house, a physical trace of history, is a threat
to history itself: 'ce qui a duré des siècles, et qui aurait duré encore
des siècles, est donc condamné' (BN III 58). The hostile and
threatening nature of the modern world is confirmed for him when, in
the wake of yet another sonic boom, a mirror in his study falls from
the wall and crashes down on a place where he often sits:

> A tort ou à raison, cette chute fut attribuée à l'ébranlement causé
> par par les avions qui passent le mur du son au-dessus de
> Malagar. Je le crois quant à moi, car il y a bien d'autres signes
> que ces murs séculaires et lézardés ne résisteront pas toujours à
> cette loi indéfiniment violée. (BN III 533)

The booms become a sinister warning of impending catastrophe: 'ce
mur du son quotidiennement violé au-dessus de notre tête par les
aviateurs de Cazaux retentit lugubrement comme l'annonce d'un
malheur qui n'aurait pas encore de nom – signal d'alarme pour une
catastrophe inconnue' (BN III 339).

He sees the world he knew being dismantled and obliterated,
and the one which replaces it a strange and alien landscape from
which all signs of humanity have been eradicated. In May 1964, he
tells of a walk across the fields near his house at Vémars north of
Paris, to inspect the building of the Autoroute du Nord, a key element

in de Gaulle's strategy of *aménagement*. Mauriac makes his visit with a mixture of fascination and trepidation, capturing as he does so the hubristic spectacle of modernisation:

> Hier nous allâmes à pied, à travers un paysage à demi détruit (je reconnaissais un morceau de haie, un lambeau de chemin), jusqu'à ce lit d'un fleuve inconnu, creusé de main d'homme, et où aucune eau ne s'engouffrait encore: c'était le chantier de l'autoroute du Nord, paysage éphémère et étrange comme d'une planète inconnue. Les Martiens, s'ils existaient, seraient moins dépaysés, débarquant tout à coup sur cette terre défigurée et éventrée. (BN III 477)

In evoking his reactions to the scene – reactions which his readers are doubtless invited to share – Mauriac makes skilful use of a variety of effects. His vocabulary of destruction and physical violence ('lambeau', 'morceau', 'défigurée', 'éventrée') is combined with the antithetical deployment of a river metaphor to evoke the trench dug for the motorway ('ce lit d'un fleuve inconnu'), which underlines the diametric opposition between the natural world and the world being created by man. Finally, the reference to disfigurement in the closing sentence personifies the land, Mauriac describing it as the victim of a brutal and bloody attack.

It is the eruption of such tangible signs of modernity into familiar and enduring environments which gradually force Mauriac into the uncomfortable realisation that the destruction and mechanisation of the world around him is driven by the very man he celebrates as France's saviour. The construction work Mauriac sees on the outskirts of Paris (the building of the motorway, or the development of the new airport at Roissy) is an indication that de Gaulle's 'certaine idée de la France' was expressing itself above all in the form of the physical transformation and modernisation of the nation. Finally, in July 1966, and only a short time after Mauriac's defence of technocracy, comes the painful recognition that the Gaullist regime and its policy of *aménagement* are in fact largely responsible for his growing sense of loss and alienation: 'dire que c'est sous le règne de De Gaulle que les pires attentats auront été médités contre cette France dont il ne se faisait une certaine idée que parce qu'enfant il s'en était fait une certaine image' (BN IV 297). Two months later, he will lay the blame for his malaise with de Gaulle's technocrats: 'cette indifférence, ce mépris d'une technocratie sans entrailles pour les êtres de chair et de sang que nous sommes, je commence à ne le plus pouvoir souffrir' (BN IV 312). The sense of anger and bewilderment he articulates here will linger throughout the remaining years of his life, as he increasingly feels himself to be a stranger in a troubling new land:

> Je ne lis rien, je ne vois rien, je n'entends rien qui ne me donne la sensation d'être un homme déporté sur un continent où il ne retrouve que des traces de ce qu'il a cru, de ce qu'il a aimé: dépaysement absolu, dépaysement sans remède' (BN IV 311).

Throughout the 1960s, therefore, Mauriac becomes preoccupied both with the remodelling of the world around him, and the threat to the past and to history this brings with it. As Bracher has noted, Mauriac dwells on the crisis facing the 'vieille France' familiar to him, the provincial and essentially rural world in which he is most at home. He highlights the threat to rural life brought about by mechanisation and migration, by the destruction of the natural world, and by the loss of age-old rhythms and practices.[20] The topos of memory appears ever more frequently as he expresses his concern for this destruction: he recalls scenes from his past life, and depicts rural life as it unfolds around him at Malagar, underlining as he does so the essential timelessness of its modes of existence.

Mauriac is also concerned by the threat posed to cultural memory. He sees evidence of wilful amnesia and historical ignorance among the younger generations, content as they are to live for the present moment: 'cette Nouvelle Vague est sans mémoire pour ce qui l'a précédée: "Hitler? connais pas…" Elle vit dans la minute présente et se moque de vos manies, de vos phobies' (BN III 357).[21] He imagines a future in which, such is the accumulation of collective memory, the response of each new generation will simply be to wipe the board clean, to obliterate what has gone before and to start afresh:

---

[20] Bracher, *Through The Past Darkly*, ch. 5.

[21] Mauriac is alluding here to a film by Bertrand Blier, released in 1962. The historical amnesia of which Mauriac is increasingly aware can in fact be seen to be inscribed into the project that does most to define the new generation. All those aged thirteen or older at the start of the Second World War were excluded from the *Nouvelle Vague* survey as they were felt to be 'chargé d'un passé qui ne portait pas d'ombre sur les moins de trente ans' (François Giroud, *La Nouvelle Vague*, p. 21).

L'encombrement dans la mémoire humaine sera tel qu'il faudra
bien que les œuvres disparaissent en même temps que leurs
auteurs et que le premier geste de chaque génération, à son entrée
dans la carrière, soit un coup de torchon sur le tableau noir. (BN
III 42)

That Mauriac uses the literary domain as his point of reference here is
telling: it is a clue to a further anxiety accompanying his reflections
about the threat to history and the amnesia of the present, namely a
growing concern over the chances of his own survival in the cultural
memory. For if the past generally is under threat from a 'coup de
torchon', then so too, inevitably, is he.

Throughout the 1960s, Mauriac receives repeated
confirmation of his significant place in the cultural order. He
continues to enjoy the celebrity status consolidated in the 1950s,
making regular appearances on television chat shows and discussion
programmes, or being the subject of photo-spreads in *Paris-Match*. He
is solicited too by the foreign media, telling at various points in the
Bloc-notes of visits made by foreign journalists and television crews.
Following the departure of a German television crew in 1967, he
reflects on his willingness to collaborate with the media and play the
role of celebrity, and recognises that central to it is what he terms 'ce
désir de laisser une dernière trace, une dernière image de moi-même –
comme si les films n'étaient pas destinés autant que notre corps de
chair à l'ensevelissement, à l'oubli' (BN IV 427). Mauriac's desire to
leave some lasting trace of his activity and existence is reflected too in
his decision to donate his manuscripts and correspondence to the
Bibliothèque Jacques-Doucet in Paris in the mid-1960s: 'il y aura là
désormais, confié à l'Université de Paris, un fonds qui s'accroîtra, je
l'espère, au long des années à venir. Je me suis ainsi prémuni contre la
dispersion de cinquante ans d'écriture' (OA 807). Doing so, moreover,
allows him to witness the exhibition of which he is the subject at the
library in 1968, an exhibition which provides a tangible sign that
something of him will remain (BN V 14-18).

So while in the 1960s, Mauriac might relinquish his status as
an intellectual in the eyes of many, he continues to be a valuable
commentator on contemporary events, thanks in particular to the
perspective he offers on a France undergoing rapid and decisive
change. Mauriac's perspective is that of the *arrière-garde*, those being
affected by, and living through, the change imposed on them by those

leading the drive for modernisation. The distinctiveness of Mauriac's voice during this time lies in his non-synchronicity, the fact that he is out of step with the rhythms of change.[22] His sensitivity to the effects of *aménagement* both on the landscape and the modes of existence it supports allows us to grasp the trauma of modernisation, a trauma from which France has still yet to recover. Mauriac's pessimistic vision of a changing world is accompanied by his growing uncertainty of his own place within it. The final years of the *Bloc-notes* are pervaded by Mauriac's sense of being a relic or remnant from another time. Or, as he puts it in 1966, he is like the last of the mammoths (BN IV 328), wandering in an increasingly alien landscape and heading inevitably for extinction. Yet even as extinction beckons, he remains a significant and relevant voice, and it is precisely his status as the last vestige of an older order which makes him so.

Some concluding remarks
In many ways, Mauriac's gloomy assessment of his posthumous chances of survival in the cultural memory has proved to be quite accurate. His critical fortunes in the years since his death have fluctuated, his place and role in French literary and cultural history increasingly in danger of being forgotten by anyone other than a committed band of *mauriaciens*. Or, as a rather apocalyptically-minded colleague once put it, Mauriac may simply be one of those unfortunate literary figures who fall from the cliff of mainstream critical interest, jostled over its edge as more exciting and more 'relevant' characters arrive on the scene.

However, the present study has set out to remind us precisely of Mauriac's role as a significant member of the literary and intellectual fields in France throughout the twentieth century, and of the need to consider his position and activities if we are fully to understand the forces at work on French culture during this time. Mauriac's complex career is at once intriguing and illuminating. It is intriguing for the twists and turns it takes, from right to left politically, from novelist to intellectual, from radical agitator to establishment hagiographer; but the contention of this study has also been that Mauriac's particular trajectory brings to light the more general

---

[22] On non-synchronicity, see Ernst Bloch, 'Nonsynchronism and the Obligation to its Dialectics', trans. by Mark Ritter, *New German Critique*, 11 (Spring 1977), 22-38.

mechanisms at work in the field of cultural production, and the changes which have shaped that field across the century. His varying fortunes as a novelist remind us that an activity which often appears mystifying and magical, and which is often actively represented as such by those with an interest in sustaining the myth of artistic creation, is dependent – perhaps more than we like to acknowledge – on contacts, choices, constraints and perceptions in the social sphere. Similarly, his transformation from novelist to intellectual is made possible not just by an inner epiphany or coming to consciousness, but by the accumulation of sufficient symbolic capital on Mauriac's part, and the reconfiguration of the field around a new understanding of literary excellence.

Ultimately, perhaps one of the most notable aspects of a consideration of Mauriac's trajectory is that our sense of the social and cultural mechanisms at work in the artistic realm comes as much from Mauriac himself as from a Bourdieusian reading of his career. We have seen at various points that Mauriac has a good feel for the rules of the game he has set out to play, even if – as his repeated attempts to rival the *NRF* with his own review suggest – he sometimes lacks the acuity and resources to play it as well as his peers. He has an acute awareness of the power of the *NRF* in the inter-war period, and of what it meant to be recognised by them; he identifies the relationship between the choices he makes in the literary field and the dispositions which inform them; he is aware too of the complex set of qualities and motivations which turn him into an object of desire for *L'Express*. It is for all these reasons – his dramatic and revealing trajectory, his demystified understanding of the cultural realm, his powerful and effective interventions in the political realm – that Mauriac deserves to be read and remembered still.

Bibliography

I. Works by François Mauriac

'Aux lecteurs', *La Table ronde*, April 1954, 126-127

Bloc-notes, ed. by Jean Touzot, 5 vols (Paris: Seuil, coll. "Points", 1993)

Le Cahier noir (Paris: Desclée de Brouwer, 1994)

De Gaulle (Paris: Grasset, 1964)

D'un bloc-notes à l'autre, ed. by Jean Touzot (Paris: Bartillat, 2004)

L'imitation des bourreaux de Jésus-Christ, ed. by Alain de la Morandais (Paris: Desclée de Brouwer, 1984)

'La Jeunesse littéraire', *La Revue hebdomadaire*, 6 April 1912, 59-72

Mémoires politiques (Paris: Grasset, 1967)

'Notre raison d'être', *La Table ronde*, August-September 1949, 1235-1240.

Œuvres complètes, 12 vols (Paris: Fayard, 1952)

Œuvres romanesques et théâtrales complètes, ed. by Jacques Petit, 4 vols (Paris: Gallimard, coll. "Bibl. de la Pléiade", 1979-85)

Œuvres autobiographiques, ed. by François Durand (Paris: Gallimard, coll. "Bibl. de la Pléiade", 1990)

La Paix des cimes: chroniques 1948-1955, ed. by Jean Touzot (Paris: Bartillat, 1999)

Les Paroles restent, ed. by Keith Goesch (Paris: Grasset, 1985)

Paroles perdues et retrouvées, ed. by Keith Goesch (Paris: Grasset, 1986)

Souvenirs retrouvés: entretiens avec Jean Amrouche (Paris: Fayard/I.N.A, 1981)

II. Correspondence

Claudel, Paul and Mauriac, François, *Correspondance (1911-1954)*, ed. by Michel Malicet and Marie-Claire Praicheux (Paris: Minard, 1988)

Gide, André and Mauriac, François, *Correspondance (1912-1950)*, ed. by Jacqueline Morton, *Cahiers André Gide*, 2 (1971)

Mauriac, François, *Lettres d'une vie*, ed. by Caroline Mauriac (Paris: Grasset, 1981)

—. *Nouvelles lettres d'une vie*, ed. by Caroline Mauriac (Paris: Grasset, 1989)

Mauriac, François and Duhamel, Georges, *Correspondance (1919-1966)*, ed. by Jean-Jacques Hueber (Paris: Klincksieck, 1997)

Mauriac, François and Paulhan, Jean. *Correspondance (1925-1967)*, ed. by John Flower (Paris: Editions Claire Paulhan, 2001)

Mauriac, François and Rivière, Jacques. *Correspondance (1911-1925)*, ed. by John Flower (Exeter: University of Exeter Press, 1988)

Paulhan, Jean. *Choix de lettres*, ed. by Dominique Aury, Jean-Claude Zylberstein and Bernard Leuilliot, 3 vols (Paris: Gallimard, 1986-89)

Proust, Marcel and Gide, André. *Correspondance autour de* La Recherche, ed. by Pierre Assouline (Paris: Editions Complexes, 1988)

Rivière, Jacques and Alain-Fournier, *Correspondance (1904-1914)*, ed. by Alain Rivière and Pierre de Gaulmyn, 2 vols (Paris: Gallimard, 1991)

Servan-Schreiber, Jean-Jacques, Unpublished correspondence with François Mauriac, Bibliothèque Littéraire Jacques-Doucet, fonds Mauriac

——. Unpublished correspondence with Pierre Mendès France, Institut Pierre Mendès France, Paris

III. Reviews and articles on Mauriac's work in the *NRF*

Arland, Marcel, 'François Mauriac, *Ce qui était perdu*', *La Nouvelle Revue française*, 204 (September 1930), 407-412

——. 'François Mauriac, *Le Mystère Frontenac*', *La Nouvelle Revue française*, 234 (March 1933), 519-521

——. 'François Mauriac, *La Fin de la nuit*', *La Nouvelle Revue française*, 258 (March 1935), 449-451

——. 'François Mauriac, *Les Anges noirs*', *La Nouvelle Revue française*, 271 (April 1936), 586-588

——. 'François Mauriac, *Les Chemins de la mer*', *La Nouvelle Revue française*, 308 (May 1939), 875-880

Crémieux, Benjamin, 'François Mauriac, *Le Baiser au lépreux*', *La Nouvelle Revue française*, 103 (April 1922), 495-497

——. 'François Mauriac, *Thérèse Desqueyroux*', *La Nouvelle Revue française*, 164 (May 1927), 683-689

——. 'François Mauriac, *Asmodée*', *La Nouvelle Revue française*, 292 (January 1938), 147-149

Du Bos, Charles, 'François Mauriac, *Le Désert de l'amour*', *La Nouvelle Revue française*, 140 (May 1925), 936-944

Drieu La Rochelle, Pierre, 'Mauriac', *La Nouvelle Revue française*, 331 (September 1941), 343-350

Fernandez, Ramon, 'François Mauriac, *Genitrix*', *La Nouvelle Revue française*, 125 (February 1924), 224-227

—. 'François Mauriac, *Destins*', *La Nouvelle Revue française*, 175 (April 1928), 541-544

—. 'François Mauriac, *Le Nœud de vipères*', *La Nouvelle Revue française*, 223 (April 1932), 758-762

Grenier, Jean, 'François Mauriac, *Journal (II)*', *La Nouvelle Revue française*, 287 (April 1937), 342-344

Guérin, Jean [Jean Paulhan], 'A propos du "François Mauriac" de Sartre', *La Nouvelle Revue française*, 306 (March 1939), 535

Prévost, Jean, 'De Mauriac à son œuvre', *La Nouvelle Revue française*, 198 (March 1930), 349-367

Rivière, Jacques, 'François Mauriac, *Le Fleuve de feu*', *La Nouvelle Revue française*, 122 (July 1923), 98-101

Sartre, Jean-Paul, 'M. François Mauriac et la liberté', *La Nouvelle Revue française*, 305 (February 1939), 212-232

Thibaudet, Albert, 'François Mauriac, *La Chair et le sang*', *La Nouvelle Revue française*, 87 (December 1920), 941-943

—. 'François Mauriac, *Préséances*', *La Nouvelle Revue française*, 96 (September 1921), 358-359

Vaudal, Jean, 'François Mauriac, *Plongées*', *La Nouvelle Revue française*, 295 (April 1938), 671-673

IV. Other sources

Alain-Fournier, 'Une enquête sur la jeunesse littéraire', *Paris-Journal*, 5 April 1912

Barthes, Roland, *Mythologies* (Paris: Seuil, coll. "Points", 1972)

—. *L'obvie et l'obtus* (Paris: Seuil, coll. "Points", 1982)

—. *Le Bruissement du langage* (Paris: Seuil, coll. "Points", 1984)

Beauvoir, Simone de, *La Force des choses* (Paris: Gallimard, 1963)

—. *Les Belles Images* (Paris: Gallimard, 1966)

Benda, Julien, *La Trahison des clercs* (Paris: Grasset, 1927)

Benjamin, Walter, *One-Way Street and Other Writings*, trans. by Edmund Jephcott and Kingsley Shorter (London: Verso, 1997)

Berne, Mauricette (ed.), *Sartre* (Paris: Bibliothèque nationale de France/Gallimard, 2005)

Blandin, Claire, 'François Mauriac, "pierre angulaire" du *Figaro littéraire*?', *Revue des lettres modernes*, série François Mauriac, 6 (Caen: Minard, 2003), 39-59

Bloch, Ernst, 'Nonsynchronism and the Obligation to its Dialectics', trans. by Mark Ritter, *New German Critique*, 11 (Spring 1977), 22-38

Boltanski, Luc, *Les Cadres: la formation d'un groupe social* (Paris: Editions de Minuit, 1982)

Bothorel, Jean, *Bernard Grasset* (Paris: Grasset, 1989)

—. *Celui qui voulait tout changer: les années JJSS* (Paris: Robert Laffont, 2005)

Boschetti, Anna, *Sartre et 'Les Temps modernes'* (Paris: Editions de Minuit, 1985)

—. 'Légitimité littéraire et stratégies éditoriales', in *Histoire de l'édition française*, vol. 4: le livre concurrencé, 1900-1950. Ed. by Roger Chartier (Paris: Promodis, 1986), pp. 481-527

—. 'Le mythe du grand intellectuel', in *Le Grand Atlas Universalis des littératures* (Paris: Encyclopaedia Universalis, 1990), pp. 244-247

—. 'Des revues et des hommes', *La Revue des revues*, 18 (1994), 51-65

—. 'Un universel singulier', in Ingrid Galster (ed.), *La Naissance du 'phénomène Sartre': raisons d'un succès 1938-1945* (Paris: Seuil, 2001), pp. 265-283

Bourdet, Claude, 'Mauriac et le gaullisme', *France-Observateur*, 2 July 1955, p. 5

—. 'Mauriac, l'action politique et nous', *France-Observateur*, 16 July 1955, p. 5

Bourdieu, Pierre, 'Genèse et structure du champ religieux', *Revue française de sociologie*, 12 (1971), 295-334

—. 'Le couturier et sa griffe: contribution à une théorie de la magie', *Actes de la recherche en sciences sociales*, 1 (1975), 7-36

—. 'La production de la croyance', *Actes de la recherche en sciences sociales*, 13 (1977), 3-43

—. *Le Sens pratique* (Paris: Editions de Minuit, 1980)

—. 'The Field of Cultural Production, or: The Economic World Reversed', trans. by Richard Nice, *Poetics*, 12 (1983), 311-356

—. *Questions de sociologie* (Paris: Editions de Minuit, 1984)

—. *Choses dites* (Paris: Editions de Minuit, 1987)

—. *Raisons pratiques: sur la théorie de l'action* (Paris: Seuil, coll. "Points", 1994)

—. *Les Règles de l'art: genèse et structure du champ littéraire* (Paris: Seuil, coll. "Points", 2nd edition, 1998)

—. *Langage et pouvoir symbolique* (Paris: Seuil, coll. "Points", 2001)

Bracher, Nathan, 'Mauriac and the Spanish Civil War: Ethics and Aesthetics of Commitment', *Romance Notes*, 33 (1993), 297-304

—. 'Mauriac and Decolonisation: Civilisation, History, and National Identity', *Contemporary French Civilisation*, 18 (1994), 167-187

—. *Through The Past Darkly: History and Memory in François Mauriac's 'Bloc-notes'* (Washington, D.C. The Catholic University of America Press, 2004)

Camus, Albert, *Actuelles: écrits politiques* (Paris: Gallimard, 1950)

Canérot, Marie-Françoise, 'Le premier *Bloc-notes*, ou une tragédie toujours palpitante', *Cahiers François Mauriac*, 9 (1983), 111-126

—. *Mauriac après 1930: le roman dénoué* (Paris: SEDES, 1985)

Cartier-Bresson, Henri, *Tête à Tête* (London: National Portrait Gallery, 1998)

Casseville, Caroline, 'Mauriac et la critique sartrienne', *Nouveaux Cahiers François Mauriac*, 1 (1993), 77-95

Chapsal, Madeleine, *Envoyez la petite musique* (Paris: Le Livre de Poche, 1984)

Charle, Christophe, *Naissance des 'intellectuels'* (Paris: Editions de Minuit, 1990)

Chochon, Bernard, *Le 'Bloc-notes' de Mauriac: une poésie du temps* (Paris: L'Harmattan, 2002)

Cocula, Bernard, *Mauriac: le 'Bloc-notes'* (Bordeaux: L'Esprit du Temps, 1995)

Contat, Michel and Rybalka, Michel, *Les Ecrits de Sartre* (Paris: Gallimard, 1970)

Cornick, Martyn, *Intellectuals in History: The 'NRF' Under Jean Paulhan, 1925-1940* (Amsterdam: Rodopi, 1995)

—. 'Jean Paulhan et la résurrection de la *NRF*, 1953', *La Revue des revues*, 29 (2001), 30-53.

Davis, Colin, *Lévinas: An Introduction* (Cambridge: Polity Press, 1996)

Debû-Bridel, Jacques, *La Résistance intellectuelle* (Paris: Julliard, 1970)

De Gaulle, Charles, *Mémoires de guerre* (Paris: Plon, 1954-59)

Dine, Philip. *Images of the Algerian War* (Oxford: Oxford University Press, 1994)

Du Bos, Charles, *François Mauriac et le problème du romancier catholique* (Paris: Corréa, 1933)

Dulong, Delphine, *Moderniser la politique: aux origines de la Cinquième République* (Paris: L'Harmattan, 1997)

Einaudi, Jean-Luc, *La Bataille de Paris: le 17 octobre 1961* (Paris: Seuil, 1991)

Fouilloux, Etienne. 'Intellectuels catholiques et guerre d'Algérie', in Jean-Pierre Rioux and Jean-François Sirinelli (eds), *La Guerre d'Algérie et les intellectuels*, *Cahiers de l'Institut d'Histoire du Temps Présent*, 10 (1988), pp. 53-78

Flower, John. 'Mauriac's contributions to the *Nouvelle Revue française*', in John Flower and Bernard Swift (eds), *François Mauriac: Visions and Reappraisals* (Oxford: Berg, 1989), pp. 117-131

Gide, André, *Journal (1926-1950)*, ed. by Martine Sagaert (Paris: Gallimard, coll. "Bibl. de la Pléiade", 1997)

Gildea, Robert, *France Since 1945* (Oxford: Oxford University Press, 1996)

Giroud, Françoise, *La Nouvelle Vague* (Paris: Gallimard, 1958)

—. *Si je mens....* (Paris: Stock, 1972)

—. *Profession journaliste* (Paris: Le Livre de Poche, 2003)

Gosselin, Monique, 'Le *Bloc-notes* de 1953 à 1961: une oraison publique'. *Cahiers François Mauriac*, 17 (1990), 58-94

Higgins, Lynn, *New Novel, New Wave, New Politics* (Lincoln, Ne.: University of Nebraska Press, 1996)

Jamet, Michel, *Les défis de 'L'Express'* (Paris: Cerf, 1981)

Judt, Tony, *Past Imperfect: French Intellectuals, 1944-1956* (Berkeley, Ca.: University of California Press, 1992)

Kuhn, Raymond, *The Media in France* (London: Routledge, 1995)

Kuisel, Richard, *Capitalism and the State in Modern France* (Cambridge: Cambride University Press, 1981)

Kushnir, Slava, *Mauriac journaliste* (Paris: Minard, 1979)

Lacouture, Jean, *François Mauriac* (Paris: Seuil, coll. "Points", 2 vols, 1990)

Lang, André, *Pierre Brisson* (Paris: Calmann-Lévy, 1967)

Lévinas, Emmanuel, *Totalité et infini: essai sur l'extériorité* (Paris: Le Livre de Poche, coll. "Biblio", 1996)

Louis, Patrick, *'La Table ronde': une aventure singulière* (Paris: Editions de la Table ronde, 1992)

Maulnier, Thierry, 'J.P. Sartre et le suicide littéraire', *La Table ronde*, February 1948, 195-210.

Mein, Margaret, 'François Mauriac and Jansenism', in John Flower and Bernard Swift (eds), *François Mauriac: Visions and Reappraisals* (Oxford: Berg, 1989), pp. 147-167

Mendès France, Pierre, *La République moderne* (Paris: Gallimard, 1962)

Mollier, Jean-Yves, 'La revue dans le système éditorial'. In *La Belle Epoque des revues, 1880-1914*, ed. by Jacqueline Pluet-Despantin, Michel Leymarie and Jean-Yves Mollier (Paris: IMEC, 2002), pp. 43-55

Monférier, Jacques, 'Les "Billets" de François Mauriac dans *Sept* et *Temps présent* (1934-1940)', *Revue des lettres modernes*, série François Mauriac, 3 (Caen: Minard, 1980), 67-80

Montheillet, Georges, 'Mauriac et Camus: la justice et la charité', *Travaux du Centre d'Etudes et de Recherche François Mauriac*, 32 (December 1992), 27-45

Morin, Edgar, *Les Stars* (Paris: Seuil, coll. "Points", 1972)

—. *L'Esprit du temps* (Paris: Grasset, 1962)

Ory, Pascal and Sirinelli, Jean-François, *Les Intellectuels en France: de l'affaire Dreyfus à nos jours* (Paris: Perrin, 2004)

Perec, Georges, *Les Choses* (Paris: Julliard, 1965)

Pinto, Louis, *Pierre Bourdieu et la théorie du monde social* (Paris: Seuil, coll. "Points", 2002)

Praicheux, Marie-Chantal, 'François Mauriac et l'Académie française', *Nouveaux Cahiers François Mauriac*, 8 (2000), 267-281

—. 'Le journaliste François Mauriac: une question de tribunes', *Revue des lettres modernes*, série François Mauriac, 6 (Caen: Minard, 2003), 19-37

Reid, James, 'Mauriac: The Ambivalent Author of Absence', *Studies in Twentieth Century French Literature*, 11 (1987), 167-188

Rioux, Jean-Pierre, *La France de la Quatrième République* (Paris: Seuil, coll. "Points", 2 vols, 1983)

Rioux, Jean-Pierre and Sirinelli, Jean-François, *Histoire culturelle de la France*, vol. 4 (Paris: Seuil, coll. "Points", 2004)

Ross, Kristin, *Fast Cars, Clean Bodies: Decolonisation and the Reordering of French Culture* (Cambridge, Ma.: The MIT Press, 1995)

Rostow, Walt W., *The Stages of Economic Growth: A Non-Communist Manifesto* (Cambridge: Cambridge University Press, 1960)

Rotman, Patrick, 'La diaspora mendésiste', *Pouvoirs*, 27 (1983), 5-20

Rousseaux, André, 'La vie littéraire', *Revue universelle*, 15 February 1939, 484-485

Sapiro, Gisèle, 'Salut littéraire et littérature du salut: deux trajectoires de romanciers catholiques', *Actes de la recherche en sciences sociales*, 111-112 (1996), 36-58

—. *La Guerre des écrivains* (Paris: Fayard, 1999)

Sartre, Jean-Paul, *Situations, I* (Paris: Gallimard, 1947)

—. *Situations, II* (Paris: Gallimard, 1948)

—. 'Le Prétendant', *L'Express*, 22 May 1958, pp. 8-9

—. *Situations, VIII* (Paris: Gallimard, 1972)

—. 'Mauriac vu par Sartre, propos recueillis par Jean Touzot', in Jean Touzot (ed.), *François Mauriac, Cahiers de l'Herne*, 48 (1985), 44-52

Scott, Malcolm, *Mauriac: The Politics of a Novelist* (Edinburgh: Scottish University Press, 1980)

—. 'Mauriac and the Raising of Dreyfus', in John Flower and Bernard Swift (eds), *François Mauriac: Visions and Reappraisals* (Oxford: Berg, 1989), pp. 133-146

—. *Mauriac et De Gaulle* (Bordeaux: L'Esprit du Temps, 1999)

—. *Mauriac et Gide: la recherche du Moi* (Bordeaux: L'Esprit du Temps, 2004)

—. 'Pour recevoir le journalisme de François Mauriac', *Revue des lettres modernes*, série François Mauriac, 6 (Caen: Minard, 2003), 151-187

Serror, Serge, '*L'Express* et l'opinion publique', Unpublished Mémoire de DEA, University of Paris, 1960

Servan-Schreiber, Jean-Jacques, 'Réponse à François Mauriac', *L'Express*, 13 August, 1959, p. 3

—. 'Un homme dans l'espace', *L'Express*, 13 April 1961, p. 5

—. *Passions* (Paris: Fixot, 1991)

Sirinelli, Jean-François, 'Mauriac, un intellectuel engagé', in André Séailles (ed.), *François Mauriac entre la Gauche et la Droite*. (Paris: Klincksieck, 1995), 145-158

Siritzky, Serge and Roth, Françoise, *Le Roman de 'L'Express', 1953-1978* (Paris: Atelier Marcel Jullian, 1979)

Sorum, Paul Clay, *Intellectuals and Decolonisation in France* (Chapel Hill: University of North Carolina Press, 1977)

Stora, Benjamin, *La Gangrène et l'oubli* (Paris: La Découverte, 1991)

—. *Histoire de la guerre d'Algérie (1954-1962)* (Paris: La Découverte, 1993)

Stallabrass, Julian, *Paris Pictured* (London: Thames and Hudson, 2002)

Touzot, Jean, *Mauriac avant Mauriac* (Paris: Flammarion, 1977)

—. 'Quand Mauriac était scandaleux...', *Œuvres et Critique*, 2 (1977), 133-144

—. 'François Mauriac chez les "hommes-sandwiches" (1925-1935)', *Revue des lettres modernes*, série François Mauriac, 3 (Caen: Minard, 1980), 21-37

— (ed.), *François Mauriac, Cahiers de l'Herne*, 48 (1985).

—. *Mauriac sous l'Occupation* (Bordeaux: Editions Confluences, 1995)

—. 'Les trois avatars de la revue rivale', *Nouveaux Cahiers François Mauriac*, 8 (2000), 199-210

Viala, Alain, 'Effets de champ, effets de prisme', *Littérature*, 70 (May 1988), 64-71

Vian, Boris, *Manuel de St-Germain-des-Prés* (Paris: Toutain, 1950)

Vidal-Naquet, Pierre, *La Torture dans la République* (Paris: Editions de Minuit, 1972)

Vinan, Richard, *France, 1934-1970* (London: Macmillan, 1996)

Weiner, Susan, 'The *Consommatrice* of the 1950s and Elsa Triolet's *Roses à crédit*', *French Cultural Studies*, 17 (1995), 123-144

Welch, Edward, 'A "Catholic Novelist" in Context: Suggestions for a Reassessment of the Work of François Mauriac', Unpublished doctoral thesis, University of Oxford, 2000

—. 'Commitment, Commodification and the Dawning of Image Culture: The First Years of *L'Express*', *Web journal of French Media Studies*, 4 (2001) (http://wjfms.ncl.ac.uk/express.htm)

—. 'Le carnaval perverti de François Mauriac', in Edward Welch (ed.), *Masque et carnaval dans la littérature européenne* (Paris: L'Harmattan, 2002, pp. 39-53)

Winock, Michel, 'Mauriac politique', *Esprit*, December 1967, 1004-1014

—. *Le Siècle des intellectuels* (Paris: Seuil, coll. "Points", 2nd edition, 1999)

Index